DROWNING ON DRY LAND

PLUMBING THE DEPTHS IN LADBROKE GROVE, SWANSEA AND SAN FRANCISCO

RAY ROUGHLER-JONES

BONE

First published 2010 by Bone

Bone is an imprint of Tangent Books
Unit 5.16 Paintworks
Arnos Vale
Bristol
BS4 3EH
0117 972 0645
www.tangentbooks.co.uk
richard@tangentbooks.co.uk

ISBN 978-1-906477-40-0

Printed by HSW, Tonypandy, Wales

Editor: Ian Bone
Design: Nick Law

Special thanks go out to: Ian Bone & Anna Chancellor for giving me the balls to finish the story. Piers, Tanya and Nicky Kentish Barnes for letting me use their computers and anyone who either jogged my memory or provided a photograph. Every single day of my life I have needed help of some kind, to try and list all the people who have aided me here would take longer than the writing of the book, they know who they are, and I love them all.

Bone is interested in publishing radical biographies and autobiographies both contemporary and historical. If you have an idea contact Ian Bone at www.ianbone.wordpress.com or localnews4us@yahoo.co.uk

This book is dedicated to my long-suffering mother Cassie.

Contents

1. Taffy was a Welshman, Taffy was a Thief

I'm entering the Café de Paris in Leicester Square; on my arm is Ines de la Fressange, Muse of Karl Lagerfeld, Top model at Chanel and soon to become the 'Marianne' of all France. A few steps behind is my girlfriend Kirsty accompanied by Gilles, who, in turn is right hand man to Lagerfeld. We've just come from the opening party of the new Chanel store in New Bond Street and I'm about to hit the dance floor with the most beautiful woman I've ever seen in real life.

None of this is because of my own endeavour, but nonetheless good company for a bloke who as little as seven years earlier was living on speed in a poxy high-rise flat in Swansea making ends meet by thieving, fiddling and the odd bit of low–end drug dealing. Let me take you through how all this came about.

I'm from Swansea in South Wales, born in 1951. My father Tommy was a civil servant and my mother Cassie, as well as being a housewife, took on cleaning jobs. I was delivered at home in an old three-storey house on the Prince of Wales Road in the Greenhill area, which was primarily the domicile of second-generation Irish Catholic immigrants. It was a dark old house, with a pitch black hearth for the cooking and heating, there was gas lighting and an outside toilet. This may sound archaic today but that's the truth of it. There were all sorts back and forth through the front door, but I couldn't tell then if they were friends, relatives or just lodgers. Back then my granny ruled the roost, I can't remember too much about her, but there are photos of her holding me as a child. I was told later that she wouldn't have anyone else holding me, except her, not even my mother. That's probably stretching it a bit, but I was without doubt the apple of her eye. My father was considered a bit of an outsider by my mam's four brothers and sister.
He wasn't from around these parts, he hailed from Tairgwaith or 'up the valleys' he was also Welsh speaking, which believe it or not was quite alien in most of Swansea.

Like my sister Linda before me, I started school at three. St. Joseph's infants, where we were taught by nuns to read, write and to fear the Lord. This was the school which took care of my education through to 11 years of age, by which time we knew the Catechism backwards, the Mass in Latin, and how many people had died for our sins. When I was about five, my Mam and Dad were given a council house on a brand new estate. My mother was over the moon, the house was pristine, and for the first time in her life she lived in a place with electricity throughout an inside loo and a bath. In the old house one had to bathe in front of the fire in a tin bath (cue violins). She must have been happy with life, but we weren't very well off. I gauged this by the amount of sweets other kids, and not just the Italian ones whose parents had a café or sweet shop, seemed to have compared to myself.

By the time I was ten or so we'd moved back into the area we'd moved from. The street, which was, and still is one of the roughest around there, was barely 500 yards from school. This was great, no more bus to and from school, and all my mates within spitting distance. Football was the order of the day, and although I was very mediocre as a player, I was the numero uno expert on the why, when and wherefores of the game. Being indoors never entered my mind; I only went home when I had to. I was well liked, I think, by all the boys, but due to my father's bedtime rules I always seemed to rise much earlier than my oppos, and I'd always be annoying their parents by calling on them early in the morning, or while they were eating. Years later a couple of them told me that their mums thought I was a bit of an oddball. Consequently, I spent a lot of my time wandering around on my own, scoring goals and breaking world records in my head. In 1961 my sister Margaret appeared. Can I blame some of my misdemeanours on being the middle child now?

1962 was a time of rejoicing in our house. For some remarkable reason I'd passed my Eleven Plus. Not only was I the first person in our family to do so, I must have been the only one to do so in the history of Colbourne Terrace. Mam was chuffed, and my father even uttered a few words of encouragement and prattled on about opportunity and career prospects. All I thought about was a chance to play rugby (I had to be better at that than I was at football) and what present I was going to get for passing the exam. It must have been tight, but they got me a push bike, gold in colour and brand new. I'd only recently learned to ride, but on the first day I got it Julian Till and myself went off to places I was unfamiliar with, but hey, who cared? I had wheels man.

We landed up on the road that brings all traffic to and from Swansea called the Jersey Marine. Pedalling along I thought the outside part of the tarmac seemed quiet compared to the side I was on. I didn't know then that I'd ventured into the fast lane. Almost immediately I got hit by a car. I was knocked ten feet into the air, and landed head first on the grass verge. I was stunned but not unconscious; the driver of the car was as white as a sheet. When he realised I was all right he settled down, I told him I was fine and off he went. Maybe I was a bit hasty there, maybe I had done some damage, because now when I think back, I often pinpoint that moment as the possible start of my anti-social phase, which never went away. At the time I was more worried about my bike. It was knackered, beyond repair, kaput. My dad went back to the shop, James Bond was the name of it (no kidding) but he couldn't help, so I'm back on Shanks' Pony. Never mind I had a new school to look forward too. The first opportunity for me to wear long trousers and free of having to go to church or confession every five minutes, and lying about it when you never went.

Dynevor Grammar School was the premier seat of learning in Swansea at that time, and this is where I landed up. It was a rude awakening. There were boys here whose fathers were doctors, lawyers and other important things. These kids seemed to like going to school, and never moaned about the homework, in fact they revelled in it. I wasn't used to that one bit. There were young boys having grown up conversations with teachers. One boy I'd see regularly conversing with the mighty Meredith Hughes, headmaster of this establishment, turned out to be Rowan Williams. He went on to become the Archbishop of Canterbury. What chance me here? I was a wrong 'un from the start. Fighting, giving lip, going around the town pinching and hanging around the snooker hall, or the record counter in British Home Stores. Obviously this golden educational opportunity I had been given was not taken too seriously. We got some hefty clouts off the teachers too, but if you really fucked up, you'd be sent to the head or deputy head. In St. Joseph's we had our fair share of whacks with the cane, but that was meted out on the hand, here they gave you six of the best across the arse, which is ten times worse. So I wanted out. I got around my mother, that was easy enough, but the old man wasn't having any of it. He was definitely right, but I'm at the bottom end of the class here, and I hate the place. So what's the point? My father finally relented after one call too many from the school for him to attend and discuss my misdemeanours. He eventually bowed to the inevitable, and before you know it, after two years, I'm back at St. Joseph's.

The Greenhill, Waun Wen, Brynmelyn and Hafod districts, which surrounded St. Josephs were football mad. It took up all of our time, playing it or talking about it. Swansea has a good reputation for producing top talent. John and Mel Charles, Ivor and Len Allchurch, Cliff Jones and Terry Medwin were just a few local players who went on to international acclaim. Our gang had some good players, Billy and Anthony Screen both became professionals, Tony (Gypo) Williams had trials for a number of clubs, West Ham included, Peter Popham was really good, but any thought of him making it went awry one afternoon down Ashleigh Road when he got his leg broken in a nasty tackle. Bobby Smitham was tricky, he turned into a good player when he got a bit older and stronger, but as a kid was considered too small, and was overlooked by the Swansea Schoolboys. The one who proved to be the best though was Gypo's younger brother Stephen. He was running rings around grown men when he was little more than a toddler. You would have expected him to go right to the top, especially when he was snapped up by Arsenal. He progressed to be captain of an Arsenal youth team that included many of the players who were in the Double-winning side of 1971. Then his father (and mentor) died in tragic circumstances. I don't know if this had anything to do with it, but his form, and perhaps, application dipped afterwards. Of course we all supported the Swans, but we were rarely, if ever, treated to top-flight football down the Vetch. In fact, we seemed to be doomed to mid table in Division 2. Then something strange happened, and for our lot it was the greatest footballing thing that had ever come our way, it was the 1963/64 F.A. Cup run. It all started innocuously, a 4-1 win against lowly Barrow in the Third Round. The next tie was against Sheffield United at Hillsborough. This was tough, but Swans managed a draw up there. In the replay at a packed Vetch Field, Swans hammered United 4-0. There was Cup fever in the air after that, and when Swans drew Stoke in the Fifth Round loads of Jacks made the pilgrimage to the Potteries for the game, myself include. I jumped the train, had to, I could only afford the ticket to the game. Luckily, this didn't cause any problem, and again we came away with a draw (2-2). The Vetch was heaving for the replay. If ever a crowd carried a team to victory surely this was it. Swans won 2-0. I think local lad Herbie Williams got one with a thunderbolt free kick. We're in the quarter-finals.

Everyone in town listened in anticipation for the draw. Swans name came out after Liverpool. Yes the Liverpool of Shankly, Ian St. John, Roger Hunt, Ron Yeats and Peter Thompson. The only connection us boys had with these household names is when we were pretending to be them in a game up St. Joseph's Park. Not many held out much hope for the lads, but hey, we're there.

Thousands left town that morning. I wasn't one of them. We waited anxiously for any snippets of information that came filtering through. Incredibly Swans were holding their own against Anfield's finest. Then it got even better. We fucking beat them 2-1. Unbelievable. In the Sunday papers the next day, every report gave Swans keeper Noel Dwyer ten out of ten. Many say to this day it was the most remarkable display of trench war goalkeeping ever seen. But he wasn't on his own out there, all the boys played out of their skins.

The Swansea Evening Post was full of the Cup run. One day it was manager Trevor Morris talking up their chances, and extolling the virtues of team spirit. The next it was team coach Walter Robbins pictured holding a football under the headline 'As sure as I'm holding this ball we will win the cup' or words to that effect. There were player profiles as well. We had our own connection with some of them. Reggie Draper, whose name wasn't Reggie (he was given that nickname when he was a small kid. He'd bomb around on his pushbike and people would say "look out its Reg Harris". Reg Harris was a top British cyclist) had a brother in the team. Derek Draper was our inspirational inside forward. His nickname was Didi, a reference to the great Brazilian forward. Defender Brian Purcell was a cousin of Terry Purcell who was in my class at school. There were imports in the team, but it definitely had the feel of a local team back then.

It seemed like the whole town went to the Semi-Final at Villa Park. We got lucky in the draw. Preston North End were in our division, so there couldn't have been much between us on paper, and taking into account the way we had been performing, confidence was sky high. High anxiety reigned in our street that Saturday afternoon. We were out there kicking a ball about, waiting for news. A kid appears "Swans are one up at half time!" We were 45 minutes from Wembley, 45 minutes from the greatest moment in the history of Swansea Town AFC, 45 minutes from the greatest moment in our lives. Preston pulled one back, and it was nip and tuck all the way. Then with next to no time remaining, in atrocious conditions, the Preston defender Tony Singleton hoofed a ball, in no particular direction. It took off into a rainy sky, came down with snow on it, and careered over Noel Dwyers outstretched hands into the net. What a gutter. We were all heartbroken. Spare a thought for inside forward Jimmy McLaughlin. This Irish forward had been instrumental in our march forward in the cup, imagine how he must have felt, not only did he score our goal; he hit the woodwork three times. We'd fallen at the last. The long suffering Swans supporter would have to wait a few more years, and for the arrival of John Toshack at the Vetch before they sniffed success again. With a team consisting of Welsh lads Jonathon Charles, Robby James, Allan Curtis and Wyndham Evans, Tosh did the unimaginable; he took the Swans to the old First Division.

I must have learned something at the grammar school because back at St. J's, I'm so far in front of the others that they bump me up a class. Either that or there are some thick fuckers here. So in essence,

I'm learning the final year curriculum one year early, and I'm still top of the class, which helped a little when I got into trouble I guess, but I was still getting my fair share of the old corporal. I'd taken up with another miscreant who'd been expelled from elsewhere: Leonard George Cullen, who was trouble. Early on he had this plan, his father would deposit £5 a week into Leonard's bank savings card, most kids got a few bob off their parents to put into this scheme, normally four or five bob a week, which would be divvied up at Christmas, so five pounds was quite a lot, ten fags only cost two bob back then, so to a kid a fiver was a fortune. Leonard's plan was to nick the old man's fiver, and for me to forge a signature on his card. Sounds easy. In school we had these old-fashioned pens that you had to dip into an inkwell, messy fucking things they were, I was about to sign the card with one of these, when a huge blob of ink ran off onto the bank card. What a mess. It was raining outside, so we decided to 'on purpose' drop the card and stamp on it, and then back to the radiator to dry it out. Jackson Pollock would have been proud of our handy work, Leonard's old man wasn't so impressed, and he wasn't daft. He told Len that in the morning he'd be going down the school to sort it out. Leonard panicked and decided to 'go on the run' this entailed taking up residence in a Douglas builder's bus that was parked opposite Monty's Café where we spent most of our time. I took some grub over for him. This lasted two cold nights. On the third morning us two useless 'aipoths' were on the flipper machine in Monty's when he spots his parents getting out of a car and approaching. He ducked behind the machine. His parents asked "Have you seen our Leonard?" I said no, but my eyes gave the game away. His mother spotted him, grabbed him by the ear and dragged him out of the café. Leonard's father Bernard was a well respected man in the hardest circles of Swansea life, but I'd rather face him than his mother, I can tell you.

Another example of how Leonard's schemes backfired was the school leaving exam. The teachers did all they could to help the boys get through and although there was a science exam, there was no science facility in our school, so the teachers let everyone know 'what to expect' on the theory side of the test. If you could get through that part of it, you'd get a pass. Leonard somehow got hold of the paper from the teacher's desk. Armed with this knowledge Leonard achieved a mark the teachers wouldn't have got. When it came time for us to get the results, most of us had passed, the teacher said "and we have a scientific genius in our midst, Cullen come here". This was Jack Hartigan feared by many a schoolboy, who'd make it absolutely clear he hated Leonard, whenever he got the chance. He marched Leonard back to sit the test again. This time instead of the 70 percent he got first time around he scored exactly ZERO. Leonard got what was inevitably coming to him. But that was that. In a couple of week's time he'd be leaving school to take up a job as a career criminal.

Killer Morgan was another of my colleagues around this time. He was about my age, but I don't remember him attending any school, ever. Killer gained his name when, after winning a fight, he left the defeated boy lying across a railway line. It was soon evident to all, that this particular line had been closed for a couple of years, so the vanquished lad was in no danger, but 'Killer' got stuck with this moniker, and it was a hard one to live up to. Killer's game was a mixture of shoplifting and walk-in thefts, by day anyway. He liked to enter a pub the minute it opened, when, by his way of thinking, the landlord always had something to do. Sounds daft, but he was successful at getting hold of fags, spirits and sometimes even the 'float' out of the till. I suppose at night he had something dodgy going on as well. Killer had a colostomy bag fitted from a very early age, and wasn't embarrassed about it, or where he'd empty it. Whatever the reason for the bag, I knew, even at that young age, drinking alcohol wasn't a help. But Killer drank from his youth, all the way up to his early death. Doctors had obviously warned him of the dangers, but his whole personality was centred around him being a game lad who wouldn't shy away from any pursuit with an edge of danger involved, and with his obvious internal problems, drinking was one of them. He made me laugh one afternoon in the Gower pub, he was selling a pair of shoes to this woman, she was half pissed, but even so, a blind person could see that they were both left footed shoes. Not her. She forced them on, said, "They'll be all right, just need to be broken in a bit," and gave Killer the money.

My last year at school should have been a breeze, and in many ways it was. I'd done all that years work the previous year so was given all the good jobs that were available: corridor boy, which meant ringing a bell whilst running through the school at full tilt to signify a change of lessons, running down the shop to get fags for the teachers and, the best, taking messages to Sister Angela down the girls school, which was separated from the boys. It was also my task to call out the teacher to dole out the cane when wrongdoers had been sent 'up the corridor' for a beating. If some little kid came up there and it was Jack Hartigan's turn with the bamboo, I'd make a noise similar to a caning, and tell them to go back to their class blowing their little mitts. Lunchtime I'd be a dinner monitor, you would help the women over the dinner hall, and at the end of the sitting you could eat as much as you wanted. Some would sniff at school dinners, I loved them, out of all the food scooped out up there, Semolina was the only thing I couldn't swallow. Every morning I'd be up at seven, out soon after to deliver the papers, then over to Ivor's for three or five Woodbine to carry me through the day, then school kept me busy until 3:45pm, when I had to deliver the early Evening Post, home after that, quick tea, over the quarry for football, then out and about looking for trouble or girls with Dai Badger and Percy Beddows. On a Saturday night I used to sell The South Wales Echo, the local pink paper for sports fans, so I was never idle. I had these little jobs, and was always looking for others, running errands, cutting grass, I even put my name down to be an altar boy, no money in that you'd think, but when I heard that Leonard had his name down for it, I guessed there must be a fiddle somewhere along the line. But then as now, I never had any money, and I didn't drink or gamble then.

Priests at St. Joseph's Church must have noticed a decline in the number of 14 and 15-year-old boys attending confession. We were meant to go at least once a week, no one I knew ever went anymore, to get around this you'd find out off a younger kid or maybe a girl, which priest had been conducting the confessions the previous Friday. With that name fixed in your head you were ready for the very real prospect of being singled out by a teacher who would ask "Who's been to confession this week?" All hands aloft, Leonard Cullen's among them. The teacher would then single out a pupil and ask what time they went, and who did they see? The 'who did you see' bit was easy, but if the time you said coincided with the time this teacher was there praying for salvation, and it was a lie, look out. Anyway the church seemed to be concerned about the lack of attendance from said age group, so devised a plan to bring the confessional to you. Father Findlay was the venerable chap who got the ball rolling. He turned up one Friday afternoon and set up his stall in an empty classroom. It was either going to be me or Gally who were going to go first, because at that time it was considered that we had the least to lose by missing a lesson. Gally used to go to mass and confession back then, so he didn't need as much saving as me, so I was first. This was slightly different from church confession, there the priest was behind a screen, and here you were face to face with your confessor. Fuck it, let's get it over with.

The first question he asked didn't come from any religious text that we'd ever learnt. He pulled out his cigarettes, lit one up and said "You smoke don't you?" Obviously you'd reply "No Father" he wasn't having that. "Have one if you want" Is this guy having me on or what. "It's OK, take one" Why not I thought, he was smoking Senior Service, top of the range. So I smoked my fag whilst chatting away, said my confession, picked up my penance and off I went. I told the boys and as you can imagine for the next few weeks anyway, our class was closer to the Lord than ever before,

I stuck with Percy Beddows, especially when he claimed he knew of a girl who took on all comers. We went along there one evening to see which way the land was lying and joined the queue. This was not on some bombsite or over the beach, but right there in the passageway of this game girl's house. Some say, that on occasions, while she was entertaining the troops, her father would bellow from the front room "Hurry up out there, I want my tea." As you can imagine this girl wasn't big on looks, but hey, who learns to ride a bike on a Claude Butler? I have no big memory of this event, just glad to get it out of the way. I dressed it up a bit when I related it at school, to a class full of virgins though. They hung on my every word. But if truth is told it was shite. One thing though, if I was ever asked "Do you remember your first time?" I can answer "Well if I ever forget, there'll be ten others who can remind me." A few years later, when I was picking potatoes down on Turnbull's farm, I went for a drink with one of the other pickers. His wife turned up at the pub later, and it was that same girl. They seemed to be getting on all right. Odd couple though, he was like a gypsies dog while she carried plenty of condition. She didn't know me. Why should she, out of the hundreds? Her teeth were an unpleasant sight I remember, seemed to have some green vegetation growing in there.

Percy Beddows was the second best fighter in school. Try as he might, he couldn't topple Ken Jones and grab the crown. Percy had left school by now, and was working for a coffin maker on Oystermouth Road, right beside the nick. Whenever we went out at night Percy carried a bit of a reputation with him and consequently was forever getting into scraps. Win or lose he'd always put up a good show, but if he came off second best and was marked up a bit, he made us swear that if his father asked what happened, we were to say Percy had won, otherwise his father would have given him another hiding. I must have been fit back then. I was on a curfew of sorts and had to be home by a certain time, always cutting this fine; I had to run up Constitution Hill most nights. This a fucking steep incline in the centre of Swansea, in fact when they had stages of the Tour of Britain running through Swansea they had to bike it up there. When they swung the corner at the bottom of the hill and saw what was in front of them, en masse, you could hear 'oh fuck' from these gallant pedallers. I was always at loggerheads with my old man now, and couldn't wait to leave school myself and clear off somehow.

2. In the Army Now

I started the procedure of clearing off by foolishly going to the Army Information Office in Castle Street. Before you know it I'm sitting a test to enlist. I had a fast head in those days, and the test was easy. A couple of weeks later I'm back to find out the results. I could tell by the guy's reaction that I'd done well, he told me the options open to me, and before you know it I'm signed up to join the Royal Army Pay Corps. How hard can this be? Working out people's pay, a piece of cake, a cushy number, thought I, WRONG. I was dispatched to a place called Worthy Down, near Winchester in Hants and I hated it from the start. Cleaning, preening, bulling, drilling, scrubbing floors, running and jumping. You got used to that a bit, but the schoolwork was harder than school. Bookkeeping, map reading, geography all things I couldn't get my head around. I'd palled up with a boy from Llanelli called Con, we both signed up for the rugby, but the team was shite, and we'd get hammered regular. Even when it came time to pick a weekend sport, I got it wrong. For some reason I chose canoeing, how hard can that be? Well the army is meant to make a man of you, so there was none of this meandering along a lazy river where the warm wind blows; it was the Exe, Wye and Severn in the dead of winter. On one outing on the Wye, as the grown up N.C.O. was leaving the canoe he and I were sharing, he managed to dislodge the boat from the bank, and there am I floating toward the middle of the rapid river, backwards. I stretched my arm out backwards to retrieve his paddle, in the process I capsized the canoe, everyone was shouting this that and the other from the bank, I had hold of the canoe, but I would never have got me and it back to the bank, so I let it go, and swam for safety. When I was safely ashore the N.C.O. Larry Pickard said, "Why didn't you save the boat?" He actually had the hump. Later on we spotted the remains of our canoe in a thousand pieces downstream, it had been dragged in to the weir.

Whenever people mention the Rhone River in France, I always pipe up "I canoed on the Rhone, from Lyon to Avignon" as if it were some romantic interlude in my life, it was horrible graft. This was my first time abroad, and although I have some good memories of it, they are superseded by the sheer arduousness of all that paddling. There was a minor road accident during which some things got misplaced' including my passport, there was talk of me being left behind to wait for a replacement, this never happened though, and I paddled till the end. Having moaned so much, I should tell you that arriving at the bridge at Avignon by boat is a fabulous experience. Back in camp my schoolwork wasn't improving but the other parts of the regime were getting easier. I quite liked the drilling, the gym work was getting better, we nicked a few footballers for the rugby team and things were looking up, and my running had improved to such an extent that it would probably got me into the cross country team anytime soon (cross country was at weekends, no more canoeing) but I still wanted out. This time the old man wasn't having it at all. He was right again. But I pressurised my mother, and in the end, my dad washed his hands of it. So I'd managed eight or nine months serving her majesty. Thinking back, it would have been mighty different now if I'd stayed put, but I was fifteen and being a soldier was about the unhippest thing in the world. When I was there the older lads would talk of exotic postings overseas, cushy jobs in all corners of empire, and I thought for a very short time that if I'd stuck it out I would eventually be on easy street. One morning I was reading a piece in the paper about soldiers killed in Northern Ireland, two of them were from the Pay Corps, pen pushing doesn't exclude you from the bullet of the enemy, if you're in uniform, you're a target. Nowadays, with so much military action all over the globe, I doubt anywhere can be classed as a cushy posting.

Back in civvy street, the old man has read me the riot act, get a job, and pay digs money every week or else. I got a job clerking in the British Transport Docks board, in the dredging department. I didn't know then, and still don't know, exactly what the function of the Dredgers were, but they seemed to be playing a vital part in ensuring that sand was moved from one place to another. My boss was Captain Armstrong, an old salt, who didn't seem to know what I was doing there either. He was all right though. I did have a few tasks to carry out, sending messages back and forth to the ships, and taking the odd telephone call, but that was it. There was an old typewriter in my little cubby-hole. It didn't work, and the last person to resurrect this machine was me, but through a mixture of boredom and a lack of fags, I gave it a go and eventually got it operating. On this I would compose shite poetry and send it off to this girl I'd met in Worthy Down. The rest of the time I'd go walk around in the town centre.

I had little or no fashion sense back then, I loved soul music though and would go round Dai Badger's to listen to our fave Stax performers, Otis, Rufus and Carla Thomas, Booker T and everyone's favourites on the dance floor Sam and Dave and Wilson Pickett. Some of my contemporaries had a little bit of a mod thing going on as well, Georgie Thomas would utilise his father's clothes to cut a dash. His brother Tom, Paul Grey, Johnny Wilson, Bello and I suppose Kingo were one little posse, another camp had Tony Thomas, Glen Ellis and others, Tony's' brother Vince was 'Top Face' for me. He'd been to London, knew about the Flamingo and that, and what 'Blue Beat' was all about. Vincent, Mudge and Jiffy Pennock were the elder statesmen of the Mod thing. There was one guy who I never got to know, Vincent and those knew him, Tony did as well, but I never met him personally, but I saw him one Sunday afternoon strolling along Lion Street. His name was Bernard Black, and I had never seen anyone so well dressed in my life. He must have looked out of place in this part of town, but he had on an immaculately tailored suit, a shirt with a detachable collar, collar studs, club tie, tie pin, cuff links, a rolled umbrella and the shiniest shoes I'd seen outside a sergeant major's locker. If I aspired to anything right then, it was to be able to dress like this guy. Don't think I quite made it, but I looked all right. There was a little team of scooter boys as well, Dai Holmes, Harty, the other Bello, with Corgi riding pillion, they'd be buzzing round on the Lambrettas in their Parkas. More often or not all these different 'gangs' would land up in the same venue. There wasn't that much choice. I got bored at the dredging office, and had the opportunity to join Jackson the Tailors. The money stunk, but you could get your three-button, single-breasted, 14-inch vent with ticket pocket mohair jacket, and your parallel 12-inch bottom mohair trousers for a song. No money in the pockets, but cutting a dash. Search around the 'old man' shoe shop in Union Street for a pair of Brogues, or better still pair of black Oxfords, and you're all set.

There were a few places to go and dance to all this soul and ska stuff, most notably the Glanmore jazz club, where every now and then a visiting artist would appear, the biggest crowd pleasers were Ronnie Jones and the Q set, and The Alan Bown Set. Ronnie, who was a black American dude, would kick up a storm doing covers of our favourite tunes, whereas the Bown Set would do more original stuff, and, I think nursed hopes of a rise to a higher league. It never happened for them though, or for that matter for their fabulous singer Jess Roden. I believe he even had a go at becoming the singer for The Doors, What chance you got there? There were local acts to entertain us as well. Best of these had to be the Eyes of Blue. Apparently they'd won one of those NME competitions. These were nationwide events, and if I'm not mistaken the 'Eyes' beat Yes into second place. The Eyes looked like pop stars to a man – and they could really play. Ritchie, Gaz, Taff, Wyndham, Phil Ryan and Pugwash are the incarnation I remember. They were superb, and for the time, happening. Girls loved them. They got a deal and were set for take-off. Then someone must have taken too much acid or something. The single they released 'Supermarket Full of Cans' was atrocious. I'm not sure if that was the death knell for the 'Eyes' but they never made it. They were terrific live. Bad management done for them I guess. For other live talent St. Benedict's was an option. We'd get down there to see The Dream, with Martin Ace and Deke Leonard, who went on to become 'Man', Spiv had a good little group as well, called Human Leg. Tommy Goss fronted a nice little outfit called the John Smith Committee. Tommy was a great singer, and the band was tight enough. Over time Tommy would get his name put up to join numerous bands, and so enhance his career, but nothing came of it. Tommy certainly had something going for him. I believe, in his case, he would have never have left Swansea for long anyway. Too much of a mush.

The West Cross Country Club was another good one for dancing. Cruising along Mumbles Road in Tony's frog-eyed Sprite car, smoking spliff and laughing our bollocks off. We're getting further away from Swansea now. And you'd be meeting a different kind of bird too. Don't get me wrong. Nothing wrong with our girls, but this was novel for us, and I guess, for them. Girls love a dance and most of us would be first out there on the floor. Moving further along towards the Gower, we'd be at the Langland Bay Hotel and Redcliffe Hotel in Caswell, where Tony and Stevie Miles had pallied up with some of the locals, who knew how a surfboard worked. There was C.P. Russell, Steve, and Simon, who tragically died in the tide. They were a good bunch, and the lot of us would make the pilgrimage to Crossways outside Bridgend, which was a good dance joint owned by Swansea born, British and European boxing champ Brian Curvis.

I was doing all right in the tailors. The boss liked me, so did the customers, and I was picking up on the measuring of customers for suits. I'd met a girl called Lynne; she was my first proper girlfriend, and although she lived in Blaen-y-Maes, which is a rough old neighbourhood, her family could almost be described as having a middle class lifestyle, owing to the fact they owned a very profitable shop. Her father Roy used to 'get to know' at the dogs, and her mother was a real blonde bombshell, who it was easy to have fantasies about. At the time drink never entered my world, I'd take speed and smoke a bit of spliff, in fact you sort of looked down on the boozers. I just wanted to be 'up' and on the dance floor. Lynne liked a drink, so not to be anti-social I'd have a few halves of lager; this became a lot more at weekends. Lynne and I had been caught in bed together by her parents. They stopped us seeing one another, and this was the beginning of the end of our 'courting', she finished it. I tried to win her back, I even sent her a record of Harry Nilsson singing 'I Wonder who's Kissing Her Now'. Here is a song that would make Stalin cry, but it cut no ice with Lynne. I've got to admit it knocked me for six. I started drinking too much. I even started drinking of lunchtime; I hear it all the time at meetings nowadays, how innocent fun in the pub turns into full-blown dependency in next to no time, and before you know it, it has taken over your whole persona, I blamed it on a broken heart back then, and it would take me another thirty years before I recognised the problem for what it is,. I started missing work, but the boss always bought my excuses, but I was losing interest.

Then along comes Steve Northampton with a plan. He thought it would be great to take a trip to Europe. Why not? I got one of those cardboard passports, and we were off. Our plans weren't really thought through because by the time we hit Calais, I, at least, was skint. So we hitchhiked and bummed around France, up into Germany, without much plan of why or where we were going. I don't think we actually begged, but we relied on the kindness of others. I don't remember which country's border we were at, but they weren't letting us in anyhow, so we had to turn around and head back from whence we came. One scary night, we'd crept into a barn for some kip, after a short while we hear dogs barking and voices, then a torch shines on us held by a guy, who had in his other hand a gun. We put our hands in the air. The guy understood some English and soon realised we were no threat. He invited us in to the farmhouse gave us some grub, washed down with Schnapps and let us go back to the barn to kip. Even our youthful optimism had disappeared by now, so we had to get home. Problem was not many were giving lifts to the likes of us. Steve had a hairstyle like Robert Plant. It was blond, and hadn't been attended to lately, I don't remember bathing that often myself, so we must have looked like a right pair of ne'er do wells. Frustrated by our lack of lifts, we had a row, one of us stormed off, so now I was alone. No money, and, as I soon realised, no passport, Steve had it. Now how's this for luck? Two days later I eventually get a long lift, the guy is going all the way to Paris. He drops me off somewhere in the centre. As I step out of the car I hear "Ray" It's Steve Northampton in all his hippy glory. He's already worked out how, through the Embassy, how we can get repatriated. So, we are on our way home.

I'm in the doghouse with the old man at this stage. So I have to sneak in and clean up while he's out. I've no money, so I went down to Jackson's to see if they owed me any. I couldn't believe the welcome I received. The manager asks where I've been and all that, and then he tells me that in my absence, I'd won a nationwide competition as the best/friendliest salesman in the country, the prize was a fortnight all expenses paid holiday in France. Fuck my luck. It was too late for me to take the prize now. As I wasn't around, they'd given it to the runner up, who came from up north. The boss wanted me back; in fact he made up a story for me. Then the area manager came along and said that, if I wanted they would send me to one of the Oxford Street shops in London and groom me to be a manager, which sounded great to me. Then a week or so later the boss get's the sack. He wasn't 'fiddling' he'd just left some of his mates take suits, with the promise of payment. These geezers might have paid him eventually, but that made no difference, he was gone. The new guy was a different animal all together, and he wasn't having me. Even if I'd shone, my days were numbered with him. So one day I just didn't turn up.

3. Thieving and Drugging

I'm on the dole now, and drinking too much, the old man on my case about rent, my mother lying on my behalf, and no money coming in. At that time Ken Richards enters my life. I'd known of Ken by reputation for a few years, we went to different schools, but he had relatives and friends around our way. Ken was the best footballer of his age group in Swansea. When he was fifteen, the school team he played for swept all before them. They were so good that ten of them went on to make up the Swansea Schoolboy team, and quite a few made the Welsh team. Ken was the odd one out. As good as he was the powers that be couldn't overlook the fact that he was a bad boy. His failure to make these teams obviously destroyed any chance he might have had at becoming a professional footballer. Ken was a thief, no ordinary thief mind, what he could do with a football paled into insignificance when you saw the tricks he could do with carrier bag and baggy anorak. When it came to making things disappear from the retail outlets of Swansea and surrounding area, he had no equal. TVs, stereos, a tray of rings, cameras, watches, you name it. I started hanging out with Ken, not only for the thieving, we were mates. We had a lot in common. We'd talk for hours about revolution, darts, football and the Velvet Underground. The drug scene around Ken wasn't very healthy though, as I'll reveal later.

I tried to be on all sides, dressing and dancing with Tony and the lads, thieving and drugging with Ken. Work had taken a back seat by now, and I was always at loggerheads with the old man. I went to stay with Mavis in his high rise in Brynmelyn, which was cool, if you could cope with his rendition of an old Al Stewart number which was his party piece on the guitar. The 'nickings' were cropping up with regularity now. The drugs were fun, but now due to the lack of a few quid, you'd be mixing Mandrax, Secanol or Tuinol with the drink. You might have thought yourself invisible when you went out 'shopping' in that state, but you stuck out like Mumbles lighthouse to the store detectives. It didn't help that these people knew you by your first name either. What was the point of legging it? They'd just call the cops, give them your name, tell them what you nicked, and you're nicked. Back then people were being convicted of big offences on peoples say so. The Magistrate is never going to take your word against a store detective. So I wasn't far off a prison sentence myself. I managed to get away from it somewhat when I met Edie, she was having a rough time with some boy friend when I first saw her, he'd be ignoring her, and me and her would throw darts, flirt around the oche, and dance like mad at the West Cross.

A couple of weeks later we were stepping out. It was great, Edie was very outdoorsy, she swam butterfly for Wales, played netball at a high standard, and loved to shag. We had some good times, got a flat together, but I was always skint. I didn't want to get nicked now, apart from the lack of money, I was doing all right. But she worked you see, they get a bit resentful, and before you know it she's gone back to her folks. Well we all knew that's the beginning of the end. And so it was.

Pressure was building on all sides for me to get a job, and I found one. They were taking down these towers over in Llandarcy, and I'm on the demolition team. There seemed to be gas everywhere around and about, because at least once a day a siren would go off, and everyone would abandon ship. Some of these disruptions went on for so long we had time to go to the pub. Edie worked here, in the offices. She was friendly, but nothing else, I suggested a quick one behind the Gasometer, but she acted as if she didn't understand. Yeah, remember what I said about her and the great outdoors. On about the third day, they've got us working in the bowels of some huge silo thing, I was whistling away merrily, when a big brick, which has been dislodged from the top of this monstrosity hurtles earthward, in the process, it collides with my hard hat, fractures my arm, and crushes two of my toes. I was lucky. Who said hard work never killed anyone. TWATS. So my latest career move has been scuppered. Edie called at my mothers and gave me sympathy shag, fair play to her; she probably had a new geezer by now, so it was just the one off. It won't be long before I'm back on the bag, hanging round at Kens or accompanying Leonard Cullen on his forays into anything that's not nailed down.

All my life I'd considered my old man to be a socialist and an atheist. Our family, apart from dad, were Catholic, and from what I could gather, they all believed in God. My old man wasn't having any of that, thank you very much, so it was somewhat of a surprise when I heard he was going to become a catholic himself. We must have been talking at the time, because he confided to me the reason behind this drastic transformation. St Joseph's School, our family's alma mater, was in need of a caretaker; my father was in need of a job. The problem was that the school only employed Catholics. I knew this to be true as regards the teaching staff, but for coal shovelling? Do me a favour. But rules are rules, so if he wanted the gig, he'd have to get baptised. Fair play to the old man, he's always had a job, and he wanted this one, and the house that went with it, so he went through with the ceremony, and got the job. When he'd left the 'Valleys' and come to Swansea, he'd gotten a job at the Mackworth Hotel, that's where he met my mother. He was a barman there, so capturing a job in the Civil Service, which he did do soon afterwards, was obviously a step forward. He was on the Pneumoconiosis Panel for a few years, this place dealt with miners who had contracted this disease after years breathing in the shitty air down the pit. Then a move to the DHSS, which again, I guess, was an upward step. I seem to remember him being up to his neck in union activity at this time as well, so what happened. He was obviously quite ambitious, took the work seriously etc, so how come he's now a caretaker. I'll never get to the bottom of it, but know one thing for sure. When he was working in the Pensions department at the DHSS he held a job that could be comparable to any teaching post, now of course he'd dropped down the social ladder, and whereas before the teachers could be considered as peers, they were now of course his bosses. This must have hurt the pride, but it wasn't something he'd ever admit to.

I can't believe that he'd had a visitation from the Lord, and his humour toward me had improved on the advice of a higher power, but around this time we were on reasonable terms. He was friendly with another caretaker called Aubrey Maynard. I knew Aubrey by sight; his brother Billy owned the local fruit and veg shop on Carmarthen Road. Anyway, over a pint Aubrey and my father got to talking about me, and my lack of work. Aubrey suggested that I apply for the job as caretaker at Dan-Y-Graig School, which is across the River Tawe from where we live, and a place I was not too familiar with. I went there for an interview and got the job. Fair play to Aubrey, he was getting on a bit by now, and he had a dodgy leg, but he came over there with me and talked me through the finer points of boiler maintenance. In fact he lit the thing for me, all the time talking me through the process. Then I was left to my own devices. On about day three, the fucking fire went out. Try as I might, I couldn't for the life of me re-ignite the damn thing. I tried everything. I couldn't raise Aubrey, none of my mates had any ideas, and I was bolloxed. What does a man do when the going gets tough? He legs it. I couldn't be arsed at the time. I just went to the pub. I kept a low profile the rest of that day. The next afternoon, there it was, all over the Evening Post 'Children sent home from freezing school' The article went on to quote one lady as saying "They've got this young man working here, and I don't think he knows what he doing." Darn tooting I don't.

Bryan Gallivan used to sit beside me at school. Somehow he'd become a sought-after roadie. When he came home to Swansea he'd regale us with tales of the Chass club, and 'Strat' (Tony Stratton Smith) and nights down the Marquee. The Marquee is a holy grail for any aspiring Mod, and I would love to go there myself. Gally was living in London and working with a group called Van der Graf Generator, who were on tour with Geordie folksters Lindisfarne. He invited me along. It soon became apparent that out of the two, Lindisfarne were the more 'likely' Van der Graf were like toff hippies, very light on laughs, whereas, the Lindisfarne boys, were well up for the crack. They could all play, and eventually did gain national recognition. 'Fog on the Tyne 'was very big for them.

But the best times with Gally was on his days off. He always had some plan, and every morning, he'd spike you with acid. This was good clean acid. You could go anywhere on it. We went to the zoo, I've never paid so much attention to our furry friends, but I recommend it. We went to gigs, the movies, all over the shop under the influence. Gally had a flat in Powys Square. I got lucky with the girl downstairs on about the second night. Gally said "Don't get carried away, I think she's working her way through the building."

One evening we're hanging out, a bang on the door, Gally let's in two students who lived upstairs I guess. They wanted to know if Gall would swap them some acid for what they had, dope tea. Not much of a deal you'll agree, but Gally is a generous soul. These two come back later with their herbal concoction. I want nothing to do with it. After some pressure I relented. I'd been grooving along nicely up till this point. Then my world collapsed around me. I was on a bad trip. It was not fucking nice. I wanted to jump off the balcony to get rid of the worst horrors I'd ever had. Gally grabbed me. He literally had to hold on to my sorry arse for a couple of hours, until I landed. Moments later, the dope twats from upstairs, who Gally had shown the door earlier, were hammering the door down. They were freaking out now. "Leave the twats out there to suffer. Fucking hippies."

On one of my last outings with Gally we had an odd encounter. By now he'd left Van der Graf Generator, and was employed by none other than ace axe man Jeff Beck. He took me over the rehearsal place with him. Beck is obviously a legend to my mates and me. He was in The Yardbirds, and had had Rod the Mod singing in one of his bands. I stood in the corner, out of harm's way watching Beck as he manipulated his guitar to produce shit-hot blues music. In his band at that time was Bob Tench on vocals, and the formidable Cozy Powell on drums. Gally had done his bit for rock and roll that night, so we were off to the pub. He pulled up the van at a red light, a Rolls Royce pulled up beside us. The window of the Roller slowly opened, and then a figure appeared from within holding a water pistol. It was Keith Moon. He had us pull over. He asked Gally if this was a band's van. Gally told him about Beck. Moon asked after Jeff Beck's well being, and then invited us to a club.

At the door of said club Moon was greeted like a star, which he was, but inside it soon became apparent that he's totally bonkers. He's all over the gaff, dancing, shouting and bawling and annoying women. One group of girls were having nothing to do with him, whoever he was, and they made this double clear to him. Moon got a bit nasty then and his chauffeur had to pull him away. He eventually joined our lot in a booth. Some food arrived for him; he didn't even look at it. He soon got bored with this arrangement and promptly jumped onto the table and started dancing over the plates. I think someone came over and told him to calm down, but he's not going to listen to any of that. Is he? Gally was our governor, and he'd had enough of all this shit, so he got us out of there, and took us to the pub, which was much safer, and a lot more fun. He could get you murdered that Moonie.

4. On Remand

Apart from that freak-out incident I had a good time in London, and thought I might move there soon. But for now I'm back on the Swansea merry-go-round. Then I get nicked twice in a week. You don't really want bail if you've been nicked twice in a week whilst on a suspended sentence. Why? Because everyone will think you're a grass. I know today some people get bail on murder charges, but then it was the norm to be held if you were already on bail for another offence, however small. I got remanded in custody. On remand you're in the cell all the time, it was all right for me, I could get on with a bit of reading, nothing heavy, just time swallowing crime novels, you could have a newspaper sent in to keep up with the news and you had the crossword. Not so good for Hoskins though. He couldn't read and write, I gave him help in that department. I'd help him compose letters to his wife. The embarrassing part was reading out her replies. Must have made him happy though, he'd leave my cell singing 'And I Love Her So' or some other Jim Reeves song, very badly.

If you had to be in the nick, this was the place to be in, if you were a boy around town. It was like the pub, without the girls or the drink. Apart from the Valley boys, you'd know everyone in there. Hank, Kingo, Dicky and Zoogs running the gym, Big Dai Murdoch, Mickey Baker, George White the Glasgow Rangers supporter, who made me take a picture of Kenny Dalgliesh off my cell wall, Sharpy, whose cell you couldn't enter for the fear of catching Silicoses from the dust exuded by his constant sandpapering of his matchstick creations. I had a good cell mate, Dai Crocker, we played cards and draughts to while away the hours, and we even had a keep fit regime. I think Dai had done the lot, Borstal, Detention Centre and now, not for the first time, prison. So the keep fit thing was normal for him, granted in other institutions he had use of a gym, in here we did our push ups, sit ups and burpees on the cell floor, and, again it ate up some time. Another thing you soon find out is that all is not what it appears. The big hard man walking around the remand wing, you find out, after he's been sentenced, and disappeared down below, turns out to have been there for robbing and beating up old women, or worse. On the other hand, a bloke about twenty was in there for shagging his bird, she was fifteen and three quarters, but he was branded a nonce by some dull cunts, and set upon. The major antagonist in this attack was a bloke who was awaiting trial for rape, but he was 'one of the boys', and the general consensus was 'She asked for it'. He got found guilty. The guy who was caught with his girlfriend got a sentence too, but I believe he's still married to the girl.

I had one unhappy encounter in there though. The remand wing was easy going. You'd be in and out of each others cells all the time. One morning I'm in George White's talking cobblers when the screw pulls the door closed locking me in the wrong cell. I thought nothing of it, once they do the count, I thought, they see the mistake and put it right. The screw let me out all right, but as I passed him, he landed a right-hander straight on my jaw. Nearly sparked me out it did. This horrible Bastard was called 'Nicker' Price. Old-school screw, hobnailed boots, bulled-up toecap and guardsman style slashed peak on his hat. I heard later that he got his name not for nicking cons, but for nicking off cons. I wouldn't be surprised. I kept out of his way after that, until that is, after a trip to the dentist when I was haemorrhaging blood all evening in the recreation room. This no–good cunt wouldn't let me go to the medic and get it seen to. So I had to sit there swallowing blood all evening. I used to pray that something horrible would happen to this no–good twat. It did. Apparently he got nicked for robbing the prisoners' grub and selling it on the outside. Hooray. Hope he's fucking dead after suffering excruciating pain.

There's no work on the remand wing, so finding ways to ease the boredom was a problem. You could have a visit every day, and the visitors could bring you provisions from the outside, but it was still a long day. Up in the morning the first thing you'd check was if any of the other boys had been captured overnight. Gary Taylor made an appearance. No stranger to the inside of a cell, Gary was a career criminal. On release from prison he'd be up to no good immediately, I don't mean the following day or week either; he'd be at it on the way home from the nick. I was standing in a pub one afternoon talking to Gary and others, Gary disappeared never to return. When the landlord returned from the cellar we soon knew why, the till had been rifled of every penny. Gary's confinement this time was down to breaking and entering a chemist shop (now being called canteens). He wasn't too pleased because this sort of behaviour had been targeted by the old bill as something that's getting out of control, so Gary, with two arms and legs length of previous, was expecting a hammering from the beak. He was housed in the next cell to mine. A couple of days into his stay, a thump, thump, thump began resonating from his cell. Best not to ask. It turns out that he'd smuggled a barbell and a weight from the gym and was tunnelling his way out through the twelve-inch wall, two storeys up. The remand wing was so busy that summer that three to a cell was the order of business, this worked in Gary's favour. Two beds running along both walls was the norm. But this overcrowding had enabled him to position his bed across the back wall facing the street. I don't know where the nightshift screws were during this. The noise was fucking loud, every night bang, bang, bang. Everyone on the landing seemed to know what was happening, and when cell searches were announced I for one thought the game was up for Gary. The screws entered his peter, he said, "Fair cop, there's a hole in the wall" to which the screw said, "Yeah, we've heard that one before" and walked out of the cell. Every morning, walking by his cell, it was all you could do not to look in that direction. I must admit I had seen the hole in its latter stages, and you could see the outside wall through it. Fuck knows what occurred after that, someone must have grassed because Gary got tumbled. He had six months added to his sentence, was put in the stripes of an escapee, and was accompanied by screws everywhere he went, and was searched about 50 times a day. Just to make matters worse, the long sentence he was expecting didn't materialise. I wouldn't say it was a waste of time though; it kept many a con amused. Gary died young.

Trouble was brewing over in 'D' Hall. This is where they house cons on their first visit to the nick. I'd missed it because I'd been on remand for so long they probably thought I'd already met my fair share of bad influences. What with all the barbiturates flying around outside, it was inevitable that some would find their way into the nick, usually through the remand wing. Before the powers cottoned on, one way of doing it was to load up a works (hypodermic) with diluted downers, and inject the contents through the plastic top of a bottle of squash. Anyway, when this arrived in 'D' hall someone (it was probably Kingo) had the bright idea of spiking the screws' tea with it. Needless to say, after tea break the screws were dropping like flies. Deep sleep was induced. All through the night, the cons over there had a right old knees up. When the shift changed next morning, the new screws were greeted by the sight of their colleagues pole axed all over the wing. This is serious shit. Whether he was guilty or not, Kingo became the target. The way I heard it was, they came at him, and he picked up a mop. And landed a beauty right on an advancing screw's chin. He was quickly overpowered however, and was given a right good hiding, which included a broken jaw,

It's so boring down the nick that a project or two are always a good call. Some make knick knacks. Some study or do crosswords, and a lot of folks down there kill time talking absolute bollocks about girls they have not shagged and big jobs they'd never been on, nothing so mundane for Dicky and Zoogs in the gym. They hadn't been wasting time. They'd been productive. They were manufacturing homemade hooch. Everything was in place for this drink to come out of hiding when one Dai Murdoch became a bit impatient, and attempted to take a bottle back to his cell. Within sight of his goal, Dai let's slip of the bottle, which goes landing wise, and smashes to pieces. I would have drunk it, so would plenty of others, but the smell of it was appalling. To make it worse the screws got wise to it, and as far as I know that was the end of the Xmas hooch.

After serving three months on remand I was taken to court. I was hoping to go home that day on time served, the judge weren't having it, six months. He said, so it's back to the nick to serve the last month. Now I'm in the real prison for the first time. Any optimism that had been present on the remand wing was washed away with the reality of having to serve one's time. If you had a month to go, you'd better keep that to yourself. I managed to get a job on the Works party; this was just doing maintenance and painting around the place. It kept you out of the cell, and if the civvy screws wanted to do a bit of overtime, you worked in the night too. Staying out of one's cell was worth a hundred times more than the coppers you would earn. Then it's time to go home. You take with you the vow never to return, and another useful skill, the ability to be pleasant to people you don't even like, especially sociopathic hard nuts.

All promises of 'never again', last until the first piss up, and drug binge. It's not just a case of changing your regime, you could sever ties with the criminal element in your midst, but if you did that you'd never see anyone socially, everyone I knew was at it in some shape or form, so before long you're back to normal, searching for a fiddle or a chance opportunity to make your life easier somehow. I've heard it called 'Like wanking on speed' in other words going nowhere fast, with a very disappointing outcome. The likes of Ken and Leonard must hate the sight of me. There they are going along very nicely, and then I turn up. I'm out and about with Leonard one day; we've made our way into an office where the money (if there is any) should be. He's having a gander about, when the phone rings on the desk beside him, footsteps approach, the two of us dive for cover in a cupboard. A woman enters and answers the phone. We're shitting it in this tight space when she starts to talk. The poor thing had a speech impediment, "Neff, Neff, Nefinatelly" I know it's cruel but holding in the laughter all but killed us. Gratefully she replaced the receiver, and we were out of there. No money of course.

I don't disbelieve these boys for one second, when they tell me about the nice touches they've had. Trouble is I'm never around when these occur. I'm out with Ken late evening, last chance of a few quid before the shops shut. He knows of one he's had previously. At the Co-op in Oxford Street the girls at each paying station emptied the contents of their tills and put them in a paper bag ready for the two guys to come around and collect all the days' takings. So the plan was to get hold of one of these in the food hall. I had to distract the girl. The slightest distraction was enough for Ken, his hands were as fast as Ali's when it came to thieving, so he soon had it up his armpit, and we were away, out the back of the Co-op, through Castle Gardens, down the side of the Castle and down the Strand. We eventually thought it safe enough to stop and check our haul. We opened the bag to reveal two pounds of bacon! I've got to be a jinx. Even when I managed one of my own it almost ends in disaster. A certain jeweller in town had an outside display window, showing off a very smart array of Rolex watches. I'd found out one could open this up with a thin screwdriver. I was with D, I slid the glass back, and he made his move, grabbed the watches, and was gone. This was right in the centre of Town, so no sense in hanging about. We met up soon afterwards; he'd stashed the booty, but now couldn't remember where. Five hours later, with darkness descending, we fell over them, which was a relief. But why is nothing ever straightforward?

While drugs now took much of Ken's time up, we still had some fun. He told me the story about the time he'd nicked a leather football out of a shop window. Ken always nicked a football, nothing new there, but this one was special. He told of how every panel on this ball was a different colour, nothing unusual in that these days, I don't suppose, but back then it must have looked psychedelic. Every club in the country has its player who's dubbed 'he's here, he's there. He's every fucking where' and the Swans were no different. In our case the recipient was wing half Vic Gomersol. Like many players who came to join the Swans from other clubs, Vic stayed on in Swansea when he finished playing. He had some sort of back room job down the Vetch. To cut a long story short, Ken spotted Vic in town and asked if he wanted to buy a football. Vic thought it was a joke until Ken pulled this belter from under his jumper. Vic turned white "where the fuck did you get that?' Ken told him and Vic retorted "We just got that ball made special like, it's to be presented to Ivor Allchurch next week." Well, one mention of Ivor's name was enough for Ken to hand it over, and the ceremony took place as planned. Ivor Allchurch was thought by many, me included, the best player to ever don the Swans shirt. This would make for great arguments in the pub, some for, some against. One or two might even plumb for Mel Charles. Mel was a fabulous player who went off to Arsenal, a few years ago I found myself in his company, and asked him a question he'd probably been asked a million times "Mel, who's the best footballer you've played with, and against?" Without hesitation he replied "There best I've played with is my brother (John Charles, the greatest Welsh player ever) and the best I've played against was Pele." Fucking hell, of course Mel was in the Welsh team that got beaten 1-0 by Brazil in the 1958 World Cup. " I had to mark him," he paused looked around at the company and said, "I didn't do too bad against him" and the people at the table old enough to remember nodded in agreement, "but he was the best I've ever come across." What a story that is to hear on a wet afternoon in a Sandfields pub. Ken thought it would be a great idea for us lot to go on 'tour' This consisted of four of us taking off in a hire car and go on a thieving holiday. In those days loads of the shops would give cash refunds. They could get a little shirty about it, but Glenys was very persuasive, so nine times out of ten-she come up trumps with the cash. We'd hit Marks. Woolies, B.H.S., Littlewoods, and all the other department stores in each town. You're not making fortunes here, but it's a nice way of seeing the country. We managed to eat well, drink well and stay in reasonable accommodation every night. We got nicked one time in Bristol. They all got weighed off the next morning; I on the other hand, had to traipse back and forth to Temple Meads three or four times. I thought it was going to be a custodial, but in the end they decided on a suspended sentence.

5. The Curse of the Drinking Classes

After the Bristol thing, to be on the safe side I got myself another job. There seemed to be tons of factory work going about. By now I'd realised that a career-defining occupation was beyond me. Factory work was the lowest common denominator, apart that is, from the bins. John Locke and I went down to the bin depot to ask about work, our theory for working there was based on this assumption. On the Kingsway in Swansea is the Swan pub, we'd get in there early most days as it was very handy for the Coral betting office, but regardless how early you arrived there, you would never beat the bin men to the bar. They'd be supping away in the Bovega lounge long before you ordered your first drink. "You'll land up on the bins" was the scary scenario teachers would extol when you were messing about in school, so it wasn't exactly a dream ticket, but hey, getting in the pub at opening time has its advantages.

Locky and I went for the interview. It went something like this "Can you start tomorrow?" you'd answer "Yes" and the guy would say "Be here at 6:30" and that was it. Next day we're at the depot waiting to be allocated a truck, the boss says "You two, go over there to Fireball XL5" all the trucks had pet names. Over there we started chatting to our new colleagues "Nice early finish today boys?" I asked "Not bad" he replied "We should be finished by 4 O' clock" Fuck off. I looked at Locky, we both had the same thought, let's get out of here, so we legged it. It turns out that those guys in the Bovega were career bin men, with plenty of years on the clock. I managed to get a job at Mettoys up in Fforestfach, now this place must be desperate for manpower, when I arrive Corgi's working there, as are Hank and Kingo. They put me together with a hand operated fork lift truck, on which I'd transport the raw product to the women on the assembly line, which they'd turn into toys I guess. The other three had jobs on the furnaces into which they'd drop these ingots of metal to be melted down. I didn't fancy that. When I'd pass by there I'd notice red hot molten metal flying all over the place, it looked dangerous to me. Hank and the others didn't seem to care. No wonder, they were on acid most of the time, and if not that, they'd be stoned on something else.

My sex education was added to at this time. I'd spotted this girl hanging around with Kingo. She had a Cher vibe about her (well this is Swansea) and her name was Susan. Kingo didn't seem to be involved with her so I seized the opportunity and asked her out. On the first date it soon became apparent she wasn't one of these "I don't do it on the first date" girls. We went to the Castle cinema. Cinema was a cheap night out them days, even I could afford it, but I insisted we sneak in around the back way. The film was shite so we got straight on to 'necking'. The Castle cinema in those days boasted these loving couples seats, so you didn't have the inconvenience of the armrest getting in the way of the grope. The Berlin Wall wouldn't have stopped this girl. She was completely oblivious to anyone or anything around her, so before you can say "action" we're flat out 'at it' on the floor. This was novel to me; I was intrigued. On subsequent outings we did it in shop doorways, Lewis Lewis store was a favourite, in phone boxes, on buses, over the beach, but never in a bed. In fact, we never did it inside any kind of residence at all. The closest we came was a quick knee trembler outside her front door when I took her home one night.

I must admit to being a bit baffled by this young lady. We hardly spoke to one another, I knew very little about her background apart from where she lived, which is unusual for me, because I thought that my chattiness was one of my best assets, but she wasn't complaining so I went along with it. This went on for at least two months, and we covered plenty of ground the pair of us, then we stopped seeing each other. Rumour has it she decided to accept the offer of an engagement ring from her ex. I saw her outside Marks and Spencer in Swansea a few years back. She looked much the same. When she spotted me she gathered the children (her kids or grandkids?) like a worried mum would have done during the last war, when the air raid siren went off. I don't know what she expected me to do or say to her.

For some unfathomable reason I'd been asked to be a witness for some 'ne'er do well' at the Crown Court. I told my story, no one believed a word, but I'd done my bit. I was well dressed this day as I happened into Sherman's betting shop opposite Swansea hospital. I was talking some bollocks or other with the manager in there, when I was approached by, who I was to find out soon enough, the area manager. "How would fancy a career in the betting shop trade?" he asked, "You're just the type of young man we're looking for". Blimey! This was unbelievable; he hired me on the spot. No interview, no record checks, just turn up on Monday to start the training. I knew quite a bit about betting by now. I'd spend most of my afternoons in one shop or another, so couple that with a decent standard of maths I was soon ready to be placed in a shop of my own.

It was a little shop situated in my manor, very close to my Mother's house. So every morning about eleven I'd stroll through St. Josephs Park and head for 'my shop' Honeymoon period over, it was time to put my mind to the more serious task of finding the 'fiddle'. It soon became apparent that the dog racing held the key. Nowadays the cameras that photograph and record all bets are pretty much foolproof, back then you could get a ten or fifteen second 'edge' This meant that in a dog race you could let them go around at least two corners before you'd quickly put the bet through. If you'd done a little bit of homework, you had a good idea that if so and so hound was leading by then, he should see it out to the line. This should have been played a lot more subtly, and would have been rewarding, but being the dozy git that I am, I'd still be betting on everything else as well. In fact gambling had become fulltime for me by now. After work, home for tea, then up to the dog track, then finish the night off in the Casino. I was a disaster waiting to happen.

The way I was going at it, it was inevitable that the till was going to be short from time to time. For a few months by robbing Peter to pay Paul, and by putting my wages straight into the till I kept on top of it. But it's just a matter of time. One week everything collapsed around me. I started out behind with the till, then the dog thing wasn't playing the game, and I was right down with the takings. I had about £200 when it should have been about £1100. I didn't know where to turn. It sounds like not much dough now, but in the early Seventies it was hard to get a Grand, even for drug dealers, so I was fucked. I left £100 indoors and went up the dogs with the rest. I'm probably the worst judge when it comes dogs, I don't know how the hell it works. Some fellas can talk you through a race before it happens, and when it does happen, they're spot on. I couldn't tell you which one of the six dogs was going to lead up if you held a gun to my head. Fortunately for me, one of these race-reading types was with me this night. It was pissing down. This seemed to only add to his opinion on the outcome of a heat. Following his every word, that night I bet seven out of the eight winners. Impossible. But it happened. I raced back to the shop, put the till straight and went for a curry. The guy came to collect my takings the next morning. After he looked at the bookwork, he knew something didn't add up, but it did.

Two or three weeks later I'm in the shit with the money again. Salvation arrived this time in the form of robbery. I'm on my way through the park one sunny morning when two chaps jump out of the bushes. One of them sets about me, whilst the other grabbed the moneybag. There had been talk of an attempted break in at my house the night before, but the dog wouldn't stop barking. So they must have put it on hold until the next day. I was shaken up, but wasn't exactly heartbroken, as the bag was well 'light' I got the third degree off the old bill. Everyone could smell rat. But hey, I'm the victim here. Hell how many warnings does one person need? It's just a few weeks later, it's a Friday, and the Area Manager pays a surprise visit. Oddly enough, although there's a shortfall, I have it covered mentally. One of the punters owed £70 and I would have made up the rest by Monday, the day it was due. They'd all had enough of me by now, so before I could try and blag my way out of it he said. "If that money is not back here by tomorrow (Saturday) I'm calling the Police." There was no way I could get my hands on it by morning, even after the punter who owed called around with the money. It was time to disappear. I told them at home I'd had enough of it. The next day, with a few belongings in tow, I was on the coach to London.

6. London Calling

Paul Grey one of the boys from Swansea was holed up in Chelsea, so I got in touch. He and a few others had rental accommodation just off the Kings Road. The first night up there I got lucky with a girl. What with all the grief and the fiddling and gambling back in Swansea I hadn't had much time for that sort of business of late, so it made a nice change. We were boozing in the Markham Arms, and got in with these Canadian girls. They were, surprisingly, a good laugh. I gravitated toward the lithe one with the short dark hair. They came back to the flat. This gaff had a huge sitting room, and between the two of us, we covered every inch of it. I wouldn't consider myself an athlete in this department, but this girl was giving off a gym teacher vibe, so I felt I had to make the effort. I was quite happy with the result, and she didn't seem too disappointed, so I was a bit miffed when she uttered: "Pity it didn't last a lot longer, I would have taught you a trick or two." Big headed git. Probably used to shagging Mounties.

The next day, another surprise surfaces, the lads were behind with the rent, and have to do a runner. Paul's friend says he'll put us up at his place, so we're on the move again. The next day they go off to work. I spot a few pounds on the side there. I decide to borrow a few quid for a bet. I had no right to do this but when you gamble you think it'll be OK. Of course it never is. So before you know it I've done the lot. Not a huge amount of money, but not mine either. What a cunt. I can't face anyone, so I leave a note telling Paul the story, and that I've cleared off to Ealing. I manage to track down Ron Paris who was in Dynevor School a year ahead of me. I can't imagine why he'd moved up to London, but here he was, thank God. There was space, so I could stay. The next day Paul and the 'money' guy turn up. I'm embarrassed for Paul. He's done me a favour and I've shit all over his doorstep. All I could do was apologise and say I'd sort it out soon. I arranged to meet them the next day on the Kings Road. When I got there the guy was telling me how he'd been saving up for a projector. I walked into Boots and nicked one there and then, and gave it to him. Not the best outcome, but a start nevertheless. I never thought I'd bring this up again, but this is one of the shittiest things I've ever done, and I think I should own it.

The squatting scene in Ealing is pretty well organised. And you soon find out you're spoiled for choice as regards getting your head down. I think Ron went back to Swansea soon after I arrived, so Paul Durden and myself were on the hunt for somewhere to stay. We met a pair called Gilda and Andy, two London girls who used to frequent the Three Pigeons. So we all moved in together. Us two lads find a couple of mattresses and fling them in our rooms. The girls on the other hand had theirs themed to a hippy specific quicker than you can say 'Ricky don't lose that number' which they played incessantly. It wasn't quite a 'She had a snake for a pet, and an amulet, and she was breeding a dwarf, but she wasn't done yet, she had grey green skin, a doll with a pin' vibe, but it wasn't far off. When they weren't on the Leary trip, they were definitely on the beery tip. Paul and I were seasoned pub dwellers, but try as we might; there was never a time that we beat these girls to the pub. We never had any scenes with these two, but they were good company. Little did I know at the time, but lurking in the wings was a mate of Gilda's called Jed. She turned up at our place one night and that was that, she's my girlfriend. I don't think the words 'I don't do it on the first date' ever crossed Jed's lips. She might have said 'I will not do it in the pub toilet with a guy a minute after I've met him" but I doubt it. I wake up in the morning and she's in bed beside me. She's pleasant enough. She's on the rough side of attractive, but hey, that's me too. I think there might have been a cup of tea and a slice of toast handy, but by opening, we were in the Kings Arms, on our first date. I should have realised this was going to be tricky. When I was coming back from the loo, the barman pulled me to one side and said "Is that bird alright?' I said, "I think so. Why?" He went on "Well she's just eaten all the daffodils out of that vase on the table" Fuck sake! When I asked her why, she just said, "I'm fucking starving"

Jed had had a hard life. I found out she was a low-key hooker from when she was fifteen. I don't know what went on, but her and her sister, who was even younger, were doing something for the pleasure of some Indian geezers out Southall way, don't ask, I didn't. It also turns out that she'd had a child along the way, which was now in care. She obviously was working towards getting the kid back, in her head anyway. But this scene around here wasn't the best place to start. And what help was I going to be? We got on great some of the time. She loved sex, and was good at it, and was never shy about letting you know when she was in the mood. I've heard and read about the way certain girls let their partners know that they feel a little randy. Agony aunts go through a whole catalogue of seduction techniques for women to try on their partners. I tell you one thing; they should take a leaf out of Jed's book. One of her favourites was "I don't 'alf fancy a punch up the knickers." This always worked for yours truly. Give it a try.

Jed would disappear on occasion, which suited me. Howard Griffiths would turn up from time to time. On this particular occasion he'd come up to London to attend a rock 'n' roll extravaganza at Wembley. Did I want to come along? Are you kidding me? Whatever cobblers I come up with in the pub about my likes and dislikes in music, you know, trying to be hip and clever, meant fuck all when it came to the legends of American rock and roll, and the bill at Wembley was choc a bloc with some of the biggest names imaginable, short of Elvis himself. The day started quietly enough. A few British acts did their thing, and then high excitement, next on legendary Seattle political rockers the MC5. I knew about this bunch from Durden. I'd heard Kick out the Jams and the rest round at his, and the energy catapulted out of the Dansette, and made you feel ANGER, so I waited with baited breath for their arrival on the stage. Talk about anti-climax. Of all days to pick, the Five chose this one to change their image from rebellious leather and denim clad agitators, to American comic hero caricatures. Talk about the bloke who turned down the Beatles, this was up there with the worst decisions in Rock history. Not that many in the audience would have been au fait with the Five anyway. But if they come across as a hard-working outfit they might have given them a chance, but dressed as the Silver Surfer and the like they had no hope. I don't think it lasted one song before the audience close to the stage, who were mainly Teddy Boys, started hurling all and sundry at the stage. This was taken up shortly afterwards by what seemed to be everyone present. Bottles, cans, the ghost of Stanley Matthews and even the lead of Pickles the dog rained down on the band. A bad day indeed for the MC5, one from which they never recovered.

As night fell the big guns started arriving. Everyone is pissed, but very little trouble after a long day guzzling in the sun. It was a bad night for Little Richard though. He came on to rapturous welcome, but immediately went weird. He's on top of the piano, giving out some of his trademark hollers, but all the time two of his people are holding his legs for fear that he might jump off the piano into the audience. I'm not talking an Iggy or a Kurt Cobain vibe here, I'm talking suicide. He was off his face, and his minders were afraid. So Richard never delivered, but hey, he's delivered plenty over the years. No such problem for the next act. I was about to witness the best thing I've ever seen on stage, before or since. Accompanied by the diminutive landlord of the Black Raven pub onto the stage, Jerry Lee Lewis took off his jacket, handed it to the landlord guy, went to the piano, adjusted the microphone, and said "This is The Killer speaking" and you could feel the hair stand up on the back of 70,000 souls. Top of the bill was Chuck Berry, he had the crowd in his hands from the opening chord, he was brilliant, but The Killer, oh boy.

After the show, we, like everyone else started making our way home. Why is nothing ever straightforward? Find car, get in, drive off, and go home. Not us. Howard was absolutely legless, and his driving was giving plenty of clues to prove this. He said he couldn't drive, and on top of that he mentioned that the car was nicked. His plan was to pick up a couple of hitchhikers and let them, if they were capable, drive. Implausible you'll agree, but it did happen. These two twats jumped in, they're heading in our direction, and say they can drive. This was bollocks, they were worse than Howard. It was scary, and was sobering me up quicker than a stomach pump. I have no idea where it came from, but I said "Stop the car, I'll drive." I've been behind the wheel of a car only once before, but I thought I can't be as bad as this twat at the controls, so I took over. Howard mumbled something like 'It's straight all the way' so I did this. I wasn't bothering to stop at any lights even if they were red. After about three infractions I heard the siren behind me, he flagged me over, he stopped, and I pulled in behind him. The cop got out, I followed suit. I hadn't walked two yards toward him, when to my horror, my car was on the move, it tippy toed down this incline, and hit the cop car up the arse. I've obviously no licence, I'm pissed, and the car is stolen. The Swansea thing is hanging over me, my first inclination is to leg it. While I'm making a futile effort to remove our car from his he asks about where we've been. I've told him the story; in fact apart from the nicked car part of it, I've almost told him the truth. He says "who's the real driver of this car?' From the bowels of the back seat Howard pipes up "Me" The copper says "Well get behind the wheel, and fuck off home." Luckily for us this copper was not typical of the Seventies, when, if you were the same sex as the person the cops wanted for a certain crime, you stood a good chance of getting nicked. What a fucking day.

Jed was acting up a lot lately; she'd fly off the handle at the drop of a light switch. Then without warning she'd disappear after storming out. She did this one time whilst her mother was visiting. Problem was she had the only key. So this left me and her mum locked in. OK for me, I could climb out the window, and over the wall, not so easy for Jed's mum though. So I had her there for a couple of days. She was all right, but I don't think she worried too much about Jed's relationships, I think if I'd popped the question, and she was an attractive woman, she wouldn't have had any qualms about shagging her daughter's boyfriend. So here's the scenario. On the second day I'm out through the window to get whatever she needs from the shop. Then I leave her indoors while I get on with whatever I have to do to keep the wolf from the locked door. Then when night falls, it's back over the assault course to home and hearth. Jed's mum was coming on a bit strong by now, I'd had a few pints, and so it wouldn't have taken anything to lower my defences. We got to chatting, when the door opens, its Jed back from wherever. We weren't caught doing anything, but the vibe was such that Jed smelled a rat. But what could she say or do anyway? She's been on the missing list. Her explanation was typical; she'd been to see this ex of hers, Mick Bell, to see if she still had feelings for him. She became tearful after that, begging forgiveness, and telling me about the lousy shag she'd had with him. Charming. I just want to go to bed. It's late, but Jed, still smelling a rat about earlier, insists that her mother leaves. And that's what happens.

I'm in the pub a few days later when a guy comes on to me and offers me a pint. Fucking right. Turns out it's this guy Mick Bell. I'm sensing trouble but he's beering me up. Jed came up in conversation, but not that much. Before you know it we're like two old mates. At closing he says "come back to mine, I've got plenty to drink." He didn't live far away, so I went with him. It was true about the drink. He even had a bottle of whiskey that we never got around to opening. About two o clock I got up to leave. He wasn't having that. "Stay here" I looked around to see if his wife seemed ok about it, she wasn't bothered, so I decided to stay. "Where shall I kip Mick?" I asked "Oh fuck it" he says "come upstairs with us". In for a penny, thought I. Upstairs the three of us pile into the double bed. Mick's missus is not a bad sort, in that blonde with black roots sort of way, so when he starts guiding me towards her, I was up for it, then it dawned on me what he was up too. Jed must have told him that he was useless shag, and now he'd brought back this other guy, who was seeing Jed, to shag his wife so she could do a comparison job. I think sex should be an uncomplicated thing, so after I'd thought this through, any amorous ideas on my part had disappeared. I told him I weren't having it. He turned over and went to kip. On the first snore I whispered to his wife to come downstairs, she did, and we had a good time on the sofa. I slipped away after that. And I nicked the bottle of whiskey on the way out.

My days with Jed were numbered. She was my partner in crime, so to speak, and ever giving in the kip department, but she was fucking nuts. I got back to our place one afternoon and she'd wrecked the gaff. An old cliché, but it was as if a bomb had gone off. I tracked her down to someone's house around the corner and she acts as if nothing's happened. I go berserk with her, and demand she go back there and clean it up. I thought that was reasonable, but she still wanted to ruck about it. She wanted me to hit her. That was it all along. Now I like a bit of physicality on the shag pile, but I'm not going to belt a bird just to prove how much I love and care for her.

Got to get out of this.

Time has come for a trip to Swansea. I haven't seen my mother in ages. I get a few quid together, and I'm all set. Now Jed wants to come with me. I don't know what drugs I was on at the time, or whether I was having some kind of breakdown, but I agreed to take her along. Perhaps I have gone mad. The day dawns, we pack our stuff in one bag, and we're off. We had only gone as far as Ealing Broadway when she goes off on one. I don't know, or care what it's about, I've had enough. I dump her stuff right there on the street, and run for it. Any money we had was in my pocket, and I was gone, straight to Paddington, on the train, and on my way.

I popped into a pub when I got to Swansea just to let a few know I was back in town. I had a pint, and then went to the family home. My mother was in. I asked where the Old Man was; she said, "He's in the Prince with your friend." It was true. I nip into the pub, and there's my father having a bevy, and chatting away to Jed. A lot of people might think me mean to leave her in London with no dough, but listen; here she is drinking with my old man, after finding out where I lived, and getting to Swansea without any cash. She can look after herself. I wasn't going to go off on one in front of the folks, but I did ask her later how she managed to get here. She explained that she'd gone back to the house, grabbed the bottle of whiskey I'd nicked off Mick Bell, gone to Paddington, hopped on the train, chatted up the guard and travelled down in the guards van with him, having the occasional drop of Scotch. I bet that's not all he got.

So Jed's in Swansea. My Mother and Father think she's great, and I'm spending all my time trying to think of ways I can escape from her. I'd normally disappear, and she'd go drinking with my father. One evening she came looking for me though. I was in the Griffin Bar, in company. She found me there and started creating. I told her we were all over, and exited with the people I was with. We managed to cross the street, when through the darkness a bottle whistled passed us and hit the window of Swansea Goldsmiths. Over the years armed robbers and smash and grab merchants had driven up onto the pavement outside this shop, jumped out with sledgehammers and failed to make a dent in its window, Jed managed to do it with a bottle from thirty yards away. The alarm went off, and the police turned up in a flash. Touch wood, they saw no bottle, and bought our story about stumbling and bumping into the glass. But that was it for Jed and me. I sent her back to London the next day, and haven't seen her since. I bumped into someone who knew her a good while later, and they said she'd settled down with a bloke, and gotten her child back. Good for her.

7. All the World's a Stage

Back in Ealing I moved in with John Cory and his girlfriend in West Ealing. This gaff was well sorted, all the amenities in working order, and more importantly, safe. Howard Griffiths even found me a job. He'd recently been working as the house carpenter at the Regent Theatre in town. Howard always had things to do, and places to visit, so he was ready to pack it in. He put a word in for me, and when I met the Manager, the interview couldn't have gone more sweetly. The main reason being that he loved Swansea, and had spent his honeymoon down the Gower. So I'm in like Flynn. The Show that was on at the time was called 'Let My People Come'. It was diabolical, someone trying to cash in on the 'Hair' phenomenon. It was basically a sex show with music. Howard stayed on a few days to show me the ropes. The stage was quite sparse, just a couple of velvet covered boxes, which had to be moved around the stage from time to time. This was part of my job, and I got it right pretty quickly. The nudity was a bit unnerving for me at first, but you get used to it. The daytime part of the job was general maintenance around the theatre. If anything needed fixing I'd call one of my mates up to give me a hand, because I'm just not handy. I got away with it for a while. I was making 'friends' with the performers, and had my scene moving duties down to a fine art. So much so that I could stretch my time in the pub from seven minutes before the interval, through the interval to six minutes into the second half, so life was ok.

The cast were a mixture of gay men and straight women, who were finding it difficult to crack the West End or had given up trying. The songs were something else, 'I'm Gay' 'Come In My Mouth' and one whose name I can't remember that went 'I know a man who's got a cock that's twice as big as his. It's sloshing round within my cunt, at least I think it is'. Throughout this number, one of the cast Johnny Worthy, would have a piece of string in his hand, the other end of which was tied to his ample appendage. Another song, sung in an Andrews Sisters stylee was unbelievable. Titled 'The Cunnilingus Champion of Company C' it was a parody of the more familiar

'Boogie Woogie Bugle Boy of Company B', which I believe was a morale boosting song that the sisters sang for the troops during world war two. This went like,

They say he came from Memphis; maybe it was Saint Jo,
And where he learnt to chew the pussy, we'll never know,
When asked if he could demonstrate his skill with the cunts,
He said he couldn't do it; he nearly killed someone once,
What a blow, what a way to go,
He was the cunnilingus champion of company C

Classy huh?

There were all sorts of sexual shenanigans going on, and I guess the cast's remit was to make it appear spiritual. I became pally with the dresser. He came from Porthcawl, and was the campest geezer I'd ever met. But lo and behold he had a gorgeous girlfriend. One night we were around his house, myself, him, his girlfriend and a guy from the cast called Graham. Graham was the hunk of the show, and unashamedly gay. After plenty of drink, we were all rolling around on the bed. Porthcawls' girlfriend was pissed, and bang up for it. The dresser wasn't bothered; in fact he was egging her on. In a perfect world she would be shagging Graham, but he wasn't having any of that, so that left me. I'm ashamed to admit I never took the opportunity of a lifetime that night. She was a knock out.

I don't know what it is but if there's someone around and about who I think has more chance with a certain girl than me, I immediately back off, and by the same token, if I think a girl is out of my league I do likewise. Back in the late Sixties early Seventies in Swansea, a beautiful girl hit town. She had been Miss Whereversshecamefrom, and was a stunner. I could kick myself now for being such a twat in her presence. I'd see her in the dance hall and she'd say to me "Don't go home without me" and I'd take her home, go inside and try nothing and leave. When her parents came to visit she insisted that I come out with them for the day. But the biggest sickener was when she said come around to my flat, we'll have a drink, I'll get changed, and then we'll go dancing. She had more than one room in that flat, yet she decides to strip naked and change her clothes right in front of me. I still didn't take the hint. What a mug. But it's understandable when I think about it. I've never known if a girl has taken a fancy to me, unless they've told me right out, or, after a drunken snog maybe, it's so obvious, even to me. But that body language stuff is way above my head.

Meanwhile back at the Regent, I'm muddling through. I've got it all down pat. Then one evening the electrician comes running into the Phoenix pub where I spend my time. "You'd better get back there quick" I do this, and when I arrive in the auditorium I am met with a scene of carnage. The whole front row of the stalls has collapsed, and there are people all over the gaff, in various states of shock. The manager says, "Where were you?" I made up some yarn, which he didn't believe for a second. "Right I'm going to move them back for tonight, tomorrow I want this fixed". To be fair I did turn up early the next morning, I did what I could to rectify the problem, but deep down I knew my efforts would be in vain. Sure enough, during my break that night a message arrived at the Phoenix that the same thing had happened. I didn't return that night or any other night for that matter. I'd strung it out for a couple of months, had money in my pocket for the first time in ages, so I couldn't complain. So endeth my career in theatre land.

On a trip back to Swansea it soon becomes apparent that I'm of no interest whatever to the Old bill. The bookie thing has gone away. I don't for the life of me know why, but I decided to spend a lot more time there. I didn't have any plans, nothing new in that though. It was quickly back into the old routine of drinking, gambling, thieving and drug taking. My parents had moved into a place right in the centre of town by now. They were now the caretakers of a shopping arcade, and had the rooms above. I stayed there, which was very handy for observing and participating in any skulduggery that was occurring. The drug thing was fucking a lot of people up now. Burglarizing chemists had hit epidemic proportion, and a lot of people were dabbling with the sort of medicine of the addictive kind. It was a bit weird at Kens place with all the comings and goings, and, whereas previously he and I would have a laugh, things had alas become a lot seedier. I didn't mind the downers and the speed scene, but the Diamorphine, Ritanol, Dicanol trail left me cold. I've always been quite coward anyway when it came to drugs, if I was ever offered a pill, I'd always bite it in half first off, just to gauge the strength. I'd had my fun with Acid so I'd steer clear of that too. Hash had lost lustre, because now it just made me paranoid, which just left the speed, which I loved in pill, powder or any other form. People around Ken had gravitated toward the needle too. Fuck that, got enough problems already.

Me, Mam and sister Linda

Me, Mam and Linda in Singleton Park,
Swansea in about 1954

Scruffy git, me outside the house in Colbourne Terrace 1961

Me, and the old man at the house in Colbourne Terrace

8. The Arrival of Punk

No sooner am I back in Swansea than I see a poster advertising a gig. The Sex Pistols live at Pandora's Nightclub. I hadn't seen them yet, but the punk thing was busting out in London. Not that I'd seen much of it mind you. I was in the Nashville one night, and I was wearing Carole's leather jacket, which Howard had covered with the metal tops off beer bottles, it looked hard man. This, with the drainpipe jeans and sneakers, must have given me a look that may have confused the American girl I was talking to at the bar, "Are you a Punk?' she asked. Well at the time I guess no was the answer, but I said yes anyway, it might have led to a leg over. It didn't. So punk was on the move. But in Pandora's? Jesus. I did my best for the band on the night of the gig; I went around many a pub letting people know that the next big thing had hit our small town. No one was impressed in the slightest, so I headed down there on my own. I bumped into Jacko Miles en route. Our crowd called him Jack the Hippy. Nobody was further from being a hippy than Jack. He was Elvis, He was Vince Eager, He was even Gene Vincent, but he was no hippy. I didn't go into detail with Jack about the Punk movement, I just told him to come to this gig. So off we went.

They can say what they like, I can tell you now, there was no fucker there. Okay, perhaps a dozen or so, but that's it. The whole thing bewildered Jacko. "What the fuck have you brought me to here," he said. "Hold up, the band will be on soon." Five minutes later it happened. The curtains began to open; the stage started revolving, revealing John Rotten lying on the floor with a microphone in his hand. Before the band even kicked into gear, Jacko shouted, "Get up you lazy bastard and do some work." Normally, I guess, Rotten would have had a put down for this. But seeing this Teddy Boy figure about five feet in front of him, and only about 12 people in the audience, he must have thought 'Why bother'. The Pistols played OK that night. But if you were there, (and you weren't) you wouldn't have thought for a second that this lots name was going to be known all over the planet.

The Clash at Swansea University a few weeks later was an altogether different ball game. Since the Pistols thing, punk had been all over the press, so the punters turned up in droves. I went down there with Hank. In the bar I spot Strummer. I didn't know him then, but I'd seen the 101ers plenty of times, so I knew enough to go onto him with a view of blagging Hank and me into the gig. Joe was big enough to pretend he remembered me from the Nashville and said he'd get us in no sweat. Hank, never one to let a favour go unreturned, offered Joe a dip into his little drug bag, which contained (probably) Tuinol, Secanol or Mandrax. Joe declined. Just as well, or he couldn't have given the shitkicking performance he delivered on that night, and on many other nights, during the Clash's rise to world renown.

I'm in the Prince of Wales pub talking bollocks with all and sundry, when I'm approached by Brian Tabraham and Stuart Myers. They'd been tinkering about with their guitars of late, and thought the time had come to make the leap from basement to stage. They asked me to be the singer. I jumped at it. If I've ever had anything approaching what people call 'an ambition' this was it. Up in London I'd taken to going to gigs of a night, and at the Nashville, Hope and Anchor and those kind of places, had seen the likes of Dr Feelgood, Eddie and the Hotrods, Kilburn and the High Roads and the 101ers get sweaty in a pub atmosphere, and, if possible, it was this type of energetic stage performance I'd be hoping to bestow on the Swansea types. We did our rehearsing at Stuart's house. With a mixture of Flaming Groovies, New York Dolls, MC5 type numbers, we were close to a set in no time. Driving passed the Hide and Skin works and the Slaughterhouse one afternoon, pondering on a name for the group, Durden, who was driving, suggested Dyfatty Flats, which were on our right. Why not? It's not too clever, and easily remembered, by Swansea folks anyway. And if we were to achieve superstardom, we'd worry about the name then. The boys could play OK, so I couldn't see any reason to put off our debut. We played in a few pubs, the Coach and Houses, which was a proper venue, and eventually at Pandora's.

Two things happened around all this. I met my new girlfriend

Kirsty, and became conscious of the Great Ian Bone. More on Kirsten P. Woodward later. Bone was a troublemaker around Swansea, in the best possible way. With his magazine called Alarm, he managed to get up the noses of every person you hated i.e. businessmen, councillors and the old bill. Alarm retailed for 2p, was a cracking read and put the shits up many a bent operator. I'd bump into him on many a Saturday down town when he was out selling the paper. I'm not very savvy on the political front, but Bone would keep me updated on the state of the nation. He was particularly informative on matters of the Free Wales Army, and their hair-brained schemes. One of them, Vivien Davies lived in our block of flats, and another, who I found out later was Dennis Coslett would be spotted from time to time in full uniform parading around the place, but no one seemed to be taking them that seriously. Bone's best stories about the FWA were about Julian Cayo Evans, who held the rank of Supreme Commander within this organisation, sounds impressive, but apparently everyone in the FWA was a Supreme Commander. I started attending Alarm meetings in some pub down the Sandfields. At one in particular, some guy was going on about some misdemeanour or other that had been perpetrated by such and such, somewhere. I was full of drink, and was finding all this a bit boring, so I offered "Fuck this, let's get out there and cause some trouble." Surprisingly even Bone was irked by my interjections. So I went to the bar. Bone pulled me up later. "Do you know who that guy talking was?" I shook my head "That's John Barker, you know, from the Angry Brigade." Fuck a duck, I'm trying to rally a few to run amok around the streets of Swansea, and in the process interrupt a person who has done his fair share in that department. Then it all became clear. The girl who was sitting quietly in the corner was Hilary Creek. John and Hilary were part of the revolutionary outfit that created havoc around London under the Angry Brigade banner. This culminated in the lobbing of a bomb through the Home Secretary's window. They'd been nicked, served their time, and were here at an Alarm meeting, listening to bollocks from the likes of me. I remember fancying Hilary Creek from her pictures in the newspapers. She was from somewhere in Swansea, but I'd never met her. She was very attractive in a hippy kind of way. But when you've got a history like hers, it's not the looks that attract you, if you know what I mean. She's in the Marianne Faithful, Patti Smith, Kim Gordon, Anita Pallenberg, Dianne Quick mould, you want to mystery shag them, want it to be a secret between the pair of you, and, if you're very lucky, get asked back for a rematch, but most of all, you want them to like you, but it never happens that way, mainly because when these women were in their pomp, I wouldn't have had the nerve to approach them, even if they weren't famous.

Alarm was causing trouble for councillors and fat cats alike. It was amazing how many people would take Bone aside, on the street or in the pub, to grass up a boss here, a trade union official there, who was fiddling this, and who was nicking that, and, that old favourite, who was shagging someone they oughtn't. I always thought Bone was treading a fine line. I would have assumed, that if these 'Targets' had managed to ascend the greasy pole unfairly, how easy would it be for them to get Bone 'silenced' He's not daft either, and must have had similar misgivings, but he saw it through. He got high-ranking officials nicked. Not just slap on the wrist nicked either, proper bird nicked. Check it out for yourself. It's on the record.

Alarm decides it's time to stand for the council elections in Swansea. All hands to the pump on this one. At first it was thought of as a bit of a wheeze, but as the campaign gained momentum, there was optimism, certainly in the case of an old school mate of mine Michael Aldron. Michael was what my mother would call 'a good Catholic'. He did indeed go to Mass, he knew the difference between wrong and right, and was always on hand to fight the corner for the underdog. And of course he looked the part. I suppose back then he'd be referred to as a 'straight', which might not cut much ice on the dance floors around town, but gave him a big advantage when he'd be out door stepping. Michael was standing for the ward where I lived. Kirsty and I went out canvassing a couple of times, but more impressively, we'd hung a massive banner saying 'VOTE ALARM' over our eighth floor balcony. No one complained about this. How could they? There didn't seem to be much objection when the Cravens had a horse on their balcony, so what the hell.

Bone was on the campaign trail himself. He'd enlisted the help of one Phil Williams. Now although people wouldn't say it to his face, he was referred to as 'Phil the Div' and was a man with a fierce reputation when it came to having a ruck. He made himself Bone's chauffeur. He had an impressive Citroen car, the one with the long front, like De Gaulle's, and to show his solidarity to the cause, had painted "Vote Alarm' across the doors in emulsion paint. All this sounds great, I'm sure you'll agree, but there is a downside to being on the road with someone unlovingly referred to as 'The Div' He could go off on one in a heartbeat. OK, he could terrify people into giving donations to Alarm, and might even be able to compel certain people into voting Alarm, but at the same he could turn on you too. Out on the campaign trail one day, Ruthy, a standard feature around and about, said something not to his liking, he put her out of the car in the middle of nowhere. Everyone in the car knew not to object, or they'd be next out or much, much worse. I don't know the results of this election off the top of my head, not that impressive in a lot of wards, but Mike Aldron did really well. He almost nicked it. On election night, after the results had been posted Bone led a group of Alarmists to the town Hall to bellow 'Fix" and demand a recount. There was lots of abuse and furniture hurled around the place. It was one of the great nights.

I was enjoying my time in Dyfatty Flats. I'd started writing my own songs. Nothing complicated, but pleasant enough. 'Trouble on the North Bank" was an homage to the long-suffering Swans supporters that were Hank, Kingo, Buller. Bobby Holland and the rest who were doing their best to enhance the reputation of the 'Jack Army' from the North Bank of the Vetch field, where First Division football hadn't surfaced (yet) in the clubs history. Then there's 'Trendy Wendy' who was number one pin up to the musicos of the town. She worked in the Virgin shop in Union Street, where she held court. All was cool in the shop, until the likes of Daido, Terry Evans and Maurice Courtney would come in, pissed, demanding to hear Donovan albums. She was a looker all right, and yours truly had absolutely no chance. So we could now boast original material in our act. I'd written others too,so before long most of the set was our own songs. I loved it. I had the words off pat, which gave me more chance to concentrate on my stagecraft. In these pages, I hope you agree, there hasn't been trumpet blowing by myself, as regards my talents. I've fucked up a lot in every department, except one. I was a great dancer. I don't mean a person who moves on stage to the music, I could actually dance. I even took the time to learn how to jive, properly. When I think of Simon le Bon, Jim Kerr, him out of the Stone Roses and the like, and hear people refer to them as 'good movers' I laugh my cods off. No, I could put on a show all right, but even if I was as good as I think I am, nothing was going to happen in Swansea.

My new girlfriend Kirsty turned eighteen, and decided she'd like to move in with me in my new flat. She came from a nice home up in Tycoch, which then, and maybe still now, was a posh area of Swansea. Kirsty's parents were good people. Her father was a Professor of Russian at Swansea University, and his wife was the perfect housewife. I used to love going up there, great food, good conversation and everything pristine. Kirsty had warned them not to 'be nosey' about my past and they never brought it up. She must have had a rush of blood to the head the day she decided to move into the flat the council had given to reprobates like me. These places had been deemed unsuitable for family dwelling, so in a short while, every rapscallion on the patch had moved in. So there it was, a couple, a band, and a place to live, doesn't sound like a lot, but a step up, sure. Then I get nicked, and then I get nicked again. I'm off to jail soon.

9. Doing Time

I wasn't banged up for a serious breach of the rules, just a culmination of petty misdoings. The points add up, and it's time to pay. In fact I got there a tad too early. When you're on this treadmill you obviously keep tabs on your wrongdoings, and this time I thought I got banged up one offence too soon. This concerns a night spent in the company of Conny Collins. We'd been drinking in the Griffin Bar, and were trying to find a way of getting down to either Langland or Caswell for a bit of dancefloor action. He decided that we should nick a car. Don't ask me why, but I went along with this potty idea. The car park outside Dynevor School was where we landed up on this quest. Little did we know that of late, every fucker has been nicking cars from there. The police had it under surveillance, and before we even managed to get into the vehicle, the cops were on top of us. They were determined to nick someone that night, and we were the unlucky ones.

Now normally when you're caught 'bang to rights' you plead guilty, because even if you've got a legitimate reason for being there, the old bill will just change their story to suit themselves, that would have meant Conny, him being the one opening said car door, pleading guilty, and me trying to fanny my way out of it. Conny had other ideas, so we both had to plead not guilty. When the evidence was presented in the court it was obvious they weren't buying Connie's story about taking a piss, falling over and as he fell his hand connecting with the car door, and it springing open. The Judge said "Cornelius John Joseph Collins, you have come here today and told us a pack of lies etc" and doled out Connie's punishment, I was found guilty as well, and so for something I shouldn't have even been near, I got a suspended sentence, so I feel a bit cheated as I stand in the dock this time. I got six months, not long if you're a lag, but I could have done without it right then. The group were doing all right; Kirsty and I were getting on well, so more going on than usual. Fair play to her though, not only was she going to finish her studies, she was about to get a job and keep the flat going.

No messing about on remand this time, straight into the population. The usual faces around the place, which made it depressing, when you consider you're becoming one yourself. I'm in a cell with a guy called Terry Jones, his brother Colin is the famous Welsh welterweight boxer, who I saw beating Kirkland Laing in London to win the British crown. Colin had his ears boxed off for most of that fight, and I'd given up all hope of him winning when Paul Grey's brother in law Roy Roberts who was sitting beside me said "He'll have him now" and as if on cue, Colin unleashed a punch of such venom, it made the audience gasp, and Laing was on the deck. He'd do the same in the rematch too. Colin was a great fighter who just fell short of world greatness. No shame in that. It's a hard fucking game. Anyway, I'm two'd up with Terry, who is the black sheep of his family, but check this out, he's in prison for robbing a horse. Not to sell or butcher or any profit making reason, he'd stolen the horse to get to the pub. In those days the pubs in Glamorgan shut and opened at different times to those in Carmarthen, so if you wanted too, and you were quick enough on your feet, you could, by crossing the border, extend your days drinking. Terry decides to do this with the help of a horse. How can you get bird for that? Twats.

Terry got out and I'm stuck with a right one from the Valleys named Keith, I didn't mind that much because I'd win all his canteen money off him at cards, I didn't mind his quaint tales of how he kept his wife's gallstones in a jar on top of the telly but I did mind when I found out he'd fed his child something unspeakable to make it go to sleep. He was moved out of sight. What about Paddy in the next cell? Married with two kids, in here for "pinching a couple of old shovels off a building site" At least I'm in here for breaking the law, trying to make a profit. How can they justify locking those three up?

Down the nick you can work to get a few bob to spend in the canteen. These jobs range from sewing mailbags in shop five, which is shite, to what is considered the best job, Governor's tea boy. There must be loads of perks in that, but hey, you're on show all the time and you have to carry the gossip all over the nick. I suppose it's a good job if you want to be known as a 'Wheel' but I wouldn't want it. The job I eventually got was the best job in the nick. After a couple of days in shop 5, sewing mailbags, and telling lies, I got sent to the Boiler House. It's wintertime. Where's the warmest place? Where do you work with an overtime grabbing civvy screw who likes to play cards most of the shift? Where do you get a shower and a full change of clothes every day? Where can you shit, shave, shampoo and shower in private? The Boiler House, that's where. During the week you were never in your cell, overtime every night. The screw was all right too. He was a northerner who'd been in the army, spent some time in Belfast. He had some stories about that, including the one about the night they caught Martin Meehan, the republican, at the border. Meehan had tried to steamroller through the armoured cars that had formed a barricade, and failed. The screw also loved his sport. I could talk sport all day back then. So I was good company for him as well. But let's not get carried away, I'm still in the shovel.

Before I got here this time, Dyfatty Flats had done a recording session for Swansea Sound. We did three of my songs. But I hadn't heard the broadcast yet. One Saturday we'd just been banged up, I turned on the radio just in time to hear the DJ say something like "and now a local band. Dyfatty Flats" And my voice booms out of the wireless. Not a soul in sight for me to tell, not a con on the landing to pass the word, not a living being in this shithole to share my moment. Fuck it. As small as it was, I know my stock would have risen if only a handful of cons had heard it. Never mind.

Kirsty was doing sterling work outside. She'd got a job at the Cricketers pub, and was coping well. Why wouldn't she? She didn't have me around to fuck things up. So at least I had somewhere to live when I got out. This was just around the corner now. The last day in the nick, the civvy screw say's to me "you'll be back". At the time I thought it was inevitable too. But as Chuck Berry said 'It goes to show you never can tell". Touch wood, I haven't been back so far.

My Mother and Kirsty met me at the gate, but I soon gave them the slip. I was eager to find out about the music situation. Apparently Dyfatty Flats had been performing live without me. It was mostly crap when I was there, but at least I had an entertainment spark in my arsenal. The geezer who did the singing was a roly-poly journalist by all accounts. Bigger things were on the horizon; Bone had decided to start a band. He had it mapped out in his head, said he had a few songs, and a name, Page 3. The premise was to upset as many people as possible in the name of the Sun newspaper. I told Bone I'd be in it. Keep me posted. It was getting near evening now on my first day of freedom. I'd seen Ken, Hank and the rest, so I was full of ale and drugs, but instead of going home to the flat that Kirsty had kept together while I was away, I decided to stay in Town. Just to prove to myself and the world what kind of slag I am, I met up with an old flame and went back to hers. Funny, I can't get the leg over when I'm fronting the band, but can on my release from the nick. How odd is that. I went back the next morning with that old chestnut, that no woman believes "I passed out at so-and so's flat." She's eighteen, perhaps she swallowed it.

10. Page 3

If I have any regrets as regard my short-lived musical career, it would have to be, how short the life-span of Page 3 was. With all the Punk bands around the place, boasting shoe shop assistants with Mohican hairdos and leather jackets, spouting insurrectionist dogma on the weekend, it was nice to be associated with someone who'd actually walked and talked on the Anarchy highway for donkey's ears. I was honoured to be in the group. At the first meeting, Bone handed over twenty songs, which he'd written in a couple of days. Knowing him he only wrote them because a band has to have some lyrical content to get the message across, so I doubt he sweated blood over the things, but I tell you what, for me, they all stood up. Political ditties, anti-sexist dirges, current affairs comedies all came alike to Ian. He was great with the words. I took these lyrics to Stuart's house. We didn't take that much time on them either, but after a day or two, we had the makings of a set.

At the first rehearsal I was flabbergasted about the number of people who were there. But I suppose Bone must have told them they could all be in the band when he'd had a few. So here they were: lead guitar, bass, drums, trumpet, sax, oboe, backing singers, exotic dancers (male and female) and a few around the edges, whom I guess, had some function or other. Now you have to bear in mind Bone's idea of a good group. Dyfatty Flats had been crowned Alarm's 'Band of the Year'. The twice I remember him coming to watch us; it was a disaster both times. On the first occasion the PA blew up, the second time he was around, I, whilst pissed out of my head and speeding, did one spin too many and crashed into the drum kit. This had not been rehearsed. After the 'show' Ian came back to congratulate us "Fucking shambles, fucking great." So stagecraft was not high on his agenda. Reaction definitely was.

It was always going to be rough with all these novice players, but after some practice, most of the ensemble recognized which song the rest were playing. I thought we'd try out at some boozer in the back of beyond for our debut performance. Ian had other ideas. He'd managed to talk the owner of Pandora's nightspot to put us on. Pandora's had a similar reputation to Jimmy Wilde's, (an all day drinkeria, populated by many a scoundrel of the highest order) but nevertheless it was a big venue for the likes of us. To add to the confusion Ian thought it would be great to put a couple of strippers into the mix. Hey. Why not, saying that though, I didn't believe for a second that volunteer striptease artists would be coming out of the top drawer. At first I was introduced to Carrie. She was six foot tall of solid frame, massive breasts and very good-looking; she introduced herself to me one night as a Page 3 stripper. Fuck me. A few nights later in the Coach and Horses pub, Bone introduces another cracker to the fold, Sherelee was plain sexy. I asked her if she was sure about this. She said "yes" and proceeded to pull her dress to one side revealing a great body. She also had a nice tattoo on her arse. "Will this do?" she asked.

On the Pandora's night, the place was heaving. They hadn't seen a crowd like this down there since 'Focus' a twenty five minute drum solo band from Holland had graced the very same stage I'm about to perform on. I'm shitting it. The musicians strike up the tune, on I rush, straight into 'Clap, Clap, I Wanna Get The Clap' a lively opener about a chap's hunt for an STD, which turns out to be a vain search until he bumps into his mother outside the pox clinic. Say no more, and don't ask me. Then everyone has a go. The girls sing 'Prostitutes' World' and 'Bitches on Heat' I sing about my shortcomings in ' I Can't Get It Up' and 'Premature Ejaculation' Then get my own back voicing 'One of the Boys' and 'Page Three Girls' only to be put back in my place by the girls singing 'Sexist Twat'. Bone sings 'God Bless you Queen Mum' and the classic 'Tory Funerals'. We all have a go at 'Holiday Homes' about setting on fire second properties in Wales (a great song) and keeping in the super soar-away Sun tradition, a tale straight off their front pages. 'John Bindon', whose life as a gangster, and the size of whose Hampton, had been serialized for weeks in that paper.

All Right it was a shambles, but we've gotten through about a dozen songs, and not a bottle thrown, hardly a boo and we haven't played the trump card yet. I'd worked my bollocks off. Honest. But I knew what was coming, so I still had energy enough in reserve to smash into the Troggs classic 'I Can't Control Myself'. A few bars in I was aware that Carrie and Sherilee had joined me on stage by the great surge from the bar at the back of the room. Hard nuts, burglars, shoplifters, and drug peddlers had all left the bar, and were now camped stage front. The girls were both stark naked on either side of me, I didn't know where to look. This had nothing to do with shyness, it was that Kirsty was stood right in front of me in the audience; it was fantastic, if there was a person in there, who earlier might have been critical of bum notes and shite singing, they weren't any more. The majority of musicians in Swansea ply their trade doing excellent cover versions of classics. If for instance a band had mastered the latest Dire Straits song before anyone else they were greatly admired. Most of the local bands churned out covers for years on end. The sadness of that is there are some shit hot players in Swansea, but a lack of ambition abounds. This was the late seventies mind you, things might have changed since. Anyway, that night we created a shitstorm, with a bunch of amateurs, and a lot of guts.

Jock McVeigh was billed in Page 3 as an exotic dancer. As a dancer he made Bez look like Baryshnikov. I knew him from the nick, when we were both on the painting crew. Bone decided that we needed some press. He telephoned the Evening Post with the sad news of Jock's tragic death in an accident abroad. The Post printed the story. When Jock turned up there two days later, Page 3 are in the paper again. Small beer some might think, but hey, were trying our best here. Bone had a bigger better plan anyway.

I'm guzzling away in the Tenby one night, when one of the strippers, Carrie, came in with her boyfriend. He came over to me. I shit it a bit, mainly because I'd been spending the odd afternoon at her place 'discussing the act' and having some fun. Now I'm thinking she's had an attack of conscience and told him about it. So I fear the worst. He said "I think you should go to the clap clinic, Carrie has a dose of something, and you might have caught it." Fuck me. What do you say to that? Peter fucking Ustinov would have been stuck for words. So was I. I mumbled something like "mmm cheers for letting me know." When Carrie and I were together, I think we were doing things normally. Maybe I'm missing out on something here, anyway when I went to the pox doctor I got an all clear.

Bone's plan was simple. He composed a letter to the Sun, pretending to be an irate parent whose two young daughters had been to a Page 3 gig. It went something like "when they got home they were physically sick by the antics they had witnessed while watching a group called Page 3 in Swansea etc" it went on "we are hoping this group has nothing to do with your wonderful newspaper" or words similar. The letter was posted, and we waited.

Kirsty had finished the foundation course and had her mind firmly fixed on a career in fashion. She had applied to a few and had been accepted into The London College of Fashion. Apart from Page 3 and the nick, I had nothing to hold me in Swansea. So it was decided to pick up sticks and move to London. The problem was where are we going to live? We wrote to different councils, up there, to see if we could blag a transfer. Someone who lived in Deptford got in touch, and it seemed that is where we'd land up. Even I didn't like the sound of that, and I'm far from fussy. Sitting in the Hanbury one night with my old mucker Tony Thomas and his lady wife Lyndsay, the subject came up. Lindsay had some high-ranking job with Swansea Council, and thought she may be able to help. She went as far as to say, "Kensington and Chelsea owe us a favour, let me find out"

As good as her word, Lindsay came up trumps. She'd sorted us a flat out in Ladbroke Grove. Although I'd lived in Ealing, and sped around London a bit, I hadn't heard of Ladbroke Grove. Then Durden told me whereabouts it was, that it was central, and was a "fucking great area". The council people gave me a set of keys, so I could go see "if it was suitable" so I shot off to London to take a gander. Perfect was my first thought. Then it became clear where I was. Portobello was round the corner. Notting Hill up the road, and we were only spitting distance from the West End, back to London soon then.

Back in Page 3 land, Bone had gotten us a prestigious gig at Swansea University. Wings had played there, so had Pink Floyd. If you were going to catch a big act in Swansea, odds are it's at the Uni you'll be seeing them. It didn't worry us any, what could we lose. No one would ever sign us in a million years even if we could play, so let's just enjoy it. This was our fifth gig, I think. And it turned out to be a mighty night. The students didn't know what to make of us as we arrived. And they certainly didn't take to our roadies, who although they knew fuck all about amps and wires, loved to have a punch up for no apparent reason. On this occasion the Cravens and a guy called Mack were our road crew, and sure enough, they put the fear of God into many a student. It's cheap at the Uni bar, so everyone was taking advantage of this. So by the time we were meant to go on everyone was pissed. Very early on it was obvious to the audience that we were very poor indeed.

Half way through the set Paul Durden activated the fire alarms, and that's when the 'fun' started. We just kept on playing. All of a sudden the fire doors at the side of the stage burst open, and in fly several of Her Majesty's fire service, armed for action. They were stopped in their tracks with the sight in front of them. Semi-clad girls, drunken musicians, and our leader, Ian Bone giving his girlfriend head in front of the drum kit. A fireman said to me "What's going on here Ray" I thought I'd misheard him, then I looked again and realized I knew him quite well. The only answer I could muster was "Fuck Knows". The outcome was that the whole Swansea University entertainment committee was fired, and when word of this gets out, Page 3 will find it very hard to get on the University circuit or Swansea circuit for that matter. In fact, the next and last Page 3 performance was outside Swansea. Whatever twat booked us into this one must have been on acid. It was a nightclub in Gorsienon. I'm used to tough nut shitholes in Swansea, but we're off the beaten track here. The music at this venue was charts with a little bit of 'The Birdy Song' thrown in, topped off with a round or two of a conga. All of the punters were pissed and so were their boyfriends, who were all well versed in that classic "are you looking at my bird" vernacular. I'd never worried about going on stage until this night.

Word arrived before we went on stage that Jock McVeigh, once again languishing in Swansea Prison, had been visited by legal representatives from the Sun. They were taking us to court to sue us over the name. We were chuffed, none more so than Bone. And who can blame him? The joy was short lived though. I don't think we'd completed a song before the punters started hurling everything in our direction. Things got so bad that the guy in charge pulled Bone aside and offered him the full amount agreed upon if we just got off the stage now. What a result. Some punters still wanted to have us, so we legged it for the van and cleared off. That was the final curtain call for Page 3. We never played again. But it's not the end of the story.

11. A Leap Across Ladbroke Grove

Kirsty loved the London flat, no sooner had she arrived than she was busying herself turning it into a home. This process has always been alien to me. I don't know why. When I visit other people's places, I'm always kind of envious if they are neat and tidy, with 'things' in them, yet I rarely make the effort to replicate what I've seen. Kirsty would trawl around the market for pieces of furniture and knick knacks. Before you know it the place is comfortable. She bought two wardrobes over there. When the guy delivered them, he shot off pretty quickly. No wonder, one of them was locked. He must have showed her the good one, and she, being trusting, thought they were both the same. Never mind. She managed to prise it open. It wasn't so bad, because inside she found £100. She coughed up £70 for them, so she was well pleased.

I'm not finding it easy. While she's at college all day I'm wandering around trying to find my bearings. I knew my old mate from Ealing, Sue Donne, worked in a shop called Rough Trade along with her younger brother Pete, and although I'd been there with Paul Durden when we'd come up to reccy the flat, I couldn't find it for the life of me now. So I'm a bit lost. If I managed to get a few bob I'd pop in a pub or two. I've never had a problem striking up a conversation, so before too long I know a few folk who will at least recognise me in future, but I wasn't making any forward moves. This is quite understandable when you consider that I've been, in the main, pretty rudderless. I don't know what I'm supposed to attempt to achieve in London anyway.

Not long after we arrived we were summoned back to Swansea for my little sister Margaret's wedding. The last thing I wanted to do was go back there after a couple of months, looking like a tramp, so I needed a suit at least. I'd been off the lifting of late, and, in Swansea time, I'd kept my nose clean for quite a while. On my wanderings, I noticed an easy touch as regards a suit. So easy in fact I could have managed a tie and shirt as well.

But first things first, I went to this shop, tried on a cracker, fitted me like a glove and was the right colour for weddings, funerals and God forbid, court appearances. I took the alarm off this garment without much problem, and then the assistant came around the corner. This was just her getting on with things; she hadn't come to keep an eye on me, or anything like that, but just to be on the safe side I placed the alarm in the breast pocket. No problem, I'll get it tomorrow.

Nicking a suit is straightforward. Wear a baggy raincoat, enter store, and put on jacket under raincoat, then armpit the trousers. I did this without a problem, and walked out. The bleeding alarm goes off. What the fuck? There's a woman shop assistant looking in my direction, I decide to leg it, so I'm gone. There was some kind of building work going on at this store, and they'd erected scaffolding outside. The assistant must have told one of the workers what was going on, because now a big West Indian guy is chasing me. I was pretty nimble back then, so I thought I might be able to outrun this guy. Just in case, I decide to dive through the moving traffic to give me an edge. I get across the street OK, but he wasn't as lucky. A car hit him. I hope he's OK, but I'm not stopping, I'm going to keep at a strong gallop till I'm clear. Imagine my surprise then, when through the corner of my eye I see this guy hot on my trail again, and he's closing fast. He caught me all right. Strong bastard too. I wasn't going anywhere, apart from the nick. I must have told this story to someone, who must have told someone else, because I've seen it in a book or magazine under the title 'Dumbest Criminal'. What happened was I forgot to remove the alarm from the jacket pocket.

I might make light of it now, but at the time it could have been disastrous. It could easily have been a custodial sentence. That would mean some god forsaken London nick. Sure enough the Magistrate took a dim view of the proceedings. Well he had to, once he'd read all the previous. I looked to him like a serial offender re-locating. Kirsty got up into the box and told him we were getting married, this did the trick. I landed up with a suspended sentence. Eventually, we found a few quid and bought a suit down Kensington market, which was more than adequate. So I looked good at the wedding.

We had a couple of days in Swansea. Down town one afternoon I bump into Ken Richards. He had a beautiful clock about his person. He asked if I knew anybody for it. I'd been away a while by now, and Ken knew everyone I did anyway, so I said I didn't. He seemed fucked up to me, everything about this encounter proved to me that Ken had lost his touch. Too many drugs I guess. Two days later I'm in the Tenby. Ken's girlfriend comes over; she says, "You better go see Ken. Not only does he say you grassed him up about the clock, but you're shagging me". I was furious. He'd been nicked because he'd been spotted on the camera. There wasn't a copper within ten miles who didn't know him by now, so he was picked up shortly after I'd left him. Being called a grass by your best friend is bad enough, but having it off with his bird. I wasn't having that. I went straight to his door. He answered, and asked me in. "What the fuck Ken," I said, and explained what I'd heard. He didn't deny saying it, he just said, "Look Ray it's the drugs." Fucking right it is. I left. I never saw him again after that. I loved Ken. What a shitty ending.

I got a part time job. I mentioned to Eddy the manager of William Hill on Portobello that I used to run a betting shop. He suggested filling in forms, and applying for a settler's job. I don't think that would have worked out somehow, but he let me be the boardman in there. It's straightforward; you just listen to the tannoy and write down all the information, odds and results etc on the big chalkboard. This was before they ever had TV in the shops, so it was important for the punters. The money was a pittance, but it kept me occupied for part of the day at least. It was also a good opportunity to get to know the natives. I started drinking in the Warwick, which was the nearest boozer to the shop. It was an Irish pub run by a bloke called Seamus. It was easy in there, nobody being flash or giving it large. It was like a neighbourhood pub you'd find in every town in the country. Good Guinness, no frills and plenty of craic. Keith Allen used to get down there. He lived just around the corner in Powys Square.

He reckoned he shagged the landlady on the floor in there one night. No one believed it. But who knows with him?

I eventually tracked down Rough Trade. For some reason I thought it was on Portobello. But of course it was on Kensington Park Road back then. Pete Donne was behind the counter, I got on with him, so I used to hang out in there after I'd finished my chalking commitment. Pete would whack the beer in at the end of the day, so I'd sit there listening to what the Independent record world had to offer. There seemed to be a lot going on in the back rooms of the shop, I didn't have a clue what it was. Recently I watched a documentary about Rough Trade, which took an in depth look at the shop and the label, but I have to say I'm none the wiser about that back room. It was great in that shop, real popular too. You'd get all your Clash and Aswad boys in there, The Slits, Rip Rig, in fact all of the West London music elite. The one who used to confuse me was a bloke called Youth out of Killing Joke; he used to wear the filthiest, once-white coat you'll ever see. You'd think that with the market outside he'd be able to find something better. I don't suppose he gave a toss. He's gone on to much bigger things so I'm told, but still has a scruffy vibe going. Takes all sorts.

I'm talking gambling bollocks with a punter one afternoon when a familiar face walks in. It was Dave Griffiths an acquaintance from Ealing. I stayed in a house with him in Western Road. He'd always be out and about, and up to no good. Then one day he announced he'd got a job. Maybe he was altering his ways. Sure. The job was driving one of those vans that transport freight from the airport all over London and beyond. Being a slippery fucker, he'd soon realised how he could make this pay. He would drive up to the office where he was to deliver the load, and get someone to sign his docket; he's then meant to unload the van. That's the part he missed out on. Leaving the Three Pigeons pub one evening I bump into him. "Be careful when you go into the house, I've put a few things in there," he said. He wasn't kidding. After giving plenty of shoulder to the front door, I scrambled in to be confronted by wall-to-wall, floor-to-ceiling, box upon box of brand new stereo systems. I didn't really have that many connections around Ealing then, or else I could have made a right few quid, but I did all right out of it.

As iffy as he was, every time I bumped into Dave I made a few quid. Now he's found me in Portobello Road, and he's bearing gifts. My guess would have been that he'd been out kiting. What he had was electric tools, which at the time were probably the easiest thing to sell anywhere. He kept coming back with more and more of these items and he'd leave them with me to punt out. I'd make my bit, and I'd meet him later in the Warwick and sort his end out. What made this even better was he insisted on buying the bevy all night as well. I wasn't around one time when he came over. He was looking around for me; he had a top of the range video recorder. He asked a few people if they knew me as an opening, which would then lead to him trying to punt this item. Johnny 600 said he did. After some jiggery pokery 600 got him a punter and everyone was happy. 600 asked him if he could get another, Dave said he'd get one by Saturday. That Saturday Dave shows up with a box. He finds 600 in Finches. Dave calls him outside. It's packed down there, you don't know who's who or who's watching, so very quickly 600 passes over the cash, and Dave the box, sweet. 600 takes the box inside to give to the punter. The punter wants a look. When they open the box they find three building bricks, "You've been had," says the punter. Now 600 wants someone to blame. So why not me? I was having none of it. I hadn't seen Dave during this period so it was fuck all to do with me. I might be shifty, but I wouldn't shit on my own doorstep. I live here now, and don't want that sort of publicity.

I never heard from Dave after that. He was spotted in a pub. Pete and Sue's sister Sal had the misfortune of going out with Dave one time, until she got wise to him. She was having a drink one night with her husband. When hubby was at the bar or in the loo Dave appeared from nowhere and was really weird to Sal. He was lucky that her husband didn't come back; he would have had a good hiding. But that was Dave Griff, weird.

Around this time Keith Allen had moved his empire to the All Saints Rd., This was the 'Front Line' of W11. The Mangrove was there, and it was the centre of many a confrontation between black people and the police. The riots of 1976 figured strongly around All Saints. Keith and Mario Tavares had set up a studio in a basement. Keith was in a band. They were called the Tesco Bombers. The Bombers used to play on a Sunday in the Apollo pub on the All Saints. This was a predominantly black establishment. Being quite new to the area I was quite nervous of going in there. This was just my own paranoia, it was cool. In the band were Neal Brown, Inigo Batterham, Sarah, Richard, and Keith on the drums. They were good, my favourite song was 'You Break The Ice at Parties'. There were other good tunes too, but hang about; it was 30 years ago, so I can't be more specific.

I started hanging around at the studio, and it was fun to watch as Keith and Mario started hatching plans. There were many projects in various stages of production. I even got involved; Mario let me record a few things I'd come up with. They never came to anything, but at least it was productive compared to hanging around the boozer and chalking up in the shop. It soon became clear that the main idea was BPR or Breakfast Pirate Radio. This was Keith's baby. The show was to be broadcast illegally around West London. Keith played all the parts himself – DJs, roving reporters and many of the artistes. When he needed to he'd rope someone in for the sketch. Best and funniest of these was Robbie Coltrane. Robbie was a new face in town then, but he was funny all right. Wacky and Zany comic Jim Barclay turned up a few times too, but mainly it was all Keith.

Keith and I went on manoeuvres one night to the White City dog track, to hunt down Stan Bowles, who was a standard dish down there. In his Harry Diamond persona Keith interviewed Stan. I would bump into Stan in the Grove when he was on his way to the illegal speiler opposite the KPH pub. I'd mention the radio station to him, and he'd ask when it was going out, then he'd rush off for a game of kaluki or whatever card games they played in that gaff. Keith and I went down there one afternoon to try and get Stan to play a game of six a side Keith had organised. Stan said he'd play. I would have loved to see the reaction on the opposition's faces if Stan had turned out, but alas, it wasn't to be.

There were many interesting characters on BPR. But Keith had excelled himself with two. 'Sex Boots Dread' the Rastafarian homosexual and, Gerry Arkwright the Northern Industrial Gay. Sex Boots songs were about his gay affairs. 'Me black and me proud and me Rastafaria, and me homosexual' went the lyrics on one. This is controversial enough, I'm sure you'll agree. But he was treading a very fine line singing them in the epicentre of black power and resistance, I can tell you. To 'up' the profile an interview with the NME was organised. The scribes had to interview Sex Boots from behind a barricade of some sort, so cleverly Keith situated himself in such a way that the writers could only see the top of his head. Only it wasn't the top of his head at all, it was the dreadlocked head of Sean Oliver from Rip Rig and Panic, who was sat in Keith's lap while the interview was conducted.

Although Sex Boots became the star of BPR my favourite was Gerry Arkwright, who'd 'cruised down South looking for big boys, and I haven't found a big one yet' Keith had dressed 'Gerry' as a butch Village People type with a touch of Northern earthiness. He also added a pair of mutton chop sideburns. This was homage to one of the regulars down the Warwick, who Keith reckoned he was based on. Next thing you know' there's to be a BPR album. Money was mentioned. Whose? I don't know. So it was all hands to the pump. Paul Durden was always good for a one liner, he'd come up with the immortal 'I'm an industrial gay, and I like it that way, fist fucking on the Firth of Forth' so he was handy. Towards the end of the recording I mentioned the Page three classic John Bindon. They got me to sing it; they liked it so much that I'm on the album. The BPR album didn't hit the charts. The people who did get hold of the cassettes wouldn't part with them, so you might think that they are lost to history, wrong, if you want a copy send me twenty quid and I'll knock you one up.

Keith's gone on to bigger things now, but I tell you what; he was shit hot back then. I used to go to his one-man shows at the Albany Empire. They were edgy and funny. One night he'd taken the complete contents of his flat and replicated his bedroom on stage. The lights go up, a clock alarm sounds and Keith rises from his slumber. He was bollock naked. He did the whole show like that and never missed a beat. What made that all the more remarkable was that in the audience were his mum and dad. Keith has a reputation around the place, and to be sure, he can at times be mercilessly cruel with the verbal, but you're always going to have a laugh when he's about. I remember an Irish guy named Sean gave Keith and me a greyhound. Full of enthusiasm we'd take this hound up to Hyde Park, we'd stand a good distance apart and let the fucker loose. It was fast all right, but all greyhounds are fast. It's whether they'll chase the damn hare, or whether they'll race at all that's important. I couldn't see this Sean character giving us a winner. Keith had a dog called Von Braun at that time, and I think this dog got a bit jealous. I'm convinced Braun took the greyhound off somewhere and lost him on purpose. I brought this up some time later with Keith. He had a darker tale. When he was staying in Powys Square the guy who lived upstairs named Colin had told him that two hippies had taken the dog off, and eaten it. That's got to be bollocks. This is 1981 London, not the siege of Stalingrad for fuck sake.

The moment had arrived for Page Three to face the wrath of Murdoch. We had been summoned to the courts to answer the charges of using the Page Three name, which they reckon they had ownership of. I went along with Keith. When we arrived in the court on the Strand, Bone was there with Jock McVeigh and some of the girls from the group. It was going to be a fun day out. This was a civil case, no bird to be dished out on this one, so no one gave a toss what the outcome was. If they handed out a hefty fine, or legal bill, so what? None of us have any money. When you're that age owing money to the courts didn't present any problem, you'd just ignore it.

Jock was determined to create some sort of trouble. Before

the show even started, he buttonholed the judge, and informed him that he and the others had spent the night 'in a brothel' why the judge had to know this I have no idea. It was true though. They weren't sampling the delights on offer at Cynthia Payne's house though, she'd just put them up because she was friendly with Jan Green. I can't imagine what the judge thought. After all the formal legal malarkey, the case got stated. The Sun's barristers told the court about how we had brought this family newspapers reputation down by using the Page Three name. He went on; sang the praises of how the Sun stood for morality and family values. Bone was our counsel and his strategy was brilliant. Every time the barrister said something good about the Sun, he'd produce a picture of some big titted boiler posing provocatively on Page Three . There was banter back and forth between Bone and their side until the judge said, "I've had enough of all this" He turned to Bone and said something like "Are you willing to change the name of your group?" Bone said yes. I think Page Four was what he suggested. The judge was happy with that, and started to wind down the proceedings. Then up jumps the Sun brief and starts asking for some ridiculous amount of money in costs (some say £20,000) the judge simply replied "Each side can pay their own costs." So to us it was a victory.

I regret now, that we didn't use this as a springboard to take the act to another level. By now Bone had kicked off Class War, his new anarchist magazine, and that was grabbing attention. In the weeks that followed, the Sunday People did a big article on him; naming him 'The most evil man in Britain' they tried to accuse him of corrupting the young. All that happened was he was selling the paper on some high street and there happened to be a school in the vicinity, so they dressed it up as something it wasn't. The People article was huge, a huge photo of Bone, huge boost for Class War and if we'd still been on the case, a massive plug for Page Three.

The dust hadn't settled on these events, when Cynthia Payne's house gets raided, and she gets arrested. It was all over the papers 'Luncheon Voucher Brothel' was one thing they called it. It was all very British and quaint. The beak thought different though, and 'Madam Sin' landed up getting porridge. What a diabolical liberty that was. The reason I mention this episode is that when she was arrested, half of the girls on duty that night, at her house, were none other than the girls from Page Three. These three occurrences, coming as close together as they did would have given us the kind of publicity that gets you up and running. And probably a record deal. Never mind.

I had a recording of Holiday Homes, Tory Funerals and John Bindon, so I thought I'd try and drum up a bit of interest. I went to see a guy named John Curd, who apparently knew about such things. He didn't seem to be that interested, but he found the Bindon song quite amusing, partly because he knew him, I think. Through the grapevine I found out that Bindon had heard the song, and thought it was a hoot. Thank god for that. He did add though, that it was five glasses that made up his trick, not the three we mention in our song. I awoke one sunny morning, looked out at the beautiful day on Ladbroke Grove, when I took a turn, there right below me, sipping a drink outside the Earl of Percy pub, is, in all his glory, TV tough-guy actor, hard-as-nails geezer, terror of the Kings Road and surrounding areas John Bindon. All sorts of diabolical thoughts entered my head. Had he tracked me down for taking the piss? He wasn't known to frequent this area. Then a girl I recognised in passing, as being a neighbour, approached him. I found out later she was a girlfriend of his. Phew!

Kirsty had excelled at the London College of Fashion. She was very good. She could make any garment, she could cut patterns, but more than that, she had imagination. When she took to the street in her own designs she turned heads for sure. So I thought, at worse she'll make a good living making women's clothes, and if she got the breaks might climb the heights in designer women's wear. However, during her last year in college she'd come under the influence of a French millinery teacher named Marie. Marie had worked for some of the best hat designers, and she saw in Kirsty the makings of another one. Kirsty loved the hat game, so much so, before you know it that is her career path.

On leaving college Kirsty had to decide where best to display her wares. A new fashion emporium had recently opened in Kensington High Street, called Hyper Hyper. It had one of these by-lines like 'A Showcase for New Designers' or something similar. And believe me a lot of the disillussioned folk in there believed themselves to be just that. By now Kirsty had gained a bit of a reputation with the old titfers. So for her to be able to fulfil private orders and stock up the Hyper stall, it was decided that I'd work the stall, while she beavered away at home.

As anyone with half a brain can imagine, Hyper Hyper was up its own arse a bit. There were some great stalls in there; sadly they were outnumbered by pretty mediocre ones, manned by people with little or no talent, who firmly believed that they had a shot at the big show. Traffic in there was pretty slow, so you had to have something a bit special on offer just to be able to cover the rent, so how most of them stayed open amazed me. Our stall was in the basement, opposite was Donald Fong shirts (very good product, not many takers) and Daniel James. Fuck knows who Daniel James was, but they were selling rubber clothes. Billy was in charge of things there, but like Kirsty he had to be away a lot of the time, to keep on top of the stock. That left Cliff. We got matey and would spend many a late afternoon having a swallow or two, to wind down from a day spent doing sod all.

There'd be the odd customer to see to, but mainly it was slow for everyone there. But at least Daniel James offered a few distractions. They sold rubber skirts, dresses and tops. It can't have passed your notice, but quite often rubber clothes are often married to sex. So the clientele over there were quite interesting to observe. The rubber dresses are notoriously difficult to get on, even after the application of the very necessary talcum powder, so there was always a fight to get into said garment. This made good viewing for a bored shop wallah I can tell you. There was a dressing room of sorts, but this couldn't disguise the contortions thrown by the hapless customers, and nine times out of ten some part of the female form would appear from behind the curtain. This was not the case when punk singer Nina Hagen came for her creation.

It was a skin tight, black mini dress. Not for her the battle of the changing room, she simply lay flat out on the floor and slid the thing on. She wasn't donning underwear this day either. Now boys I know you've always wanted to know what hair styles punk singers favoured down below, but my lips are sealed.

Along the way, stuck right in the corner was a stall that sold, I dunno, fluffy, cuddly, mumsy stuff. The girl running it had something of the schoolteacher or secretary vibe about her. Her dress sense was early 'Apprentice' chic, and she was as straight as a die. In the many off moments she'd come along and chat. She'd ask about the hats, and talk to Cliff about the rubber stuff. Cliff and Billy were regulars at Skin Two and all the other fetish type clubs in London. The girl on the end went with them one night. Curiosity or boredom I guessed. I was wide of the mark there. In next to no time she transformed herself into one of the major players in the arse-whipping scene. I was flabbergasted. I thought Cliff was having me on. Then one evening she was off to one of these clubs outside London, so she changed from her daytime clothes into her new wardrobe. Holy suffering Jayzus is the only way I can describe it. She was magnificent. Sadly though, with this transformation, went any chance the likes of me had of sampling her delights. Probably for the best.

That rubber stuff definitely seemed to have a sexual impact on the people who donned it. There is one exception though. Kirsty. When people accuse girls of dressing provocatively, and suggest that they dress that way to attract men, the stock, and correct, answer from women is "I dress to please myself" never has this been more accurate than in Kirsty's case. Of late she had gone through a change herself. She looked fab. Copper red hair, nose stud, Dennis Cockell tattoo, and an ever-expanding wardrobe. She looked the business. We had some great nights out, but I have to admit that on her rubber dress debut night I was expecting, well you know, something memorable, before, during and after lights out. I couldn't wait to get home. But alas it wasn't to be. It was back to the same old, formatted frolic I'd become used to. There was no adventure in that department. Try as I might, and I did try, I couldn't find the key. I thought I was the worst shag on the planet there for a while, now I realise it was simple incompatibility.

Bad news arrives from Swansea. Ken Richards is in a coma. Things had been pretty crap for him of late apparently. By now he had become an easy target for the highly unimaginative Swansea drug squad, and they had been on his case big time, and as it is in that life, he was almost certain to have had a court appointment pending. In the topsy-turvy world of drug taking, and finding the money to finance it, relationships suffer as well, Ken's was no different, and so things weren't going that smoothly, having said that though, this state of affairs was nothing new to him. Even if he had to do some bird, and his relationship went through a bumpy period, he'd soon bounce back. Ken had phoned Hank on the fateful day. He was 'off his nut'. At the time, one off his drugs of choice was Diaconal, which he'd take intravenously. He'd hit up five at a time. On this day, he told Hank that he'd had six hits. I don't know what effect that would have on a heavy-duty doper. But how bad can it be? He's on the phone for fuck's sake. Later he hopped into the bath for a relaxing soak. He passed out in there. The rest you can guess. He was pulled from the bath, barely alive, and consequently gone into a coma.

Kingo was in some shithole flat down around St. Helens. He'd been taking Tuinol. In fact he'd taken ten of these nasty pills. I've been known to take this particular drug in the past, and it's a hardcore barbiturate. If you took one, you knew (or didn't know) all about it. The nick is full of people, who, on Tuinol, would get up the courage to go thieving. Stumbling around shops with empty carrier bags was a red light to any security personnel, and they'd be quickly on your tail. This usually meant (a) failure to get what you were after or (b) a nicking. Kingo wasn't the best of lifters, but he managed to get hold of a bottle of spirits on this occasion. Back at the flat, he set about his prize with gusto, at the same time working his way through his cache of Tuinol. Who knows what happens in these situations, but Kingo passed out, then he died. The story goes that the house dog had had puppies a few days earlier, and these whelps were cuddled up to Kingo's body on the floor.

Kingo was a popular bloke. He was a good footballer, good company and could dance a bit. Latterly though things had gone downhill rapidly. He'd managed to fuck his arm whilst fixing some drug or other. The needle had missed the vein and hit some vital piece of equipment in his arm. This had rendered his left arm (his best arm) totally useless. One morning, a mate and I were going for a livener in the Queens pub on Oxford Street when Kingo happened along. He was going to the hospital for treatment on the arm, this wasn't the dentist or a visit to the local surgery for a sick note, this was important; this was to help him get a vital part of his body functioning again. Guess what he does? He says, "Fuck it" and comes on the piss with us. He'd lost interest in aesthetics by then. Now it was 100% drink and drugs. On the day Kingo was buried, news arrived that Ken had died. What a waste. These two boys had been under the cosh before. These binges were extreme, but hardly unique. It must have been the years of abuse had finally caught them out. Some would say later that it was deliberate; I'm not having that. It's just another story of fucked up drug taking. Hank must have felt awful, two of his best mates gone like that. Hank was about six stone and five foot tall back then, he'd taken at least as much as the other two, and must hold the world record for drug overdose stomach pumps, and he's still going strong. Must be the luck of the draw I guess. I was always lucky in the drug overkill stakes. For some reason or another whenever a dearth of goodies surfaced I was always somewhere else, out dancing or with a girlfriend. I could say 'there but for the grace.....' but that would be wrong, I wasn't in their class when it came to drug taking and my intermittent visits to their homes didn't really give rise to the behaviour that starts one on the drug dependency road.

Ken had a poetic streak. He could have been a writer, but it's difficult to concentrate on anything when you're on the constant hustle to get drugs or drug money. Ken was a fan of Dylan Thomas and the people closest to him arranged to have in buried in the same Laugharne cemetery as the Rimbaud of Cwmdonkin drive.The older I get, the more I realise how much I liked Ken. It's a pity that we weren't really on speaking terms towards the end of his life.

12. We Once Won – A Long Time Ago

If there's one thing I've always tried to keep up with its sport. As a kid I had an encyclopaedic knowledge of daft facts and figures about sportsmen of all codes. I not only new current and past discus and hammer throwers, I could tell you about dart players, table tennis champions, swimming world records and ice skate dancers. I was mad for it. You've got to realise that television coverage back then was limited, so to get these facts and figures I had to read about them. I wonder if I'd put as much effort into schoolwork I would be better off now?

I never got to see many of my sporting heroes back then. Swans were always languishing in the Second Division, so we never got to see the Greaves, Charlton, Law and the like. I did see Stanley Mathews play once. He was quite old by then, but he held his own. George Best played down the Vetch once. I think it was for an Ireland team (Under 21 or Youth) but for the most part it was good honest pros trying to earn a living. The rugby was a little better. The touring side used to visit St.Helen's, so I've watched the All Blacks, Springboks and Aussies a few times. But as much I admire the bottle of rugby players, I don't regard the men taking part as 'stars'. Today of course rugby players earn good dough, and drive flash cars, but back then they didn't seem much different from you or me. So there wasn't much hero worship there. Especially when you realise how many coppers play the game.

But St Helen's did give us the cricket. Down there I've watched most of the greats of my era. Wes Hall and Charlie Griffith, Kanhai, Kallicharan, Neil Harvey, Ravi Shastri, Slasher Mackay, Bobby Simpson, Clive Lloyd, Roy Fredericks, David Gower, Basil D'Oliviera, Ollie Milburn, Derek Randall, Kapil Dev, Barry Richards, Bishen Bedi, Intikhab, Billy Ibadulla, Roy Virgin, Mike Proctor, Sunil Gavaskar, Mustaq, Boycott, Ritchie Benaud, Wally Grout, Lance Gibbs, Derek Underwood, Greenidge, Glenn Turner, Doug Walters, Majid Khan (who was our captain),

Cowdrey, P.B.H. May, M.J.K. Smith... I could go on all night. As a kid I carried Australian fast bowler Graham McKenzie's bag from high street station to the bus, he was about eighteen, a kid himself. Standing outside the players entrance one afternoon, Wes Hall came bounding out of the ground asking "Where's the nearest bookie shop man?" I thought I was at the ground when Sobers hit his six sixes. But that was my memory playing tricks. In fact, we saw it on the telly, and ran down St Helen's Road. to see if we could find the ball he knocked up there. Having failed at that we darted off to the beach in the hope of finding the one he belted in that direction. No joy.

As great as Sobers was and how wonderful his assault on Nash's bowling might have been, I have to make a stand here for Malcolm Nash. I loved watching him bowl. When he had the new ball and there was damp in the air at the seaside St. Helen's ground, he was unplayable. I've seen him tie the best batsmen in knots on many occasions. It's also a little-known fact that Nash himself hit four sixes off an over against Somerset, and he batted at ten or eleven. My Dad bumped into Nash in a hotel bar and asked about the Sobers debacle. Nash responded by saying someone or other reminds him of it every single day of his life. But apparently it hasn't done him any harm financially.

So cricket is my number one sport. We never had a chance to play it at school. We used to mess around over the Quarry on the ash, sometimes we'd get a game at school, but that was on concrete, but never on a proper pitch. One evening around at Rough Trade, supping a few lagers, Pete brought up the idea of starting a team. Now I can run around a pub and knock a pool or dart team together no problem. We even managed a few games of football out of the Warwick. That took a bit longer though. But cricket poses a whole different kettle of googlies. There are so many different little tasks to be performed by the members. Luckily we had Pete Donne at the helm, and he would sort it, I'm sure.

So there was Pete, his mate Duncan, a Yorkshire lad who could keep wicket, Nigel House, also of Rough Trade, Kevin Allen, Terry

Rogers and me. Nets were arranged. Plenty turned up for those. Simon Roberts, Phil Rambow, Keith, Graham House a few others, there's almost a team there. The Warwick was yet to become the pub where everybody knew everyone else, so people kept to their own groups. I was on a bit more than nodding terms with John Gordon, Tom Clancy and Pam Brogan. They showed a keen interest to get involved, so join they did. There were meetings too. How are we going to raise money? Where are we going to play our home games? What are we going to call ourselves? Who are we going to play?

I arranged a friendly against some of the barrow boys off Portobello market. A nice introduction I thought, they can't be any better than us. The game was played at St Mark's Park. There's a wicket there, albeit a concrete one, covered by a mat. This was an evening game, and in those days I didn't go many afternoons without a session on the bevy, so I don't recall many of the details. I remember one incident very clearly though. Simon Roberts was batting; he was facing a guy called Frankie Kirk. Frank was quick enough. In the middle of the over he got one to lift sharply. Simon was crouching down at the crease, anyway, this ball took off and hit Simon straight in the face. He went down, blood appeared. Normally the fielders would crowd around to see if Simon was OK. On this occasion it didn't happen. Barry (who played for us later on) noticing that Simon had gone to ground outside his crease bellowed, "run him out". Is that in the rulebook? Is it cricket? The outcome is irrelevant. We proved to ourselves we could actually get a team together.

Seeing as we were based in Rough Trade, well our ever expanding kit bag was anyway, someone came up with the name 'Old Roughians.' That'll do for me. Terry had been busy; he'd been on the phone to various councils about the availability of cricket grounds. Fair play to him, he found us a ground in Boston Manor Park. A few of us went down there on a scouting mission. It was brilliant. A proper cricket pitch, right beside the canal, and, get this, our own changing rooms. This was going to be our home ground for the next few happy years. John Gordon hadn't been idle. John made top class rocking horses, so he could do good things with wood. Out of a few odds and ends he'd found in a skip, he made us a bulletin board, which we promptly put up in the Warwick. So what have we got now? Quite a few players. A name, a pitch, a scorer (Pam Brogan), a captain, a fixtures secretary, a social secretary (yours truly) all this, and nobody has missed a pint.

A very early game came against the Virgin Casuals. Edward Scarr captained this team, from the famous record company. It was a dismal day in Victoria Park, but in those days we were all mad keen to play. We batted first, wickets were dropping with embarrassing regularity, and by the close of our innings we had amassed the grand total of NINETEEN runs. Edward was charm itself, some may call it smug, as we ate the tea provided, he talked about the difficult wicket, uneven bounce and the rest of it. Most of us just wanted it over and done with. Well it shouldn't take too long now. Should it? How does one protect a nineteen run total? We had a newcomer with us. A hippy from out Ealing way, he was called Mark. He had a bit of the greyhound about him, skinny and energetic. He could bowl pretty quick too. Somehow the person at the other end managed to keep the runs to a minimum, while Mark steamed in from his. All right the pitch was iffy, but get this, Mark took eight Virgin wickets for three runs. The Casuals were routed; we bowled them out for EIGHTEEN and won the game. Edward looked as if he'd eaten something that didn't agree with him. We were chuffed, our first taste of victory.

The fixture list was growing quite quickly now. And there were always new faces appearing at the nets. We were keen to hold on to Mark, as you can imagine, but he told us he was off on a trip to New Zealand. He should have stayed put. Last we heard he'd been drug nicked big time over there, and was expecting a hefty whack off the beak.

Cricket became the number one focus for most of us back then. Equipment talk filled the Warwick beside the strains of 'Fields of Athenry'. People from all walks of life would show an interest in our progress, some wanted to join, some liked coming to games to fill in a boring Sunday, pre all day opening. It was great; some members had kids that they'd bring along. Pete and Shell had three by now, Terry and Mary used to bring T.A. along, so when Keith brought his son Alfie along, we could boast two of the worst behaved nippers ever to enter Boston Manor Park. If the weather was favourable, we'd get a hell of a crowd down there. It was well organised for my money anyway, and there were people on the committee who had even bigger plans. Club colours, youth team and possible tours outside London were on the agenda. Terry Rogers even came up with the club motto. Hope you're good at dead languages, our motto was 'Never Underarm' supposedly translated to the Latin.

Back in Hyper Hyper it's London Fashion. There were some odd shapes and sizes to be seen patrolling the stalls. Not Stevie Coppell though. I was about to ask him why was he in this basement, but thought better of it. Look out! here come a right pair. It's Boy George, who's just had a massive hit (and was seen everywhere you looked) and Marilyn who hasn't. They came on our stall. I was over the way, but could still see them. Like the two old fishwives they are, they did some cod camp routines while trying on the hats. That's cool. Then the talentless one got bored, (when he performed live there wasn't a soul there to watch him, so he should have been used to nobody watching anything he did) and flung one of Kirsty's hats to the ground. I think George was even embarrassed, but before I could say anything to Useless Bollocks, he'd gone.

Later a prospective customer approached. I'd noticed him having a good old gander at what was on offer, and he seemed very interested. He was dressed in a tight black outfit, and was sporting a ponytail. He asked me, in an accent I didn't recognise "You make zees hats?" I told him no, but I gave Kirsty the biggest plug I could muster. "Get her to call me," he said, handing me a card. At home that night I gave Kirsty the card. She turned white. "Who gave you this?" So I told her about the bloke, and what he looked like. "It must be Karl Lagerfeld," she said excitedly. Well that was the name on the card. I didn't know anything about him.

She soon filled me in. “He’s the man in charge of Chanel and Chloe and of course the Lagerfeld label.” Sounded good to me. Even I’ve heard of Chanel. She was a bit scared to phone, but she did eventually, and a meeting was arranged for the next day.

13. Lords, Bores and Builders

The Warwick by this time had become a bit of a cultural hotspot. Maybe not to the locals in the TV bar, they were in there to discuss important things like the price of beer, football, hurling and the racing results. In the rest of the pub the conversation could be loosely termed 'arty'. I didn't mind which side of the boozer I was on. I almost lived in the pub back then. I'd be among the first customers in the place. A bit early for the more bohemian type maybe, but plenty time enough to talk bollocks and horses to Tommy Stamp behind the bar. We'd sort out the horses for the afternoon, and catch up on the latest taproom gossip. I could also field questions from Tommy and his sidekick Willy concerning recent arrivals at the pub, especially the female variety.

And women did arrive all right, loads of them. Attractive, middle to upper-middle-class sorts who loved the dodgy atmosphere in this working-class stronghold. It must have been the boozer their parents had told them to avoid. This influx of gorgeousness has to be put down to the 'haircuts' – young lads, who liked a bit of sport, and loved a pint. Prominent in their number were, 'Sexy' Mark Layton, Mark Griffiths, Jim Radice and of course Piers Thompson. These guys seemed to be having a good old time of it. They were doing work in the pop video world, and for my money their presence in the pub got the girls thinking that it must be a safe place. And they were right.

Everyone eventually gravitated towards one of the two pool tables in there. The girls who played held their own. At that time one of the fashions was for girls to don skin-tight leggings, so you can imagine that when they were operating around the green baize, they'd attract an admiring audience from all corners of the room. Don't get me wrong; we had our own fabulous looking partners, Kirsty with me, Pete with Shell, Latif with the 'gorgeous' Valerie, and at the time Keith with Alison. Kevin always had one or more on the go, and you could rely on Glen Coulson to turn up with some good-looking fella. But none of our crowd would entertain the thought of performing the cue gymnastics associated with the likes of Evie Doggart and Caroline Harris.

The Warwick was perfect for the likes of me; it was just like any neighbourhood boozer anywhere in the country. It just happened to be situated bang in the middle of Portobello Road, obviously, one of the more famous landmarks in Britain I guess. Seamus, the landlord, who hadn't been in charge for very long, must have been rubbing his hands with glee when he started seeing this new crowd turning up. He was so grateful in fact, that if we needed anything in there, like a fundraiser for the cricket, or something for charity, he was more than happy to help. Out of such endeavours sprang several teams, the pool team, the quiz team, the football team, and the occasional darts team. I'll return to these pastimes later. But first, a tale of one of the oddest contests, that took place outside the Warwick one Sunday night.

Strolling down Portobello one evening, I happened upon a chap I knew in passing. He had wrapped around his person an extremely thick rope. I had to ask him what it was all in aid of, he said "It's for the Tug of War." He went on to tell me that his team, The Malvern were that very night, taking on a team from the Caernarfon Castle in a test of strength. Intrigued, I walked along with him to the Caernarfon to see what it was all about. It soon became clear to me, that as well as owning the rope, the Malvern boys had a fair amount of expertise in the tugging department. When the contest was called to order, and the starting whistle blown, it was plain to see that whereas the Caernarfon were all weight and strength, they lacked the finesse demonstrated by their opponents. In next to no time the Malvern were on the front foot (or is it back foot?). Try as they might, the brute strength of Caernarfon was no match for the Malvern pullers, in the blink of an eye they'd been pulled across Portobello Road as far as the start of the Golbourne.

To my eyes, this is Grade 'A' street theatre. I asked my Malvern man if there was a chance of us taking them on. He said, "You get a team, and we'll turn up with the rope." When I excitedly entered the Warwick with this news the regulars didn't seem to share my enthusiasm. John 'The Pipe' Gordon showed some interest. He gave me a brief history of Tug of War, and how it was a very honorable activity. He was an advocate of the technique over strength system, which I'd seen expertly displayed that very night, but apart from him, and a few drunks, people weren't exactly queuing up to join the team. I took a few names, and as with most things, if we were shorthanded we could drag a few out of the pub on the night. So I went back to the Malvern with our challenge.

The weather was set fair on the night of the 'Big Pull' we had managed to get a team together. John Duignan was in, Mel from cricket, not the biggest, but he talked a good fight, Maurice was there, he'd obviously done it somewhere before, in the fantasy world that he calls home, the rest were a rag, tag and bobtail of pub regulars, all the worse for drink. Pipe was our coach and inspiration. And from what I'd already seen, we'd need plenty of that. The Malvern team marched as one down Portobello approaching the Warwick. My man was at the front complete with his rope. People immediately were making comparisons between our squad and the opposition, and the general consensus was that we had no fucking chance. Very quickly word had got out about the contest. The street outside the pub was packed. Traffic was held up, and soon it was game on. The teams took their positions, and were warned to 'take the strain'. The whistle was blown, John The Pipe was at hand with words of enthusiasm, and tug of war chants, but in next to no time, the Malvern had the Warwick, skidding, sliding, falling over and gasping. They tried their best, but to no avail. It was over in seconds, when the last disco dance shoes, containing the feet of Gary Dempsey and Luke Coke was dragged over the line in the direction of Westbourne Park Road, the Warwick team were done for.

Seamus was outside that night. He knew that although the contest lasted less time than a greyhound race, it was good for business, so he got into negotiations with the Malvern skipper about a rematch. This was arranged for a fortnight hence. So two Sundays later, the Warwick's second opportunity arrived. As normal, I arrived early, and noticed some unfamiliar faces in the TV bar. When we were kids we used to go down Wind Street in Swansea to a brewery. Back then they still had some horses on the premises. These 'Drays' were used to haul beer, and we'd go to see them in the stables. As I looked around the TV bar in the Warwick that night my mind drifted back to the brewery visits. Seamus, perhaps worried for the reputation of the pub, had assembled a group of Navvies, curb layers, scrap merchants and road diggers who were all thick of arm and strong of back with hands like shovels. Not many of our original team made the cut that night. After the preliminaries were over and the whistle sounded and the pull began, it was the Malvern's turn to slide. 'Our lads had pulled them all over Portobello Road. John The Pipe's technical jargon went out the window that night, and brute strength won the day.

So another great night, plenty of ale swallowed, and, you'd think, everybody happy, but there were a few detractors, who didn't like the idea of a team, without any regulars involved, but fuck them. How many Mancs play for United?

As good as it was Tug of War was never going to gain the same popularity as pool amongst the locals. Pool is a great pub game. I used to spend all my time when I was a kid down the snooker hall in Castle Street in Swansea. You can imagine the appeal to a miscreant like me, and all my mates. There were all kinds of shenanigans taking place, it was dark and none of the regulars there seemed to work. They'd spend all day in there, smoking and gambling, it was great. John Terry (no, not that one) was a very good player, he was a very highly respected amateur nationwide. You could spend hours just watching him practice. This was in the days before the snooker was televised, so to watch him clearing a table was tremendous viewing. One quiet afternoon in there, Griffy Davis who along with his brother Denver were regulars, was looking for a game for money. He wouldn't be dull enough to take on Terry, whatever start he'd be getting, but when Terry said he'd play him one handed, and give him a start, Griffy's ears stood up. Once the rules of this particular encounter were thrashed out Griffy took up the challenge. No prizes for guessing who won. If a shot was unreachable Terry was allowed to play one handed with the rest, He didn't need to do this very often though, due to his cue ball control Terry could just lay his cue under his chin, and pot everything with ease, with his left arm firmly stuck behind is back. Griffy duly paid up. Of course we played pretty regularly ourselves. I could hold a cue; in fact if you clocked my stance, and the way I held my cue, you might be fooled into thinking I could play a bit. Not a bleeding hope. I got to a very mediocre standard, and stayed there. Now pool is a very different animal. It's a hundred times easier to pot a ball for a start, and with such a small area to oversee; safety play was a piece of billiard chalk.

I wouldn't say I was the best in there, not by a long way, but there wasn't a player in there that I hadn't got the better of, so I wasn't to be taken lightly on the baize. There turned out to be some good potters among the regulars, a lot of them thought themselves better than they actually were, but nothing wrong with a bit of confidence. So competition was strong. We held many a knock-out competition. Then some bright spark came up with the idea of forming a team. There were leagues out there for this sort of thing, and it was being looked into. Meanwhile, Seamus arranged a friendly match. You'd have expected a nice stroll around the corner for such a match, but that would have been too easy, Seamus had teamed us up with an outfit that played out of West Norwood. Apart from a few people who worked on London transport who drank there, no one had ever heard of the place. When it became clear how far away this gaff was, dissent struck the ranks. After much negotiating, we left the Warwick in cabs, paid for by Seamus, and headed into the great unknown. The pub was OK, Seamus loved it, he spent most of his time behind the bar there too. Just as well, as he'd promised to beer us up for making this journey to the back of beyond.

The trip was good practice for the pool team. I guess a bit of bonding went on, which would stand us in good stead for the upcoming pool season, when we'd have to visit such charming hostelries as the Pig and Whistle, the Arthur, the Albert and the Bridport. We always managed to get a team together however lairy the boozer was, but I remember the most difficult fixture to fill was the one against the William IV on the Harrow Road. It was a dive. Funny that, I was up there the other day, and there were bouncers on the door being fussy about whom they were letting in. Back in the pool days they'd be lucky to fill a snug bar. Anyway that was the pool experience of the Warwick Castle. What I'd like to do is name check a few of our players.

Sexy Mark, Mark Griffiths, Jim Radice, Kevin Allen, Simon Roberts, Charlie Dunnett, Mustapha, the brothers Chris and Ammy, Big Dave and Little Dave, Pat, Bob, Maurice ('cos he invented pool) *Joe Boy, Evie Doggart* and many more I'll wager.

With all the comings and goings in the Warwick at this time, something was needed to document all these events. Pete Donne and myself had a chat about coming up with a sort of newsletter. Primarily this would carry info on the cricket team, fixture list, how to join etc. So I came up with a few pages of bumph about the Old Roughians, a bit of pool, and a photo or two, Pete dug out a snap of Elvis and Little Richard which became the cover, and we were up and running. We had to give it a name, even if it wasn't much thicker than a fag paper. At that time toffs had found their way to the pub. Kate Bernard, who became a good mate, was friendly with a guy called Rory Knight-Bruce. Rory always seemed to have pretty girls about him, so I asked Kate what he did. She told me he worked at Tatler, so I thought a one-word name from the other end of the social scale would be great, so I called it Roughler. We were after all the Old Roughians, we were based (at least our kit bag was) in Rough Trade, so the Roughler name fitted nicely. Later on I took another leaf out of Rory's notebook, and gave myself a double-barrelled name as well. I became Ray Roughler-Jones.

With each issue the paper got a little thicker. It proved popular in the pub. I started taking a camera around with me; I got photos of all sorts in there. It just turned out that a few of them were in the public eye. So occasionally you get a pic of Strummer on one page, and on the opposite, a bigger snap of Shorty the pot man. I didn't have a clue how to put a magazine together, so I'd just bung something in where it fitted. For the first couple of issues, I'd put it together in Rough Trade, but as it became thicker more time was needed, as well as more room to spread all the stuff out. I found this resource centre out in Turnham Green. It was run by what appeared to be Socialists. There were art rooms, dark rooms, printing presses, collating machines, the works in fact. Problem was I didn't have the first idea on how to work any of them. When you see these machines in action you soon realise there are possibilities of improving your publication, and it's true, this place allowed you every chance of coming up with a decent mag. Kelvin who worked there was a great, patient bloke. But after I'd been there a few times he must have dreaded my next arrival. Don't get me wrong, I'd spent all day, for a couple of days at a time on the production, and I'd get knackered. Just because you're doing something wrong doesn't mean you aren't working hard doing it, and the frustration that surrounds fucking up is also very tiring. So in the end I had to test the patience of the comrades at the resource centre. I made sure I had a tale of some do-gooding charity work I was involved in, and I'd throw in a watered down version of what Bone was up too, so I managed to get them on my side. Poor old Kelvin, he had to oversee my work every step of the way, and in most cases, get so frustrated with my efforts, that he'd do them for me, right down to the stapling of the pages.

I'd get help on the contents for the paper as well. Luckily in the pub we had people who could knock up something of interest. Jock Scott hadn't surfaced yet with his poetry, but there were plenty about who could provide the odd limerick, Jo Jo Smith would keep our readers up to the minute with movie and music reviews, and she knew a bit of gossip, and Paul Stewart would send me cider-inspired fiction in his own inimitable Bristolian style. But the one person in the pub who kept the wheel turning was Steve Underground. Anyone will tell you that Steve had the weirdest imagination. Proof of this surfaced when he'd regale us, in the bar, with tales of being a personal roadie with Belinda Carlisle, or of the time he'd spent serving in the Rhodesian Rifles. Of course, neither of these, or many of the other stories he told, was true. He even had a picture of a platoon of Rhodesian Rifle personnel, and he'd point to the person that was meant to be him. The only thing he had in common with the guy in the photo was they were both white males. You hear all sorts of cobblers in the pub, but at least Steve's rantings were entertaining.

Steve kept his readers entertained with serialised stories, based on the novels of others. He had two running simultaneously in the Roughler. One was called 'Bunny' a spoof of the Martin Amis book 'Money' the other 'The Faked it and the Bread' based on Mailer's 'The Naked and the Dead' He'd follow the plot line reasonably accurately, he'd get the nuance about right, the only difference being that the hero of Steve's stories was none other than Glen Coulson. Glen was a regular in the Warwick, had been since the time he'd worked on the BPR stuff with Keith and Mario. When he was younger he'd been known as the Boy Wonder in the music business. He used to work for Tony Stratton Smith at Charisma records. He'd basically been in the bizz since he was a kid. He had some good tales, and an odd sense of humour which Underground used to observe from a distance. Glen would be espousing at the bar one day, and by the following week, this same tale would be coming out of the mouth of Maggio during the war. Steve was a genius in my book. He could have done writing for a living. But he was happy working on the Underground. That's where he got his name. Geddit? Another of his creations which I think could have become a winner given a bit more time was 'The Atricals" which was an everyday story of an acting dynasty featuring Keith and Kevin Atrical and their luvvy uncle. Steve could turn his pen to anything that was needed as regards filling up the paper. If someone didn't turn up with some promised article, I'd get Steve to write about the same thing, in their style.

Steve was a founder member of the Warwick quiz team. They were formed originally to enter The Roughler Grand Annual Quiz Cup. I'd placed yet another flyer on the Old Roughian notice board, and there was plenty of interest here. The response was so good that we couldn't do it in the Warwick. I had to seconder the room above the British Oak to accommodate the event. There were the Lisbon Lions, that would be Gary D, the other Gary, Peter Hamilton and Gordon Geddes, all Celtic supporters, and good on music, The Old Roughians, Lofty O'Reilly had a team of what he thought were ringers, I think the Haircuts entered, then there were a few improvised outfits who thought themselves tip-top in the brain department. I'd work hard enough to compile the questions, I can tell you. I was also the quizmaster. Anyone who was familiar with the lads from the Warwick team, knew they were up against it. This didn't stop the likes of O'Reilly and 'Trail Blazers' skipper Monologue Mick from Hackney Wick betting themselves to lift the coveted trophy (Cost £9.99p in Kilburn High Road).

But try as they might, they couldn't overcome the brainpower of the Warwick squad. Lofty tried all sorts. Bluff tactics, stewards' enquiries, and even downright, up-front, old-fashioned cheating, but all to no avail. The quiz became a popular night out. But the other teams were becoming fed up of continual Warwick victories, so when they reached their third successive final, and with it the opportunity to take home the magnificent Roughler trophy, I even tried to get them beat. I'd feed compatible, friendly questions to the opposition. They were mainly very good on the old music and sport, so I let them have plenty, while at the same time asking the Warwick stinkers on church, science, politics and the like, but they had the beating of me too. So they took the trophy home with them for good.

Steve, the two Johns and Pearce (Bud Abbot had been a founder member, but he was on the missing list having disappeared owing money to some drugsters) took the quizzing very seriously. After their gentle introduction at my hands, they decided to take it up a notch. They'd be travelling all over the shop for matches and competitions. There are financial and liquid rewards to be had in the strange world that is Quizdom. On one of these sorties I tagged along. I thought of it as my team. Don't ask me why, I'd never get into their team, barring injuries. At best, I'd consider myself a 50%er in the question answering department, and that's not up to scratch amongst this lot. The competition on this occasion was well off the manor. When we arrived you soon noticed that this was a different set of encyclopaedias to the one offered by yours truly at the Oak. This was boffin central. All the teams looked sharp. That being sharp of brain, certainly not sharp of dress. They looked like the type who turn up on 15 to one, Mastermind, and the likes, and no doubt, like the Warwick boys, had been swotting like mad. Half way through the night and 'ours' seemed to be holding their own, which is remarkable, for on these jaunts, Steve, and to a lesser extent John D, would get as pissed as arseholes. When it came Steve's turn to answer I looked over, and he seemed to be unconscious. To make things worse the question was out of the 'Stephen Hawking doesn't know this' quiz book. I thought Uh Uh, game up, and then to my amazement, Steve opened his eyes, pulled himself to the front of his chair, and nailed the answer. Not so lucky on this occasion John Duignan though. He was asked the following, "What was the first part of motorway to be built in the UK?" His answer was something like the A53 Preston by-pass. When it came time to reveal the answer, the quiz guy gave the answer as the M3. John was apoplectic. "It were the A53 Preston by-pass, I ought to know, I worked on the fooker." Now you might get away with this sought of outburst with me asking the questions, but the rules for this standard of competition were much more strict. "That'll be a two point deduction for calling out and arguing". I think his outburst cost the Warwick victory. That shows how good they were, beaten in hot company on a technicality.

I used to love all these pub games. They'd brighten up midweek lethargy. Also, it doesn't cost a lot either. Darts for instance, costs nothing at all. And why isn't it an Olympic event? You go into a pub, a church, a jail anywhere you like and ask for a show of hands from anyone who's thrown a dart. I doubt you'll get anyone not raising their hand. Then ask the same people how many of them have played beach ball (volleyball) or fenced or slid down a glacier with a tin tray under their arse, apart from Simon Roberts, Kev and Maurice (who invented all three) you wouldn't get a hand out of a pocket. Darts for the Olympics I say.

So we had enough going on to keep us out of trouble, but cricket had to take priority. We were a real club by now, and it all took organizing. There was a full fixture list. Pub regulars would now venture out to Boston Manor to support us. When the weather was good, whole families would show up, it was great. Our opponents, for the most part, were of a similar ability to ourselves. Some of the teams we entertained were called, The Serbian Sloggers, Victor Trumper, Not the M.C.C., Paddington Bears, Nelson One Eyes, Abdul Aziz, The Full Tossers, The Grim Reapers and our biggest rivals, The Barnes Breakers. One outfit we always had trouble with though was The Finsbury Co-op. They weren't the greatest exponents of the art, but they did have a secret weapon, who, on more than one occasion, bamboozled the Roughian stroke makers. This chap had a very ungainly gait, a windmill style arm action, which would confuse any batsmen when he approached to bowl, and then just before he released the ball, one would notice his eyes. When I was a kid it was called a squint. With his action all over the shop, and the eyes pointing in different directions, the least you'd be expecting is a ball that Muralithiran hadn't invented yet. So it was no surprise when you were out. Pete and I have had many conversations about 'eyes' and many theories have been bandied about, my own is, he bowled straight, and our lot got themselves out. Spooky.

From time to time we'd have a fixture, which meant we had to play outside London. We took on the Wellhead of Wendover, which was where Pete lived. This was a good boozy fixture, Kevin had found a pub in Sussex, and it was called the New Inn, which was hilarious. I'm not kidding; this gaff hadn't seen a lick of paint or any other kind of upgrade since the Second World War. There was a car dump out back, right beside the outdoor loo, and the furniture inside looked as though it had been found in a skip. The bar staff were something else again. They looked as if they'd walked of the set of The Munsters, but for all that they too were a great bunch. The game was played in a good spirit among the cowpats, and a great craic was had by all.

Our first official tour though was to my old stomping ground. The Badminton pub in the Sandfields in Swansea had gotten a team together. They were called the 'Bad', but that didn't disguise the fact that they all came from the Tenby pub, and I knew them all well. I was at school with John Morton, skipper Neil Glover, Laurence Toole, Sleepy, Brenton, Martin on the Buses, Jammo from St. Josephs, Peter Williams and the rest were all my old 'oppos. Behind the stumps was Terry Williams. Terry used to play for the Man band, but he was such a shit-hot stickman he was soon recruited by many other outfits. He was in Rockpile, Dire Straits, Meat Loaf and many others. He even spent some time playing with Cliff Richard, where you were not allowed to have the Sun newspaper about your person, for fear of dismissal. Terry was flown over to America one time to play drums with Chuck Berry. It was some birthday gig for the legendary rock 'n' roller. Terry was helicoptered from the airport to the gig, on arrival he was summoned to Chuck's dressing room. He approached the great man. Berry offered Terry a banana and said. "Who are you then?" Terry replied, "I'm the drummer" To which Chuck responded "Well you know the songs." And that was that.

Terry loved Swansea. He'd bust his balls to get away from gigs and recording and the like just to get back there to play cricket for the 'Bad'. I bumped into him one afternoon in the Warwick. He had a gig that night at the roof garden in Kensington. The International Model of the Year Show no less. Sounds good to me. Rock and Roll at its finest. You can imagine it, play the gig, come off stage, a quick Welsh wash, then on to guzzling champagne surrounded by rock star fixated, long legged crumpet of the first order. Wouldn't you? Not Terry, he said, "I'm not staying on after the gig moosh, the Bad have got a game tomorrow." See what I mean?

The Badminton players were footballers primarily, so they obviously liked a challenge, and with Neal Glover in charge there'd be no room for complacency. There was very little between the sides really. Most of our lot hadn't played much competitive cricket either, so it made things interesting. And it was a close call, but the 'Bad' edged that first encounter. There's a photograph of both teams congregated on the patio of the Tenby pub that night. If you look closely you'll see Brenton (I think) holding a lighter in one hand and my hat in the other. The crowd were chanting 'Burn the hat! Burn the hat!' I would have been a spoilsport to object (It wasn't one of Kirsty's) so they set fire to it. They collected up the embers of what was, if I say so myself, a rather stylish titfer and placed them in a tiny trophy thingy someone had brought along. This trophy became the 'Badminton Ashes' I was determined to get these back soon, but we'd have to wait a couple of years before we could bring them back to the Warwick.

14. A Brynmelian in Paris

With the success of Kirsty's first show at Lagerfeld, Karl had invited her to do the Paris Chanel show. It's a lot of hard graft for her, but the prestige she'd gain would be enormous. This time around she'd wangled it so I could go with her. When we arrive in Paris, it's straight over to the Iconic Chanel headquarters on the Rue Cambon. The staircase, the mirrors, and all that stuff we've seen in countless magazines and on the telly. Exceptionally well-dressed personnel flitting around the place, one of which took us to the hub, I guess, where Karl was in attendance. He seemed to love the job that Kirsty had done with hats. In fact, if you're adding up kisses, he must have been 'Over the moon John'. I just said hello or nodded to anyone who looked in my direction, then headed to the nearest corner to make myself scarce. There seemed to be fittings taking place that morning, and a never ending troupe of the most exotic girls I've ever seen kept passing my post in various states of undress. I didn't know where to look. Kirsty and the rest picked this up very quickly. All very amusing.

The woman Kirsty looked forward to meeting the most when she was out there was Mercedes Rubirosa. With a moniker like that, it should come as no surprise when I tell you she was a beautiful woman, and certainly, unlike the models, not a girl. Mercedes also had control over the Chanel accessories and costume jewellery department. Kirsty, like most girls I guess, adored this stuff, and Mercedes would always have a piece or two to distribute to the people who were involved in the shows. After the show she got to pick out some ridiculously priced item of clothing as well, but she really loved her Chanel trinkets. Everything Kirsty had brought along got the green light, so she was obviously very excited at the prospect of seeing her hard work on display at the top fashion show in the world.

We'd been given a hotel room. It was in the Hotel Cambon, right around the corner from Chanel. It was fantastic to be staying in this flash boutique hotel right in the heart of Paris in fashion week, and be somehow involved (in my case) and deeply involved, in hers. First thing I noticed was the mini bar. I'll be diving into that, sharpish, thought I, Kirsty put an end to that idea. She was probably right. Can't look that good for her, if I'm guzzling everything on offer can it? Clive Hadley, who had been living in Paris for a few years after moving there from San Francisco, called over to see us. He had a plan that entailed him going to the hotel reception, making up some yarn about there being a mistake along the way, and that we were going to stay at his apartment, and could we have our money back. Not a bad plan at any other time, but right now Kirsty was happy to stay in a bit of luxury, and drink in the atmosphere that surrounded this area on Paris Fashion Week.

The day of the show arrived and we set off for the Tuilerries, where it was being held. She had to get down to work immediately with fittings and last minute wot nots. I found myself backstage as well. I kept well out of harm's way. It was like a factory back there, everyone flat out on different stages of dressing the models, with Karl in the middle of it all, without a care in the world, or so it seemed to me anyway. I must admit I felt like a spare prick back there. I couldn't have looked that bad. What did I have on? Well, a pair of Levis, Redwing boots, Suicidal T-Shirt, a punky skatey jacket I'd bought yesterday, right here in Paris, all topped off with a hat made by Kirsty. But I still felt out of place surrounded by all this glamour. But on reflection, these models don't dress like this every day either, so who knows I might have appeared cool. My mind was put at ease soon afterwards, from her makeup chair, Ines, who was the top model at Chanel, shouted "Hey!" in my direction, and tipped me the wink. What can poor boy do?

The show itself was incredible, pure theatre. We were sat right at the front. I had a little nose about to see whom I could spot. I had to stop myself from gawking too much at the unbelievable Catherine Deneuve, cor blimey, if the local Gendarmerie were mind readers, I'd have been given a jolt in the Bastille. When the models appeared I saw Kirsty's face light up when the first of her hats hit the catwalk. The one she'd made that resembled a pile of Profiteroles was married up to a remarkable outfit; the whole thing looked great, and was greeted by thunderous applause. I was right proud to think that my bird was responsible for the millinery, nothing to do with me of course, but at least my total lack of support, and my outrageous antics, hadn't got in the way of her achieving her goal. The show was a roaring success. Backstage afterwards was full of the Worlds fashion press, all keen to capture anything Karl had to say. Kirsty attracted a fair bit of attention from many media people as well. You could definitely say she was on her way.

That night it was Party Down. We just followed along in the wake of these ridiculously gorgeous girls to various Paris nightspots. We didn't seem to have to pay to get in to any of them, and I haven't even bought a round yet. At the last port of call, 'Le Ban Douche" I thought it about time I put my hand in my pocket. I called up a few drinks for our company, distributed them, and hung around by the bar waiting for my change. I can't recall numbers now, but I can tell you, this guy wasn't giving me change, in fact he wanted more money. I thought he must have it wrong, but he whipped out a receipt, and sure enough, I've just bought the most expensive round in the history of ale guzzling. It wiped me out anyway. Thank God there was enough English money back at the hotel to get us from Heathrow to Ladbroke Grove the next day. The price of that round still haunts me to this day. But it was a massive experience, for both of us.

Kirsty had wanted to leave Hyper Hyper for some time. A new arcade of shops had recently opened near Portobello Green, underneath the Westway, so she went and had a gander. They were small retail outlets, but they were self-contained, with the added bonus of being able to use the back part as a workshop for the making of the hats. The front would be used to showcase Kirsty's wares. Things had been moving along nicely enough for her to be able to finance this change of location I guess. It would make me redundant though. I wouldn't be required to sell the hats now. She and one of her assistants would be on the premises all the time, so the last thing they needed was me on the premises, making the place look untidy.

The opening party for the shop, now titled simply, 'Kirsten Woodward Hats' was a good laugh. Pete Donne knew a guy called Patrick who was studying music at the Royal College, he and a few of his chums had created a string quartet, to earn an extra couple of bob whilst they were studying. So we got them along to play in the arcade. Flash food appeared from somewhere or other, and of course there was drink. The shop looked cushty and the hats looked out of this world. The press turned up along with Fashionista guests, and of course, our mates from the pub, the male side of whom were not averse to the sight of the girl who turned up with Jerry Hall. Of South American descent this girl had every moving part of her anatomy designed by some higher power simply to make grown men drool, and sigh "What lucky bastard takes her dancing"? A new beginning for Kirsty then, onwards and upwards. But you never can tell.

Hope this suit doesn't set alarm bells ringing!
Margaret gets married

Kirsty and me outside Rough Trade on Carnival weekend

Paul Durden puts the squeeze on Karin (Hooper) Hamilton

In the days before hair gel hit Swansea,
me, flat out with Dyfatty Flats, 1979

The Warwick quiz team(me, Steve Underground and Seamus Costello) win the Roughler Cup for the third time

John Duignan on the campaign trail

Ines de la Fressange knocked sideways
by the Roughler magazine

Pete Donne, owner of Rough Trade shop and founder of 'Old Roughians' with his camera-shy partner, Shelly

Landlord of the Warwick Castle,
Seamus Costello

Jock and I had the best intentions when we interviewed Shane McGowan. One guess as to what happened next

Obviously not the khazi at the Warwick,
the legendary Jock Scott takes his ease

The gorgeous Anna Chancellor with artist
Sophie de Stempel in the Warwick

15. A Right Royal Result

I'm unemployed again. Not that you would call ogling birds and getting steamed up with Cliff in Hyper Hyper real work. Although it did keep me busy, kept me out of trouble I guess. I'm still on the dole, so the rent is taken care of, but quite frankly, with all this time on my hands, I need some sort of income so I can afford to get down the boozer of a lunchtime. Salvation arrives out of the blue. An old mate called Vic shows up; he's got access to another old friend, namely speed. I've always loved my speed, and after a quick sample, soon realised this was a good one. I had my reservations about being able to sell it though. Does anyone take it anymore? It was laid on me, so there was no financial burden attached. So why not? The guy said it would be best not to cut it, that's all right for him to say, but perhaps he was right, so I only topped the ounce up to a round thirty grams. I'm so generous. I let people know I had it, and to my surprise, it began to fly out. Having sampled it plenty myself, I shouldn't have been so taken aback. Comparing this to some of the shite I'd taken over the years was a no brainer, this one was pucker. No bad guts, hardly any come down, and most importantly for the age group I was catering for, you could fuck on it. You're not going to get rich selling speed at street level, but the profit margin was plenty to keep me going.

Unlike coke dealers, a lot of whom, I think, quietly like certain folks to know what they do, like there's some glamour attached, selling 'fast' carries no cred whatsoever. I love it, all my mates likewise, but it's not the type of endeavour that gets you invited to gigs and parties which is just as well. Some coke dealers get taken in by their punters to such an extent, that they start considering them to be friends. When they run out of the posh, or, god forbid, they get nicked, and the phone stops ringing they're left with a bad taste. Most of the punters I had didn't want me as their mate, and if they ever invited me anywhere, it wouldn't be to a place this side of a Big Issue Fund Raiser. I would go about my selling in a professional way though. I laid down rules as to when and where I'd be available, and I stuck to it. I don't have to run around the place, and I certainly don't get any late night calls. In fact, I get most of my pedalling done in the early afternoon. This takes care of the beer money and a few extras. The Roughler, which by now is on display, and on sale, behind the bar in the pub, is moving along nicely too. Every time I go in there, they've sold a few, so there's a couple of bob waiting for me there.

I used to take my time in the mornings back then. I'd rise about 10:30. Do a few domestics, and wait for the phone to ring while reading the papers. When the phone eventually rang, it would normally be for me, mates, asking about what's going on, or some of my speed customers. Since Kirsty had moved to the new shop, all her phone traffic went there, so for the most part, if the dog and bone rang it was for me. One morning it rang, I was feeling chipper this day, so normally I would pre-empt the person on the other end, by bursting into banality before they had time to speak. On this occasion I didn't do that, which I guess turned out to be a good move. On the other end of the line was a lady with a ridiculously pronounced toff accent. With some of the girls I'd been meeting down the pub lately, and the way they talked, it could easily have been for me. It wasn't. In fact the lady on the other end of the phone was Lady Di. Jayzus! I thought. I was dumbfounded, but I managed to take down her message. And as you might have guessed, it didn't concern me.

Kirsty was excited at the news, understandably so. She'd been attracting some high-end clients of late, and her reputation as a milliner was soaring; but the Princess of Wales, come on. She was asked to attend Kensington Palace that same week. She even dragged me along for a bit of moral support. We were ushered in to the reception area. They weren't going to have the likes of me poncing around a place like this, so they put me in some side room with a cup of tea. Kirsty was then taken in to meet the special one. The interview went very well. Now Kirsty being a straight shooter, automatically went into kow tow and bow-and-scrape mode when she met Diana, but to her credit, Diana said she didn't have to do all that malarkey. Would Diana Princess of Wales use the word malarkey? I often wonder. According to Kirsty, Diana was charm itself, and she ordered a few hats to boot. It was just as well I wasn't allowed into the inner sanctum. I had some speed in me, and probably would have become over familiar. It's strongly rumoured that Princess Margaret used to get into the Portobello Star on occasions, but The Princess of Wales in the Warwick, which I would probably have suggested to her might have been pushing it a bit. Although thinking back to some of the clientele in the Warwick at that time, she probably would have walked in and known one or two of the punters. The big prize that came out of Kirsty's connection with Lady Di had to be the commission she got to supply the hat that the Princess wore at the Fergie and Andrew wedding. I remember that day well. I'd just run an errand to the West End, on my return I popped into the Princess Alex pub for a swift one. The wedding was on the telly in there. Diana featured prominently. I told anyone who'd listen that my girlfriend made her hat, no one was impressed, or, more likely, thought I was making it up. They had a fashion correspondent on the TV coverage that day, and every time Diana came into shot, this girl would mention Kirsty's name. I can only guess at how many people were watching this extravaganza, but it had to be tens of millions. If only the tiniest fraction of these picked up on Kirsty's name, her reputation would have been sealed. Again, I was filled with pride, and again, it was none of my doing,

So Kirsty is picking up some influential commissions. She does Lagerfeld, Chanel, Chloe, and lately she's been off to Italy to do her thing at Fendi. It's all good, but shitloads of hard work. I'm not much help to her, unless you include me giving her the smallest amount of speed so that she can work through the night. I can't even cook, so she still has the chore of feeding us both. She tried to keep me involved with things. She suggested I do a tailoring course at the London College of Fashion. I'd never become Tommy Nutter by doing this, but at least I'd be able to sew, and that would be a great help to her. I signed up for the course, and had to attend an annexe of L.C.F. at Curtain Road. This sounds a long way off for me, but it's straight through on the Metropolitan line from Ladbroke grove. The guy teaching us the sewing part of the course was a good bloke. He was Irish, and he liked a pint. Through him I learnt about 'dirty cotton' (Gnarled and twisted yarn) and 'lazy cotton' (to much thread on the needle) and I was getting on OK. The problem was my classmates. These comprised of barely-out-of-school teens, who were on apprentice schemes elsewhere, and this was part of their training. They were all still in school mode for the most part, and were always taking the rise out of the teacher. I was an old pro in that department, so watching these youths acting up was a wakeup call as to how much of a twat I was when I was at school.

These kids put me in a right mood most of the time. I was all right in the morning, but by the afternoon, when I knew the pub would be active, I lost interest. I began to miss lessons, this got worse over the weeks, and before long I stopped going there altogether. By now Kirsty was used to me doing things half arsed, so she wasn't that surprised. But with her new found professionalism, she must have thought that I was a lame fucker, although she never said it. While at the college I did manage to make a pair of trousers, made to my own measurements. They were in a nice worsted fabric, and lo and behold, they actually fitted me. I wore them often afterwards.

16. Along the Track Came Puffing

Now with Kirsty up to her neck in straw, felt and ribbons, I started living, to all intents and purposes, the life of a single man, for the greater part of everyday, anyway. Being the selfish slag I am though, if she was asked somewhere flash, with the hint of a free drink, I was there in a heartbeat. Saying that though, I served some purpose, she couldn't really go on her own. With the influx of 'beautiful people' into the pub, there was always an after hours drink or some party to attend. So more and more I'd fall into the flat in the small hours. If she was pissed off Kirsty never said that much about it. Thinking back, arguments weren't that big in our relationship really. I used to wind her up something awful, and she'd get pissed off with me generally, but she didn't bite for the main part. In her case, I guess it was controlled anger. But even the coolest reach breaking point. One night we'd had a few words, normal stuff, but I must have touched a nerve on this occasion. I reckon I would remember if it was a serious spat, but I can't. Anyway, she went potty this time. I was lying in the bed, holding up my side of this altercation, when suddenly she picked up the ancient upright Hoover that was parked in the corner of the room. This was a task in itself, as it weighed a bleeding ton. With cleaner in arms, in one movement, she hoisted the machine above her head, and brought it down to a crashing halt across my shins. Fuck that hurt. If you think you can stomach looking at my bare legs, next time you see me, ask for a gander at the scars that remain there to this day.

That, of course, should have acted as a warning of what was to come, but as ever, I took no notice. I just carried on drinking, and drugging my way through life, looking for what, I couldn't tell you. I had the paper to keep me busy, also the cricket as well as the occasional gig to promote or, in some way or other, get involved with, but to be honest this activity didn't take up that much of my time. If I had to get something done, I'd make sure I got out of bed early, get stuck in, and made sure it was finished by 1pm which was as late as I'd like it to be when I hit the Warwick. It was early closing back then, so you'd get a couple of hours in before closing time, pop in the bookies to check the results, then home for a wash and brush up, quick sandwich and out again by 5:15, fifteen minutes before opening and forty five before Kirsty came home from work. I couldn't stand being indoors. What's the point of me being stuck inside, when all there was to do was watch telly, or watch Kirsty working?

At the pub I'd be meeting all sorts of new people. Among whom was Kate Bernard. We became good mates. No hanky panky here though, we'd just hang out. She had a lot of buddies did our Kate, lots of whom were girls, toff girls. I have to admit to being fascinated by each and every one of them, and the names, I heard people being called Pandora, Tarka, Zsa Zsa, Araura, Venitia and Mandana. This was all new to me. The way they talked and presented themselves was eye opening. What made it even better was they seemed to find me interesting too. 'Street Cred' was still in the vocabulary back then. I think it surfaced during the punk thing, and still hadn't disappeared quite yet. If by street cred they meant someone who was conscious of his surroundings, knew how to avoid getting robbed or beaten up and knew a lot of the people who did the beating up and the robbing in the first place, I was their guy. Coming from where I do, street cred was the only fucking cred we had, nothing clever about it. In fact, it's a nuisance having to live of your wits all the time, gives you ulcers.

I'm being invited here and there to places which are fresh and fun for me, and there are girls about, most of whom I fall in love with in a second. It's my imagination more than anything that probably fuels the flame to these infatuations. When I was a teenager I'd meet up with girls who could smoke, spit, fight and play football better than me. I was wary of them, mainly because how do you live it down if one of these gives you a good hiding? You don't is the answer to that one. But from time to time I'd find myself alone with one. Let's say that things moved along a bit, romantically speaking, and lo and behold, before you can say 'five Woodbines and a penny box of matches' you're in a clinch, and all of a sudden this particular female football hooligan turns to jelly in front of your eyes and starts whispering sweet nothings in your ear, it feels like a sort of victory – your personality has altered her mindset from one of open hostility to one of demureness. With these toff types, you hoped the complete opposite would happen. In my dreams, I imagined these well-spoken, well-educated types with good manners and minds of their own turning into sluts of porn film proportions if you ever got them into the kip. You never know.

So there are plenty of girls around to chat to and flirt with. One or two were even heard describing me as 'Stylish and charming'. If that was true, what sort of geezers have these birds been hanging out with? My new friends took me to many a new venue. Nothing special, but nothing I'd had much contact with in the past either. House parties were big on the agenda. Not 'house' where everyone was 'E'd up, that would come much later, or house parties like the ones in Swansea either with speed, cider and pissing in the sink. No these were relaxed affairs. You were able to buttonhole some girl who'd caught your eye without having to shout over the music. I seemed to do all right. Maybe it was their good manner thing, but my yarns and gags all seemed to go down well. I got taken to any amount of clubs. The one I liked the best was the Chelsea Arts Club, for no other reason than it had a full sized snooker table in there. So yes, I'm getting out and about, broadening my horizons, and all I have to do to return the compliment, is to take them down the Warwick. Hard life, innit?

All this female attention is great. But where would we be without a boozing companion? We all need a mate or two to guzzle and swap bullshit with, someone who is on the same wavelength. Pete Donne was my best butty, and he'd spend plenty of time in the pub after work, but lately he's starting having kids. You can't stay out as much when that starts happening. In fact, most of the regulars in the pub had commitments when I think back. Some had families, and, believe it or not, a lot of them had jobs. A one-year-old child can tell you that boozing til closing, and then getting up for the graft in the morning doesn't mix. So by about nineish midweek the pub would thin out. One person who didn't suffer from any of these problems started frequenting the pub. Jock Scott had made his way from Musselborough to London on the rock and roll highway.

With his poetry and punk credentials he'd ingratiated himself with many a band, and would often appear on the bill with people who would become well known. He had an 'in' at Stiff Records and had compered the odd gig for some of the acts there. But his most notable compere gig had to be the one he did with the Clash. He'd never admit to it, but he was a mate of Glen Coulson. Jock's name would pop up in lots of Glens dreary dialogues, one time he was boring Keith Allen to death in there, and once again Jock was mentioned, so I asked Keith who this guy was. He gave me a quick rundown on Jock's antics, so I asked "He likes a drink then?" Keith replied, "Likes a fucking drink! He puts you to shame!" So when I eventually met Jock I felt like I already knew him.

Jock liked drink, horseracing, women, Piccadilly fags and music. You can't fault him on any of those choices. We eventually got to hang out a lot, and had numerous laughs along the way, blagging our way into countless parties, gigs, gallery openings and clubs. Through his connection with Gareth Sager, Jock had built up a toff fan club of his own. Gareth's group Rip Rig and Panic seemed to have a large following of well-heeled chicks, and Jock was his mate, so he was well in with them too. This crowd had the word on loads of parties, good ones too. We were summoned to attend one such event at a rich Greeks house in Campden Hill Road one night. When we got there our eyes lit up, for in the corner was a hill of drink, which no one else seemed to be interested in. It could have been a work of art. It probably was until Jock and I set about destroying it. This was a quiet affair; I figured out that it was a getting to know new people party because there seemed to be a lot of introductions going on. Not many of those were coming our way though. There was Royalty in attendance. Lady Sarah Armstrong Jones, the daughter of Princess Margaret was there. The next time I saw our hostess she said it was a pity that Jock and me didn't have a chance to talk to her, well that's true enough, for even allowing for the fact that we were mighty pissed pretty quickly, we had enough sense about us to know you don't upset the guest of honour at a party, especially a close relative of the Queen. This has nothing to do with manners. Who the fuck wants to get chucked out of a place before the drink runs out? Not so lucky the short arse geezer in the corner though. He turned out to be multimillion record selling singer/songwriter Paul Simon. Jock couldn't hold himself back on this one. He strolled over to Garfunkel's mate, stuck out his hand and said "Hello darkness my old friend." Simon took it well; the toffs didn't get it, meanwhile us two pissheads thought it hilarious.

Jock has got us on the guest list at the Greyhound in Fulham Palace Road. To see the launch of the solo career of Undertones front man Feargal Sharkey. The place had been booked for Feargal to showcase his first single, and the gaff was heaving. The new single 'A Good Heart' had had plenty thrown at it by the record company, and graciously, they had provided a free bar, so everyone was on top form. Dave Stewart from the Eurythmics had a lot to do with this record by the looks of it; he was up on stage with Sharkey when they played the song. Maybe he wrote it, I don't know. It was a goodish tune. Not as good as any Undertones record mind you. But it was a big hit later on. The vibe was so good down there, even Jock Scott ventured onto the dance floor. Turns out he was dancing with Feargal's mother. I let him carry on, while I attacked the bar. Free drink, so you're not gonna get served in a hurry, but there's plenty of time. I saw my moment, and thrust forward into the firing line. There was one guy before me, and when he called up his drink I thought 'I know that voice' so I looked to my right, and I nearly had a heart attack. Standing right next to me at the bar was Bob fucking Dylan. Jayzuz!

From the Stones, Kinks, Small Faces, Tamla, Stax, The Yardbirds, The Animals, Atlantic through to the MC5, the Velvet Underground, Family, The Flamin' Groovies to Traffic, The Faces and up til the Sex Pistols and the Clash there always was Bob Dylan. From the first time my Dynevor schoolmate, Viv Austen, played me his album, I've always been a massive fan, and have ducked in and out of his career ever since. OK he didn't write 'Her name is Rio and she dances on the sand, Rio, Rio dancer across the Rio Grande' But he came up with the odd good song. Now, with the man stood right beside me, I was dumbstruck. My heart skipped a beat, and I was speechless. All I could think to do was go and report the sighting to Scott. I got him to approach Feargel, who by now had sung his song, and must have been in good spirits, as it had brought the house down. The conversation went like this. "Well done Fergal. Look I've been dancing with your mother here. Is there any chance of an introduction to Bob Dylan?" Fergal didn't even break stride. He looked us both up and down and said, "Behave your fooling selves" and that was that. And if anybody asks me is it easy to forget. I'll say 'It's easily done; you just pick anyone, and pretend that you never have met.'

On another outing, this time at the Café de Paris, poor old Jock is worse for wear, so was I. We'd just left some gallery opening, and the wine had taken its toll. We fell in the 'Caff' after the pubs had closed. This is of course 'greedy pig behaviour' but what the hell. Jock needs a seat. He finds one, but is immediately accosted by two burly geezers, who ask him to shift. He was in the process of doing this, when the third member of this company piped up "It's OK let him sit down." This third geezer turned out to be George Michael. Now remember this was in a time when George didn't attract the weird press he gets nowadays, but right about then, there was a tabloid story going around about how George had flung a drink over someone or other. It took Jock a second or two before he realised he was on the same table as this songster, but when he did, he made to shake Michael's hand, in the process he knocked over a bottle of drink, which landed in the ex Wham singers lap. Jock was mortified, and mumbled some apology. Michael, as quick as a flash, came back with, "That's all right, I'm doing that all the time myself". He shot up in our estimation after that. I still wouldn't buy one of his records though.

My never ending search for some extra marital continues apace. Don't seem to be getting far with it though. I don't know how hard I was trying, but I was most definitely going through the motions. It couldn't have helped that most of the girls I flirted with knew I had a girlfriend, and if they ever took the time to find out, they'd soon realise I wasn't that eligible either. I made a few moves, but it was, as always, the male pursuits that seemed to take up most of my time. Pool, cricket, boozing, gambling and watching football and the rest are full time activities. Where's the spare time to chase up the birds? I don't know. It was while watching a game of football in the Warwick one night that I caught a glimpse of a girl who would have done the trick for me. I was with Keith, Kevin and some others when this tall, attractive almost aristocratic girl joined our company. Kev and Keith seemed to know her, so when she left I made a few enquiries. “Who was that?” I asked excitedly. Keith said “Funnily enough Ray, she asked the same about you.” I must have been pissed, the last person on earth who is going to play cupid for you is Keith, but because I was blinded by beauty I believed him. “Who is she then?” This time to Kevin, who is also partial to the wind up, “That’s Anna, she’s an actress, you’re well in there Ray.

So the very next day the hunt was on for Anna the actress. I interrogated everyone I bumped into, finding out what I could about her. I even found out where she lived, and walked past there a couple of times. But what reason did I have to knock on her door? None is the answer to that, so I didn’t. Not even when I was drunk. She may even have a geezer on the firm for all I know. When I eventually bumped into her socially, it soon became apparent that I had no chance. The bright toff girls have this knack of deflecting the conversation away from anything remotely approaching intimacy if they have a mind to, and Anna was no different. She knew what I was all about, and although she was very friendly, never once did she give me any encouragement in the amour stakes. So my mini stalking of Anna Chancellor came to nought. Worth a try though.

The legendary Jock Scott keeps slipping in and out of view of late. Sure, he’d turn up, shoot some pool, pass on a bit of gossip then as quick as he’d arrive, he’d disappear in a puff of Piccadilly fag smoke, quite mysterious. In a pub like ours, you’re never going to be drinking alone, that’s for sure, so Jock’s absence didn’t create any sort of vacuum, but I was intrigued as to what he was up to. Next thing you know Jock is the new best friend of Anna Chancellor. What’s going on here then? Surely not. Jock is a good bloke, you’re guaranteed a good chuckle with, but in the love stakes I wouldn’t have rated him that much above me. In fact, if it was a horse race I would have thought I could have given him a few pounds, and still beaten him to the winning post, but the day that he and Anna walked into the pub with shared domestic shopping, I realised I’d been beaten fair and square. The more I got to know about Jock, the less surprised I became, many a looker has fallen for this Scotsman's charms in the past. Some even said he caught the eye of no less a beauty than Neneh Cherry. That's top drawer stuff, right there. If the rumours I've heard are true, she was believed to have compared him to Clint Eastwood. "Blimey!" you might well say. I did. And of course Jock probably adopted a far subtler approach than yours truly in the love exchanges. I have very little in the hidden depth department, it's pretty much 'what you see is what you get' with me, Jock on the other hand would be likely to present poetry and floral pillow talk as part of his armoury. This probably wouldn't hit the mark down the White City estate, and definitely wouldn't in Townhill, Swansea, but this behaviour must work with the arty types. So before you can say 'Of course she doesn't fancy you' Anna and Jock are a couple, big time. Weeks later, Jock and I are playing pool when he announces: "She's pregnant, we're having a baby." The result was of course lovely Poppy Chancellor. Anna Chancellor is now one of my very best mates, if it hadn't been for her encouragement I don't think I would ever have given up the drink.

17. Carmen

I'd had a few, all too brief, 'romantic' interludes around and about, but these were generally late night boozy gropes, nothing that even came close to an affair, so my quest continued. By now the Warwick was buzzing, and Saturday afternoon was especially busy in there. On this particular Saturday, Kevin Allen was in attendance, and I noticed he was in the company of a very attractive blonde. She had this English Rose look about her, pale skin and piercing blue eyes. I managed to get a few words with her on this initial encounter, and seemed to get a fair to middling response, so I left it at that. During the course of the following week I made a few enquiries about her. I even brought her name up with Kevin, so I could gauge the depth of involvement between him and her. He didn't seem that enamoured by her, which isn't that surprising, as Kev always seemed to have a couple on the go back then. Why not? He was single, and young. Turns out that her name was Carmen, and half of Kevin's interest lay in the fact that he was kipping around at her house

The following week she was in there again. I noticed her standing alone, looking a bit awkward whilst Kevin was talking bollocks to all and sundry, nothing wrong in that. Talking bollocks in there was the equivalent of a membership card elsewhere. While he was holding court, I made my move. I'd played a bit of blind-side wing-forward for the school rugby team, and I put this experience to good use, as I positioned myself, unnoticed, right beside the object of my lust. It might have been due to the fact that she was being ignored, but she did seem genuinely happy to see me, so a chat ensued. I managed to convince her that a night out with me and my mates up in Soho would be a good thing to do the following Thursday. She thought it a good wheeze, so I arranged to meet her and her sister in the French House on that night.

Thursday arrived, and I'd made an effort, and felt good, I turned up alone at the French to meet the pair of them. They didn't seem to mind me not being in company, and I, full of the fast, did my best to entertain. Carmen's sister was called Bella, she was younger, of a darker hue, fit and attractive, and like her big sister, seemed to have a lot of time for the bollocks coming out of me at a machine gun pace. I'm going to give all you geezers a tip right now. If you're on a date in Soho with a girl you want to impress right into the boudoir, and feel that you're 75 per cent there, take them to Gaz's Rocking Blues on a Thursday. This may be the late Eighties I'm writing about here, but nothing alters down there to this day. The girls love it down Gaz's, it seems to dilute any shyness they may have had previously, and before you know it they're up there, dancing there pretty arses off, putting them in the right frame of mind for what you've got planned for later.

This certainly happened in this case. After we'd drunk plenty and slid the wood for what seemed like hours, it was time to leave the club, I was invited back to where they lived, which was a house in Islington, so in the wee hours, the three of us headed back there. More drink was taken, and then Carmen took a rest room break. I don't know how it came about, but in her absence, her sister had somehow steered me towards her bedroom. Everything happened double quick, by the time Carmen re-surfaced; me and Bella were engaged in a bout of naked wrestling. Carmen wasn't pleased about this, and made it clear she thought it was me and her, but she retreated gracefully, and let us get on with it. I suppose I did owe my allegiance to Carmen, but hey, a bird in the hand and all that. It was a busy old encounter, but in reality there must have been some sibling rivalry doing the rounds that night, don't get me wrong Bella was up for the cup all right, but I still got the feeling that her heart wasn't in it 100 per cent, and may have done it to spite her sister. These girls are toffs for fuck sake. Who knows how their brains work?

Morning arrives, and my bedfellow is up and at 'em. She's out the door quick time. No goodbye kisses, or talk of a rematch. I don't mind, I'm lying there trying to think of a feasible excuse I can use for my all night absence when I get back home. The old chestnut "I passed out round at so and so's" had been used so often by now, by every philandering fuck who ever played away, you'd think it would be extinct, but that's as far as this plan had gone when Carmen enters the room. Another story needed, I relied on the: "I didn't realise we were on that kind of date…" cobblers. It seemed to work. Half an hour later, after a quick cuppa, we are upstairs, this time in the master bedroom. It was much more fun with Carmen, the verbal's were ten times better with her than with the sister, who could be described as a slightly surly Goth, and for my money, she's more attractive too. Her body was a bit off kilter, but I quite like that in a girl.

Carmen was studying art at the Slade. She didn't have to do any work to finance this, so it would appear that she wasn't short of a bob or two. The house must have cost plenty, and she had a very nice car parked outside. She went to a Lady Di type school when she was younger and it turns out that her granddad had been made a Lord for his endeavours in the motoring business. She was well heeled all right. What I liked most about her was the way she complimented me at every available opportunity. It did wonders for my confidence I can tell you. For the last few years, this sort of talk was thin on the ground round at mine. In fact, Kirsty's nickname for me was 'never nicely', this didn't concern matters of the bedchamber, it was about my general half-hearted approach to anything domestic. According to her I never finished anything off properly, which was true a lot of the time, but even if I did pass muster on occasions, backslaps were still not on the agenda round at Roughler Mansions. So to be told I was wonderful in all departments by Carmen, made for a nice change. As time passed she even started complimenting me about my physique for gawd sake. At home, if any part of my anatomy was on display, Kirsty's response would be "Put it away Ray." So taken by my shape was Carmen, that she asked me to pose naked for her. So over the next few weeks she'd take up her brush and paint away, while I, for the most part, lay comatose on her bed.

I soon got bored hanging around at her house. I needed to be out and about. I told her where I'd be, and she would meet me wherever. Most of the socialising was done down Ladbroke Grove, so when she turned up it was cool, but the thought of hauling my arse all the way to Islington for the leg over and then having to come all the way back home afterwards was a bit too much. I wouldn't get home 'til very late, and that just equated to more grief. This turned into a blessing in disguise. I've always liked the more adventuress side of the old sex game, and Carmen, fair play, was up for it too. I don't know what her love life was like before we hooked up, but I was beginning to like what it was turning into now. I had nowhere to take her in W11 for any love action, so we decided to take our affair 'outdoors' this suited me fine. I hadn't felt this type of excitement since the days spent in Swansea with super shagger Susan. In next to no time we're at it down the big Scrubs, little Scrubs, St. Mark's Park or any near park, over the canal bank and behind Barclays bank. Fabulous stuff.

One night it was absolutely pissing down, I mean biblical, heavy rain, so bad you couldn't see through the windscreen, so she had to park up on Westbourne Villas, a snog turned a bit serious, and before you know it, we're outside in the pissing rain, shagging away on the bonnet of her car, right in the middle of the deserted street. Fucking great! It wasn't as daring as it sounds. Anyone out walking on a night like that would have to have had serious mental health problems, and thought they'd been imagining it anyway. As for passing cars, how could they see through their windscreens, we couldn't? I got home that night drenched to the bone, and exhilarated.

It was going to plan as far as I was concerned. A bit of slap and tickle just a phone call away. Cushty. Then I made the mistake of letting her come to the cricket down Boston Manor. At first it just seemed to the rest of the players that these two girls had become cricket fans. Pete and Shell guessed what was going on, and the rest soon realised something was up when I failed to turn up at the pub after games. Going to the pub after a game of cricket is the only reason for going to cricket in the first place, so everyone smelt a rat. Lots of the people involved were mates of mine and Kirsty, so I was chancing my arm a bit here. But at the time I didn't give a toss, I was pissed or stoned all the time by now anyway, so didn't see any harm being chauffeured back and forth to the cricket by someone who was forever giving me compliments. She even told me how good I looked in my whites, and would applaud loudly any time the ball came near me.

This affair didn't go on for that long, but it certainly did the trick. I'm not taking much interest in her world, and after the initial 'passion' wears off girls in general seek something a bit more substantial than anything I had to offer right then, so it fizzled out. Perhaps this was her first opportunity to sew her wild oats or go through a rebellious phase with a bit of rough, but she must have decided that it was time to take life a bit more seriously, I wasn't complaining, it was getting too much for me anyway. But I'll tell you what; it did the trick for yours truly. She managed to complete the painting of me before we called it quits, she had some talent, and it looked great. I didn't think I'd be seeing much of it in the future though. Think on.

18. Mr Saucy's Blind Date

It's been done many times before, but I have to admit that the talent show Keith Allen used to put on in the Falklands Arms in Bloomsbury was a good night out. What are brothers for? Nicking ideas off I guess. Well why not? By now we had a decent relationship with the Tabernacle, so Kevin Allen thought it would be great for us to have our own version in W11. We'd do the normal talent show stuff, then replicate a current television show and round it off with a band. This made for a jolly night out for the locals. It was christened Mr. Saucy's Blind Date, and it turned out to be a great success. Mr. Saucy was an alter ego of Kevin Allen; he came up with it first when he was in an advert with our old mate Fiona Dennison. Kev went up the market and bought the most ridiculous 1970s clothes he could find, glittery jackets, frilled shirts, bell-bottom trousers that would fly at half mast and platform shoes. He looked like Jim Bowen on acid. With a bit of make up to finish it off he captured the persona of a washed out, useless, down at heel quiz show host perfectly.

But primarily this was meant to be a talent show, and it became my job to find said 'talent' this wasn't as easy as you'd think. Nowadays you get tens of thousands queuing up for these television talent shows, but that's telly, and people will do anything to be on the box. We were trying to lure these folks along for no money, for a prize which hadn't been decided on yet. But I tried my best, and although not overwhelmed with entrants, we got one or two crackers. The worst, and probably the best act ever to set foot on the Tabernacle stage has to be 'Dangerous Dave Flame'. On the night of his heat, he turned up with what appeared to be his whole family, that's nice, but wait, he's on the stage now, and all the family are up there with him Before he starts his wife makes an announcement...

"Dave needs complete silence when he performs these very dangerous feats." OK, that's cool. Dave then takes over, he produces two glass bottles, places them in a towel and with a hammer, smashes the bottles to pieces. Then he picks up the towel and with the glass inside proceeds to rub towel and glass vigorously into the bare skin of his face, a gasp goes up from the crowd, Dave keeps on rubbing away. Eventually he removes the towel to reveal a face completely covered in blood. Wow, what a start. Then there were fire tricks, more glass, more blood, all performed with varying degrees of ineptitude.

By this time I'm sure the audience were worried about Dave's well being, but he carried on regardless. The finale of his act arrived eventually, Dave lay down on a bed of nails, his son walks on stage with a paving stone, he places this block of concrete across his father's stomach and chest. Then the wife gets in on the act, she hops up onto the paving stone, and does a little pirouette, Dave's son appears again from the side of the stage, this time clutching a sledge hammer. "NO" murmur the crowd, but it's too late now, the son takes a few steps forward and smashes down the hammer and breaks the paving stone in two. Dave's in trouble now, gasping and coughing he manages to rise to his feet. While he was staggering around the stage, taking his final bow to the audience, you couldn't help but notice the state of his back. It was as if someone had shot him with a machine gun, scores of blood-dripping holes were evident. And that was that, what an act, but there must be an easier way of making a living.

'Gary Glitter with a suntan' was another one, but at least he made a few quid out of his 'talents'. This glam rock impersonator was hopeless. He turned up early on the night of the show, asked what time he was on, and when he realised he wasn't on till much later, took off and busked his way around the pubs of Portobello, and made himself a nice few quid. He failed to impress the judges though. Jago Elliot had a go, but his party trick of hammering a nail up his nose wasn't easy viewing for yours truly. Jago was a good lad, he passed away recently. He had a lot to offer, which makes it even more of a pity.

Whilst the judges were working out their scorecards, Kevin, in full Mr. Saucy mode would host up 'Blind Date'. The Talent Show night had caught the imagination very quickly, and this was the highlight. There was no end of volunteers for this event, including, one evening, my friend Catherine Holy-Hasted. She had a choice of three men, and she plucked Gary Dempsey from the trio.

On another evening the coupling got a bit mixed up; don't ask me the circumstances, but very strangely Peter Hamilton's blind date turned out to be former Skids front man Richard Jobson. Answers on a postcard is all I can say about that one. For the lucky couples, a chance of two prizes, either a trip around the World or lunch for two at the Anglo Yugoslav cafe on the Portobello Road. No prizes for guessing which one popped out of the hat when the contestants took their lucky dip. Blind Date was great, at one of the shows, a vital piece of equipment was missing so Blind Date metamorphasised into 'Mr and Mrs', nobody noticed, or for that matter cared. It was just a crackerjack of an evening, everyone went home happy.

We'd dig out some band or other to finish of the night's entertainment. Most anticipated among these had to be 'The Singing Sikh'. Peter Singh is an Indian guy who lives in Swansea. On a couple of visits down there I'd often pop into the Coach and Horses pub in Wind Street. This was a good venue for live music, and the standard was better than the norm as regards local Rhythm and Blues shows. The couple of times I visited I noticed this guy in a turban, putting himself about, and trying to get up on the stage to sing with the band. I'd shout out "Give the Sikh a number" but no one was having any of it. I told Paul Durden about this guy, and he of course was intrigued. He may regret it now, but at the time of our Tabernacle shows, he was the Singing Sikh's manager. Before the show Peter made a guest appearance in the Warwick to great fanfare, this was just as well, because what he offered the crowd later was less than impressive. Everything about his appearance led you to believe you were in for a treat. He'd don the full Elvis in Vegas jumpsuit, topped off with a bejewelled turban. He looked the bizz, problem was he can't sing very well, and even if he could, he had trouble remembering the words. I spent most of my time during his set at the front of the stage mouthing the lyrics of 'Living Doll', and countless other rock and roll classics to him, hoping he would pick up on them. Nobody gave a toss in the audience though; they just got on with dancing and drinking.

The night of the 'Grand Final' arrived. The place was heaving. Kevin had drafted in Peter Richardson as a judge, he brought his new mate, the one and only Jeff Beck (minus guitar) who along with our very own Kate Bernard would deliberate amongst themselves the worth of the talent on display, Without Dangerous Dave or G.G. With a Suntan it was, for me anyway, a straight match between Vic Reeves and Powys Square Diva Andrea Oliver. Vic Reeves hadn't scaled the heights yet, but he was already a very funny fucker. In fact, in the heats because we were short of turns Vic did two acts, so diverse were these performances that both were thought worthy enough to grace the stage for the final. I have a reputation for overdoing it on the bevy, even when I'm on duty, like I was on this night. And to be sure I had plenty on board by the time the votes were cast and the result was finalised, but compared to Kevin I was like Jean Simmons in 'Guys and Dolls' he was fucking hanging. Before I could pick up the judges' scorecards, and transport them to the stage, and announce Vic Reeves as the overall winner, Kev had dived on the stage and announced that Andrea had won. It didn't make any difference, I certainly didn't jeopardise Vic's march forward, and Andrea was fantastic on the night anyway, and there certainly wasn't any prize, that I remember anyway, to quarrel over, so everybody's happy.

Mr Saucy's Blind Date was an absolutely blinding night out; anyone who attended will tell you that. It had the right mix of anarchy, audience participation and good and bad talent to keep even the most cynical soul entertained. There were no long-term relationships reported between any of the Blind Date contestants, but love was never the reason for doing it. Kevin Allen went off to do much better, so these shows were never repeated, probably for the best, I'm just glad to have been part of it, it kept me double busy that summer, and I managed to earn a few quid.

19. The Carnival is Over

If you live in Ladbroke Grove, Carnival is one of the things you can (a) enjoy (b) loathe or (c) escape from. When I first arrived here I thought it would be a major bonus to have a three-day party happening on your own doorstep. For the first few years Carnival started for me at 8am on the Sunday, when an African tribe would gallop down the Grove, waving spears and chanting some war cry. This would signal the start of a weekend of hedonism and debauchery that was never frowned upon by either resident or constable.

The street hustlers were out in numbers. They'd been stocking up on anything that may raise a buck. People would use their front steps to flog beer or food; others would sell you whistles, flags or the latest fluorescent gadget that was doing the rounds. This was all considered 'legal' by the powers that be. Back then you'd notice enormous queues outside any toilet available, more recently people have been making a pretty penny letting people use their toilet at a nicker a time. Then there were the, let's say, less legal types with their own plans for the festivities. There'd be your dips and your handbag snatchers, roaming the streets looking for an opportunity; others would turn up with experimental concoctions, knocked up in the kitchen. These were meant to resemble drugs. They wouldn't pass muster in normal circumstances, but at the Carnival they'd do a brisk trade. And of course there are those who sell real drugs too.

As my first Carnival approached, I found myself, true to form, skint. I hadn't known Pete at Rough Trade for very long then, but it doesn't take long for anyone to realise when they are dealing with me, they're dealing with someone, who, for the most part anyway, is usually brassic, and this time was no different. Pete fixed me up with a couple of boxes of dub reggae singles and albums, which, I guess, were past their sell by date in the shop. I was probably naïve about where to go to sell my wares. I set up outside the Mecca bookies on Portobello Road right opposite Tesco. Nowadays, of course you seem to need a licence for that sort of thing, but no one bothered me. I set up my makeshift table out there, and began trading. The records I had on offer might not have hacked it with the record buying connoisseur that frequented Rough Trade or even Dub Vendor, but for the reggae tourist it was grade 'A' merchandise. It must have been, I sold it all in next to no time, and had some money for the weekend.

Pete used to open the shop back then, with the door shut to the public, it was a good hangout. Then we'd usually drift around to the Warwick to catch up with people we hadn't seen in a while, then maybe take a stroll up under the Westway, to see who was performing on the stage up there. They had good acts I seem to remember. Maybe Misty, maybe Aswad, but definitely not the Clash. Can you imagine how good that would have been? They put a stop to it I guess because that area was deemed a flashpoint for trouble. I'm rambling now, mainly because every Carnival weekend is a blurred memory for everyone. What's that old chestnut? 'If you can remember it blah, blah, blah.'

So all in all, Carnival could be a wheeze. This changed for a lot of people in 1987. You get used to stories about so called 'steaming gangs' coming from outside the area just to cause trouble. These twats are hell bent on creating some sort of reputation for themselves by causing mayhem among the revellers. But even by their low standards, they went too far this time. A lad named Michael Galvin had set up shop selling cold drinks, a gang approached his stall, and one of them just helped himself to a Coca Cola. Foolishly, Michael went after him and asked for it back or the money. The thief, as brave as a lion, pulled out a knife and stabs Galvin. He was taken to hospital where he died from his wound. For fifty pence, he was fucking dead.

Michael Galvin was the father of two young kids. I was approached in the Warwick by a guy I'd seen around the place. He handed me a leaflet, 'The friends of Michael Galvin appeal fund', and asked me if I could help. I took his telephone number, said I'd love to be involved, and that I'd be in touch. On the Monday I went around the Tabernacle to have a chat to Dave, who seemed to be in charge up there. He thought it was a great idea to put on a show for this charity, and let me have the place for nothing. Good boy. It was decided that the format should be a Saturday 'all dayer'. This made a lot of sense. In the afternoon we could possibly attract the visiting types, then in the evening rely more on the local population. That said it wasn't going to be easy to keep the momentum going for ten hours. Gene October was drinking in the Warwick then. I didn't realise he had a band called Chelsea who had a reputation back in the punk days; anyway they were willing to play. World Domination Enterprise, who had just released there brilliant single 'Asbestos Lead Asbestos' were up for it, Steve Jameson the bass player was a boyfriend of my old mate Sue Donne, from the Ealing days. Everybody's favourite cowgirl Amoco Cadiz was in too. Then there were any number of solo artistes, comedians, poets etc, so after a bit of running around, the bill didn't look as skinny as I thought it might.

Billy Mac said I should call up Jerry Dammers. "He'll probably come along and do a bit of Dee Jaying at least." Jerry Dammers turning up as a punter would do for me, I'm a big fan. I used to love his band. I, along with a lot of others have tried to write songs with a social message. That's hard enough. He did it with a sense of humour, and you could dance to it as well, that takes some doing. What baffles me now is, in these days of revival tours, how can people go see The Specials without Jerry in the band. To me it's like seeing The Kinks without Ray Davies or the Floyd without Pink and the Pogues without Shane. Anyway, that's another story. I phoned Jerry, he was very apologetic, he had a gig that night in the Midlands somewhere, but he liked the vibe, and wished us all the best. Never mind.

AD/CO is a design place in Blenheim Crescent. Richard Adams the boss round there must be fed up to the teeth with the likes of me dropping in there trying to blag a professional piece of artwork to advertise our harebrained schemes. They were more than glad to help, and came up with a really good poster for the event. The reason I bring this up is that until recently I had this poster on my wall. I've misplaced it. If I still had it I could type in, very merrily, the names of everyone who took part in this event, and thank them in print. They know who they are, Oh yeah, I played live myself that day, With Latif and Chris Mustoe, so I was double busy.

By 4pm the show was in full swing. There was a decent crowd for the acts to reveal their hidden talents to. Things were going very well. For a cause like this, I like to think that these same people would have turned out if we had a show full of spoons players, but even so, you want to entertain. Don't you? Then Jerry Dammers walked in hauling two boxes of records. "I've got to be outta here by 5: 30," he said. We showed him to where the record decks were, and he was off. What a toff. He went up even further in my estimation after that. The show of solidarity shown by everyone involved was infectious, and gave me and everyone else a lift. Things went swimmingly after that, Keith even took to the mic and gave me a slap on the back for my efforts. That takes some doing, I can tell you.

The show was a success. More importantly, without the presence of household names, we still managed to earn decent money for a decent cause. Everyone was stoked. We weren't just piss heads from the Warwick (well we were really) we could do something constructive. But I still couldn't help thinking, none if it would have been necessary if it weren't for one stupid incident. I took the cash to Rough Trade; they exchanged it for a cheque made out to the charity. I arranged to meet the guy who first got me involved at the Warwick the following Monday, for the presentation. I wanted a picture to bung in The Roughler. It wasn't the busiest night, so getting someone who was in the public eye to present the money didn't seem to promising, when in strolls our old mate Vaz Blackwood. At the time he was in a show on the telly with Lenny Henry, and plenty recognised him. He was OK about it; he even posed for some photos. Then Ade Edmondson, far from being a regular, strolled in, so I asked him to repeat the dose, he agreed. I'm glad these two showed up, up until then, the choice of presenter seemed to lie between Pete the Murderer or Dog Woman.

20. They're Gonna Put Me in the Movies

Word arrives at Roughler Mansions that Peter Richardson wanted to see me. I was familiar with Peter. I used to see him perform down the Comedy Store when he was part of a double act with Nigel Planer. They were called The Outer Limits. In those days Tony Allen was involved down there. He told me that if you're willing to get up on the stage, you can get in the place for nothing, and have two free pints. Bring it on. They had a gong set up, if the audience didn't like a certain act the crowd would holla "Gong' The MC would then smack the gong, and the performer had to clear off. So if for example you went up there and started out "There was a Scotsman an English.... Gong, you're outta there.

I saw most of the comics who would go on to become household names. Keith had gone by then, so had Alexei, but Rick Mayall and Ade Edmondson were performing under the name 'Twentieth Century Coyote', Dawn French and Jennifer Saunders were a double act, even back then. My favourites were Arnold Brown and Jim Barclay, they were funny, and earned their crust, but never scaled the heights of the others. The up and comer back then was Ben Elton. It was called Alternative Comedy, and I guess it was, but me , I prefer the Scotsman, Englishman gags, that would definitely have made me non-PC down there.

Keith Allen and Peter had done some film work together. Now for their biggest project to date, 'The Bullshitters' they needed extras for a particular pub scene. Because the budget was so tight Keith thought it would be a good idea to offer free drink to the extras instead of cash. The pub was in Islington, so Jock and I got there early, and got stuck in. There didn't seem to be many restrictions as regards moving about, talking bollocks and guzzling lager, so it was just like any other day really. A nervous Elvis Costello was on hand. He had a part in this production, and he seemed to be taking it all seriously. At the time perhaps he was thinking of a career change. Who knows?

Towards the end of the day there was talk of me being needed for a very small cameo role, which, inevitably, was to take place in the karzy, when they found me passed out under a table, they turned their attention towards Glen Colson, who landed up doing it. So my first chance of celluloid stardom got nipped in the Budweiser (Stella really). So from that experience, you would have thought it highly unlikely that Peter would have anything at all to do with yours truly, but he wanted to see me anyway. Down at Comic Strip HQ in Soho, I meet up with Peter, and he talked me through the new project. It was to be a spoof on the Miners' Strike, Funnily enough, it was to be called 'The Strike'. The story revolves around a character named Paul, and his efforts to get his script turned into a movie. The Paul in question was of course Paul Durden, who was always coming up with ideas for everything, including films. Originally Paul D. was to play the main part, but I reckon they bottled out on that idea, and thought that perhaps someone with so little acting experience might find it difficult to carry a film. I don't know. All I do know is that Alexei was now cast as the 'Paul' character, and I had a small part as his mining mate, called Ray. It was a big enough part for me to be taken on location, fed, housed and paid so I'm not complaining.

Camp was set up in the small Welsh village of Banwen. This place seemed to be on its last legs. It might have seen better years back when there was some industry still operating, but now things seemed glum. They still had the Banwen Miners hunt though. That had been going for donkey's years I guess. The residents were proud of it, and didn't want anyone coming down from London with any Fancy Dan opinions on the subject. All cast and crew knew better than to broach the subject. The hub of the village was the pub. Nice boozer, they even had a boxing ring upstairs and for some it appeared to be the only access to a telephone as well.

Slowly but surely the main players arrived in this backwater. Jennifer Saunders, Dawn French, Robbie Coltrane, Ade Edmondson, Nigel Planer, whose nickname, behind his back, was 'niggle complainer', the Allen brothers and Peter, who as well as being the director was to play the lead role of Arthur Scargill. The twist was he was playing Al Pacino playing Arthur Scargill. Jennifer was playing

Meryl Streep playing Mrs Scargill. At the time I didn't know what was going on. I didn't get my head around the story until I saw it on the silver screen.

The following day was the first day of shooting, and my bit was first up. So that night I was summoned to Alexei's room to discuss strategy. He seemed happy enough, perhaps a little nervy, but not as much as me I'll wager. On the morrow everything had been set up for our little scene. They'd handed me a set of orange overalls. They were the cleanest item of clothing I've ever worn. I had to roll around the street, in puddles and the like, just to get an authentic look about me. I'm a miner for god sake. I wonder if De Niro would have thought of doing that. The action went like this. Paul (Alexei) was leaving town, script in hand, on his way to London to meet some film producers. All the neighbours were on their doorsteps wishing him good luck. I'm secreted behind the front door of a house, waiting for my cue. When I get the signal I have to fling open the door, run across the street, fall in step with Alexei, and deliver my lines. I kept getting one part of it wrong. Alexei was getting the hump. I said "Hang about, I've never done this before." Next take I got it right. The next bit was easier, I had to stuff some money in his pocket, and shove him on a bus. I had a gag to deliver. I'm no Les Dawson, so it wasn't the best delivery, but it was OK.

Alexei had to do a rant in the middle of the street after that, for some other scene from the film. It soon became clear that the Welsh accent he'd used when talking to me had been dumped. It didn't make any difference, and he was great after that.

The next action for me was a scene with Dawn French. By now all the lads had shown up. Paul Durden, Clive Hadley among them, so by the time I was called over to do the next bit, I was cool. Dawn was playing the casting director, and I had to approach her and ask for a job. I was bang on the money this time, probably because I had Durden standing beside me. There were loads of spectators out on this hot afternoon, as were most of the cast. When I'd done my bit Ade and Keith came over and told me how great I was. So that's OK. I was just relieved. I was finished for the day. Straight to the Banwen

Arms. Perfect. Back in London I had a few more bits and pieces to do. I got to deliver one great line. To the assembled 'miners' in the pub, I had to ask: "Have a guess who's playing Arthur Scargill in this film lads?" PAUSE "Al Pa-fucking –Cino!" Classic stuff.

It was all a great laugh. You might think I'm bigging up my part. Fucking right. I'm in a film. Never thought I would be. Through my endeavours, I was, for a short time anyway, on the party circuit. You'd get to meet a few faces, for sure, but more importantly, you got to guzzle plenty for sod all. There was a big party up West for a Comic Strip thingy, all the Warwick wanted to come; they'd smelt free drink. When we arrived it wasn't going to be as easy as I thought to blag everyone in. I managed to get hold of someone in charge. I'd been told on numerous occasions that I bear an uncanny resemblance to a certain Irish songster. I didn't know how true it was, but I thought I'd try it out. "Oim Feargal Sharkey from the Undertones, and these are my guests…" It must have held some water, as we all got in.

The Strike was a good film. Many said it was one of the best Comic Strip productions. It did really well. It even won prizes. It won the Golden Rose of Montreaux. Recently I had a chat with Peter Richardson, I asked him "Am I the only person you know, who'd acted in an award-winning film, and never worked in the movies ever again?" His answer was: "That's the best way Ray, go out while you're at the top".

21. The Split

Kirsty has had enough of my lifestyle. I guess she'd realised that after all this time I was beyond change. Add to this the fact that she's far from stupid, and even if she didn't have outright proof, she must have had a good idea about my misdemeanours with Carmen . If I'm coming home really late, jumping in to bed with her without taking a shower you can't tell me she didn't notice anything untoward. I must admit though than when she announced she'd be moving out in three months I was shocked. Then her plan became clear. She'd become friendly with an American girl called Erin who also had a shop in Portobello Green. I'd met this girl one night at a party on the All Saints Road. This event was gate crashed by some nutters on acid. In no time at all, these lads started hurling bottles and glasses indiscriminately at all and sundry. I half saw it coming so took the appropriate action and dived for cover. In the process I grabbed this Erin girl and got us out of harm's way. She was in my pathway to safety, that's the only reason I grabbed her, she read it differently though, and before you can say 'loonies on acid trash All Saints party' I'm a hero. Erin is good looking; make no mistake, so with my recent elevation to Galahad status still fresh in her mind I took the opportunity to invite her to this Mutoid type gig going on later that night. By the time we got there, I was pretty out of it but she was pissed. Nothing really happened, just a bit of snogging and dancing, but now with her in Kirsty's corner, I feared the worst. For instance, if Kirsty started having second thoughts, there'd be no way in the world that Erin would champion my cause.

Through Erin, Kirsty had become friends with Lucy Astor and her crowd. Lucy lived in the Mansion on the hill, a fabulous house in Notting Hill, and had offered Kirsty a place to live in three month's time. So now we'd split up, but the both of us still lived together in our flat. This was a bonkers situation. I put up with it though. Probably in the back of my mind I thought she'd never leave, and maybe she wouldn't have if I'd altered my ways, but of course I didn't. In fact, if anything I got worse. I felt that she had now given me the green light to do as I please, and I did. Little did I know how devastated I'd be when she finally flew the coop. But right then I was trying to prove to her, and myself, that I didn't give a toss. What a twat!

So the countdown was on, and after sleeping in the same bed with a bolster separating us for the last three months, the day arrived. After fourteen years my partner was leaving me. There were no scenes, just tears, and right there and then I realised I was lost. Oh I wish we'd had a kid together. It wasn't long before I took to making late-night drunken, pathetic phone calls asking her to come back, I'd be crying into my beer in the pub, and boring everyone to death with my griping. But there was no way back. She must have felt free for the first time in her adult life. Through all our time together, even when I was in the nick, I knew exactly where she was, and what she was up to. I would never have considered myself one back then, but I was probably what they call a control freak. Now of course she could do as she pleased, and it was fuck all to do with me. I saw her photograph in the newspaper one day, she was glammed up, and seemed to be in the company of that Halpen geezer, I didn't think for a second that this was her date, but it was as I feared, she was moving in swishy circles now, and I wasn't in on it. I thought it just a matter of time before she gets hit on by some well-heeled type, with plenty of money and a clearer view on the world than me.

Maurice from the Warwick was on a par with Tom Pepper when it came to tall stories. You could generally take his inside information with a pinch of salt, but on this occasion what he was telling me had a sniff of truth about it. He mentioned that Kirsty had been stepping out with a new fella, and he was far from complimentary about him. If Maurice can diss you, you must be a wrong 'un, but as I said I wouldn't take what he says 100 per cent seriously. It wasn't until Warwick quizzer Bud Abbot backed up, and elaborated on, this guy's dodginess that I believed that Kirsty was treading a dangerous path. It's none of my business, but under the banner of 'marking her card' I decided to give her a ring. She wasn't having any of it, and told me to keep out of her affairs. She probably thought that after all the time spent with me it couldn't possibly get any worse. I'm afraid to say it can. One of the messages I left for her, must have been overheard by her new partner, for a couple of days later I was having an early morning livener outside the Portobello Star when the two of them approached. They stopped, she went into the bank opposite, and he headed toward me. He's one of those wiry, big mothers who look like they're not averse to fighting. Having said that, he wouldn't have had to been extra special in the fisticuff department to see me off, but when he approached I made a pathetic attempt at machismo by getting to my feet. This was met with an aggressive "Don't stand up, I'll only have to put you back down," quickly followed by "She's with me now, you're out of the picture." He could tell I'd gotten the message, so he walked off.

I don't think we spoke after that. I'd see her about but thought better than going on to her. She'd left the Mansion by now, and had a purpose built houseboat moored up in Little Venice, the shop was going well as far as I could tell, but through my spies I heard that in next to no time the boat was gone and so was the shop and she was having a baby. We were completely estranged by this point, which was a pity, I'm sure we could have remained on some sort of speaking terms if I'd kept out of her affairs. Maybe I could have helped her out in some small way. Never know now. I'd bump in Kirsty years later, in Swansea of all places. She was down there visiting her folks. We had the briefest conversation centering on what she was up to now. Yes, she was still in the hat game, but on a much smaller scale. That didn't refer to her outlet; it meant that she didn't go in for the sort of customers that attract a hoo hah from the press. That suited her, on reflection it was always me pushing her toward the more showbizzy side of it, whereas she was just happy with the craft of the thing. She was pleasant enough, but soon took off for a fabric shop opposite.

Even later, back in London, pissed all the time, I got up one morning on a mission. I needed to go down the town hall to sort out my housing benefit. I didn't wash or care what clothes I had on, I just wanted to be the first person at the door when it opened. I was pissed off. The place had just opened when I got there, so I fired up the stairs, and bulldozed my way through the housing department door. The place seemed to be deserted, and then I was stopped in my tracks. There was one other person in there, it was Kirsty. There was no way on earth I was going to let her see me like this, so I turned tail and legged it. I've never seen or heard from her since. What I couldn't get my head around was when we met briefly that time in Swansea, she knew about me being ripped off in San Francisco. There is not one person out there who I could ask about Kirsty's whereabouts, not one. So I often wonder who among our mutual acquaintances could have told her this story, it must be someone she's sworn to secrecy I guess.

22. They've Nicked the Corner Shop

In the late Eighties change was afoot on the streets of W10/11. There were all sorts of businesses popping up to cater for the more well-heeled types, who in recent times had gravitated towards the area. There were restaurants galore, theme bars, shops selling things you didn't know how to use, and of course there were galleries. You could buy anything from Albanian cheese to Bulgarian wines, finding a place to buy ten woodbines, a box of matches and a ham sandwich was an altogether more difficult operation. One thing about the galleries though was on the opening nights at these gaffs there was always free drink on offer, so it wasn't all negative.

My connection with the art world was pretty limited. Carmen had shown me around the Slade, talked a bit about the subject, and of course she had painted me in the nude but apart from that, my knowledge on the subject was nonexistent. I had this idea in my head though that most of the girls involved liked shagging, so on that premise I thought it would be a good idea to have a gallery of our own. Lots of arty types seemed to habituate the Warwick of late, as well as others, who seemed to have a connection with that world, so a move into the gallery experience seemed to be a sensible step forward for Roughler Inc. Orlando Campbell was one such boho type hanging around the pub at the time, so I got him on board. I didn't think for one minute there was any work in him, but at least he had a better understanding of the way of the of artist than I did.

Luke Coke and Simple Simon were living in a squat on the Portobello Road. They were occupying the rooms above a shop. The shop was empty so that became the target for the first Roughler Gallery. Targeting is probably too strong a word, there were no hurdles to overcome, Luke and Simon were Warwick regulars and played for the football team, so they weren't going to object, and as for the owners of the property, they were completely off the radar back then, so we had a clear run at making the place art friendly. As anticipated Orlando wasn't much help in the decorating department, so his job was to track down contributors for what was to be a group show. On his travels he recruited his mate to help out. You'd think that this was Orlando showing initiative wouldn't you, until you realise the extra help came in the form of one Lord Patrick Conyngham. Billed as an underwater poet and re-named 'Lord Matey' by the gossip press, Patrick had entered Warwick society like a typhoon. Landlord Seamus and the rest of the bar crew were intrigued by his presence in the bar, after all he was an Irish Lord. I don't know what they expected from him, and, even when it became clear that he was a pisshead of the highest order, he was always treated well in there. I'm convinced to this day that when Patrick went to the bar to order, the bar staff would adopt a 'thumbs down the seam of the trousers' stance when they served him.

If Orlando wasn't much cop on the gallery makeover front, you can multiply that by ten as regards Patrick's input, so I had to rope in all and sundry from the pub to help with the decoration and the odd repair. Considering the canvas (art jargon already) we had to work with we managed to make a decent fist of it. There wasn't much we could do with the floor though, there were potholes everywhere, and short of bringing in someone in to skim the room with concrete, we were stuck with it. I thought I'd solved the problem when passing the Nu Line wood shop I noticed the sawdust mountain they had in there. That's it! We'll cover up the floor with this cheap alternative. They used to do it in butchers shops, so why not a gallery. It was a daft enough idea. People might even think we'd sat down for hours and sweated our mental bollocks off to be artfully constructive. Well it certainly took Orlando in. He thought it was a genius idea. My idea of genius is when you have a plethora of choices and out of a massive choice you make the apt one to suit the project, the sawdust was a 'Hobson's Choice' take it or leave it. Funnily enough the sawdust floor became the most talked about part of the show.

With decorating finished the time had come to take stock of what we had to hang on the walls. We weren't doing badly. Laura De La Mare gave us some work, Fred Ingrams, Donna McLean, Patrick bunged some of his in, Kevin Allen turned artist for this occasion then there were pictures from people that Orlando knew.

Catherine Holy-Hasted, a girl I'd had my eye on for a few weeks, offered some of her paintings, she was also more than happy to help with the hanging of the show. Would romance blossom among the water colours? You never know. So it's all taking shape, then a girl turns up with what would turn out to be the centrepiece of the show. Sophia Clist was a good girl, easy to get on with, and without pretension. The added bonus as far as I was concerned was the fact that she was sexy; she also had a remarkable piece of art in the form of two six foot high metal sculptures, depicting a man and woman dancing. It was called 'Crazy Naked Dancing' and it was great. So heavy and precarious was this piece that we had to drill holes in the floor to ensure it was safe for the drunks of Portobello, who you'd expect to attract on the opening night, to view and lean on in safety.

Whenever I'm involved in any form of work with others it's usually me getting the bollockings for such misdemeanours as turning up late, turning up pissed or not turning up at all. This time around I'm the one doing the chasing. I don't think he took much persuading, but Orlando would always blame Patrick for his absence on site. Thinking back, it was probably a blessing in disguise, Catherine did a damn good job. And we were ready to go. My passionate affair with Carmen had cooled of late, but we still got on. She was an artist, so of course I asked her to contribute something. Out of all the paintings I'd seen round at hers and in her space at the Slade, she decides to turn up with the nude painting of me, and it's fucking big, the painting that is. Luckily the pose she'd used saw me with an arm across my face, thus obscuring who it really was to the observer. I doubt even Kirsty would have thought it was me, but stupidly I mentioned to Luke, of all people, who it was. After a few you'd never rely on him not blurting out this information to anyone within earshot. Kirsty had left our flat by now, but I still held out vague hope that she might return one day. If she saw me up on a wall bollock-naked laying on a strange girl's bed it would not be good for any reconciliatory ideas I might have. The other time I was asked to sit for a painting, I did it with Kirsty's blessing. A local artist called Saffy had me go to her studio so she could paint my portrait. Unlike the Carmen 'sitting' I was sober for this one, and as it was in a studio setting I got a better understanding of the artist at work. This place had a Bohemian feel to it, with the usual mess of paint and unfinished work scattered about. In the corner was the obligatory brass bed. That came in handy I can tell you. When it was finished Kirsty actually traded two hats with the artist, and it became a gift for me.

I needn't have worried though; Kirsty didn't turn up on the opening night. I saw Luke during the course of the evening standing beside said masterpiece, whispering to all and sundry, so word soon got around, but apart from Kirsty I didn't give a toss who knew. The gallery was a success, if you gauge success in how many people enjoyed themselves. I don't think we sold anything, but lots of people had a good time and we managed not to piss off any of the artists. For the follow up show I thought it would be fun to bring in Mutoid Waste. I knew Jo Rush a bit, and loved all the stuff they did, especially the movable stuff, which they used to drive around the Grove, on many a weekend. In fact the first time I ever saw Jo Rush was when I looked out of the window of my flat to find out what was causing a commotion outside. There, holding up traffic was a chariot made up of all sorts of bits of old cars and that, being driven by a geezer in leather, with a banana on his head standing in for a Mohican haircut. Next to him was a girl with blonde hair dressed like a leading player from The Valkyries. You could not fail to be impressed with this show of automotive anarchy. I mentioned the gallery to Jo and he was up for it.

I managed to break down any resistance Catherine Holy-Hasted might have had to my charms, and to all intents and purposes she was now my 'bird'. Warning bells rang early though. It was Carnival time, and I invited her to spend some time with me down Portobello. I met her at about 12.30pm outside the Warwick and walked her to the front door. The place was packed with our lot, all very much on their way to oblivion, and I was eager to join in. As we entered Catherine said something I'll never forget. "Ray, you can't possibly want a drink at this time of day." I know. But I swear it's true. It was from that moment that she was christened by me with the new name 'Barmy Bonkers'. After a couple of pints or whatever she comes up with another classic. "Come on Ray, let's go out and follow the floats." Her first statement was spoken just to me, but this latest, ridiculous suggestion was heard by everyone. She was lucky not to have been laughed out of the pub. She still thought it a good idea though, and off she went.

The Mutoid show wasn't going to plan. I'd managed to get some flyers made up, and started putting the word about, but my heart wasn't really in. I was unhappy right then, and was drowning my sorrows big time. Not only had the Mutoids started moving their stuff in there in readiness for the show, they'd also moved in there to live. Every time I went up there to see what was going down I was met with surliness, not from Jo, but plenty of the others. I've met some of the most anti-social fuckers out there, and they can be awkward fuckers, but most had the sense to direct their anger in the right direction. I believed I was helping these people out, and on top of that had inadvertently found them somewhere to live, and I felt I was being treated like cunt, so I lost interest completely. Jo got the hump with me for not doing much PR on the event, and he was right, but the feeling I got was that they didn't need any help, so I let them carry on.

Kirsty always said that I only got involved in these enterprises to advance my credibility, and to make people think I was a good lad to boot, and that I never gave any thought to the business side of things. She must have been right. The gallery had been hard work, physically and mentally. Now if you've got a job say, and wake up with a hangover you might think 'fuck that, I'm not going in today' then you have a cup of tea, think of the money you'd lose by not going, and drag yourself off to your work. Compare this with waking up every day with a hangover, dragging yourself to work (the gallery) working hard, all without the slightest chance of making a shilling. Daft right? So why would anyone with half a brain decide to do it again? Well I did. I'd spotted a Chinese takeaway which had closed down. It was again on Portobello Road, but further up the road, in an area which our new partner Piers Thompson had christened NOGO (North of the Golbourne). If we'd encountered difficulties with the first gallery, they were nothing compared what we were up against this time. Piers was brought in for two reasons, firstly he was keen, and secondly, to my eyes anyway, he added a bit of respectability to proceedings. Piers actually worked, and he found it easy to talk to people. This last talent was the one he used to secure the premises for us. Now we had to make it look like a gallery.

Think fish and chip shop and you'll get an idea what we're up against. There were deep fat fryers, ovens, gas stoves and all sorts of machinery for the production of take away grub. A lot of these gadgets were attached to the wall with bolts, so as you can imagine taking these down was hard graft in itself, couple this with the inevitable damage we were doing to the walls whilst we were taking everything down and you'll understand. We cleared all the machinery out, and gave all the surfaces a thorough de-greasing, it was hard fucking graft, and this gave a chance to see how bad the walls were. There were holes everywhere, craters more like, and the place would need plastering. Piers' mate Hugo turned up to do a bit of skimming, he tried his best but after he'd finished, the walls resembled a skateboard ramp. There was a bloke out on the street called Timmy, the drink had got the better of him by now, but he had been a plasterer previously, and was cheap. He turned up and set about putting things right. It didn't start very well, on his first trip up the ladder he fell down, put his hands out to protect himself and collided with big shop front window. The window buckled, but never cracked, thank God, he would have been cut in half. We didn't manage to get the best finish in the walls, but it'd do for us.

I'd blagged a cracking piece of artwork out of someone or other for the flyer and poster, and excitedly headed to the Warwick to show the partners. After a couple of hours of boozing, I hadn't been as attentive as I should have been with this art. In fact I'd sat on it, doing it bad damage. Piers turned up later, I think he had the hump with me for being pissed, but when he saw what I'd done with the artwork he definitely wasn't impressed. In fact, he resigned on the spot. I thought he was overreacting, I mean I got the artwork as a favour out of a mate. I realise now, that wasn't the point. It was the unprofessionalism that irked him. So I'm left with Orlando, Patrick is still on the firm, but early on he'd hilariously announced he wouldn't be getting involved in the physical side of things this time. There's more work in still water.

One afternoon with Orlando on the missing list, and me busy in the gallery, someone told me they'd spotted Mutt and Geoff drinking in the ground floor bar. I steamed down there, as I entered these two started laughing, I went mad, picked up one of the drinks and fired it all over them. From that moment on I lost it completely for the duration of this gallery's life. I can remember two incidents only. Firstly, we'd hung an incredibly heavy painting up, it was in an iron frame, shortly after the punters arrived on the first night this monstrosity broke free of its moorings, and hurtled earthwards. When it hit the deck it was like a fucking bomb going off. I'd had enough, so the painting was left where it landed. About ten o clock that night I got a massive resentment to everyone in the room, and started throwing people out. Everyone left except a few who included James Moores and Patrick. When they took no notice of my urgings for them to leave, I locked them in, and took off for the pub. Orlando came a begging down the pub. I told him I'd thrown the keys in the canal. I was determined to leave them in there, but a few hours later I relented.

Piers and Orlando teamed up shortly after this and did some food-based parties, I think they went well. No one was including me in their plans. In fact, the word had got out that I had gone completely mad. Patrick just went about his usual business I guess. I hadn't seen him for a while, and then I bumped into him one night in Soho. My reputation, if I ever had one, was in tatters by this time, but someone had actually invited me to something that was going on at the Groucho Club. I'd popped into the Coach and Horses pub for a livener before the party, and Patrick was in there. I told him where I was going and he decided to come with me. On the way to the Groucho, Patrick announces that he's barred from the club. Apparently one night in there he decided to take a piss out of the window, spraying all the passersby in Dean Street below. Of course there were complaints, and Patrick was turfed out. He told me of this as we approached the front door. I wanted to go in, so I suppose I could have given him the swerve right then, but I hate it when that's done to me, so I didn't. There were some strange looks, but we managed to get in and put ourselves about. Patrick, who was half cut by now, spotted the well known publisher Naim

Attalah holding court in a corner of one of the upstairs rooms. "Look there's Naim, I want to talk to him about my book." I don't believe that this book existed, and I definitely didn't think that Patrick knew this geezer, but that's not going to stop him. Adopting what he considers his Byronesque personage; Patrick approaches the publisher, and attempts to strike up a conversation. Attalah was bemused, but Patrick persevered. He then decides to adopt a nonchalant air, and stretches out an arm so he can casually lean against a wall. Problem here was, there wasn't a wall, he'd placed his arm on fresh air, an open doorway, and went tumbling down the stairs. Where's the camera when you need it? That was the last I ever saw of his Lordship, they say he lives the quiet life in Ireland now, well good luck to him, he was always good value.

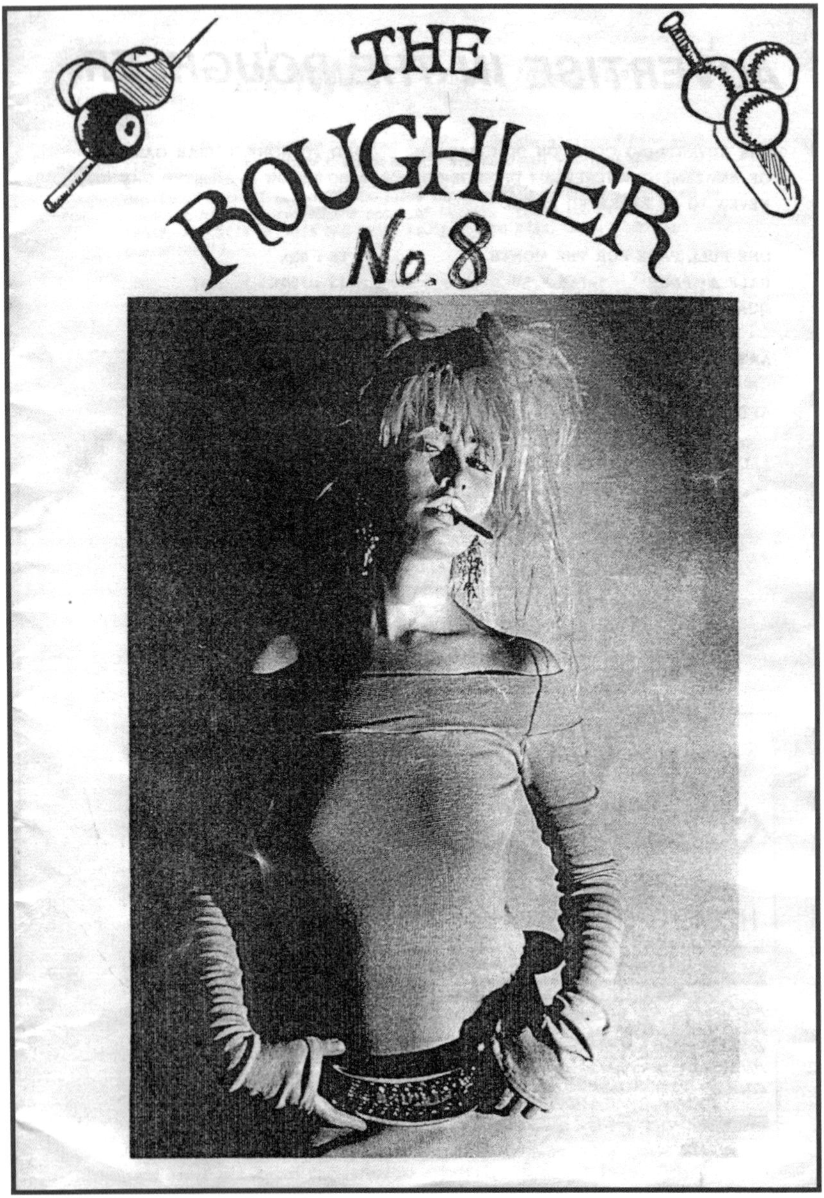

For all its rough and ready qualities The Roughler scooped some damn good cover stars such as Wendy James of Transvision Vamp…

Keith Allen on the set of Comic Strip presents…The Strike

Neneh Cherry hangs out in the Warwick

The Roughler gets a Joe Strummer exclusive

the Roughler

THE DRINKING MANS BIBLE £1

DRINK ISSUE!

Who better to adorn the drink issue than legendary
bon viveur Shane MacGowan

Cool Ken – King of the Warwick

Keith Allen mines comedy gold on the set of The Strike

The brothers Allen in directorial pose

My attempt at matinee-idol good looks while in San Francisco. Sadly, Hollywood is in LA

23. The Property Ladder

I've never had any truck with the Tories. Why should I? They've never been the party for the likes of me. But now I'm about to attempt to take advantage of one of their policies, 'the right to buy scheme'. Didn't think to tell Bone about this, I wonder why? Would I become a 'class traitor'? Well he might be a genuine working class hero, I'd like to be one myself, but even he would have to look at it from my viewpoint, and come to the conclusion that even at my most boisterous in defence of the working man, I was still a thief, and always on the lookout for an easy few quid, so why would I change now? It would have been an even greater idea to buy the flat if I was still in a relationship, that would have ensured that at least one person in this attempt to get on the property ladder, had an ounce of sense, then it would probably have been a springboard to a better financial future. Now with me on my own, I wasn't all that sure. There was a very big discount on offer with this scheme, and when I told my pals about this, to a man they said I'd be a fool not to buy. "You'll be sitting on a goldmine," was the general consensus. So I decided to look into it further.

Step one was to go to the council offices so they could talk me through it. The first stumbling block was the two names on the tenancy. When we moved in, the flat was in both our names, the guy told me I'd have to have Kirsty's name removed if I intended buying it on my own. Another motive I had for making this move was for all the wrong reasons too. I naively believed that this departure from my usual 'Devil may care' attitude might in some way win her back, so I couldn't wait to spring this news on her. This was before her new relationship had blossomed, but even so she wasn't all that keen on me visiting the shop. I called her up and explained she was OK about it, so I took the forms down there for her to sign. Thinking about it now, right then she would have signed a death warrant for Mother Theresa, if it meant getting shot of me, so I'm over the first hurdle, but she wasn't impressed. She probably knew I'd manage to fuck it up somehow. Why are girls much more farsighted than us boys?

You have to remember I'm trying to do this while I'm on the dole and am absolutely broke, so I wasn't exactly holding my breath when I visited the Bradford & Bingley on Portobello Road. But once I'd told him how much I would have to pay for the flat he said he couldn't see any problems with me getting a 100 per cent mortgage. He booked me in for an interview later that week, adding "Bring all your work and salary details along, and we'll sort this out quickly." Yeah, sure thing. Over to Pete in Rough Trade in the hope that he could manufacture a job I might be doing. I think Pete gave me a few pointers as to what I could say to these people, so I went back there with some very shaky proof of a job. It worked. On reflection this agent handed me some of the worst advice in mortgage history as regards taking a fixed interest rate, but I didn't know that then, so I signed on the dotted line.

A solicitor had to be found to carry it further; he was all right, so it's moving along. Then I hit not so much a stumbling as a brick wall. I have to get a survey done. I was under the illusion that the 100 per cent mortgage covered everything, not true. Perhaps I was not going to become the first person to buy a flat for nothing after all. It was going to cost £500 to follow this pipedream. I wasn't that surprised or dismayed, my life has revolved around setbacks and mishaps, couple that with the constant disappointments that go hand in glove with the gambling game, and you'll realise that reversals of fortune are second nature to me. Not to worry, there's always the pub, and on hearing this bad news, that's where I went.

I'd been boring my drinking buddies with this tale for many weeks now, so when I walked in the Star that lunchtime, the subject wouldn't have been that long in coming up. I told them that I had fallen at about the third hurdle, and explained about the £500. There were some half hearted mutterings about ways I might get over this set back and some dumb assed ideas about how I might raise the cash, but the conversation soon moved on to another subject, and that was that.

Joe Strummer was in the company this day. Joe had some sense or maybe had something better to do, but not long after, he got up to leave. There's no way he's going to stay in the boozer all day, talking bollocks with the rest of us. As he headed for the door he said to me "What are you doing tomorrow?" I said "Not a lot." He replied "Meet me in Bites cafe tomorrow morning, about ten". Why wouldn't I want to meet up with Strummer? So I said OK. Next day I went to Bites as arranged, ordered up a coffee and Joe arrives. He said "What's your full name?" I told him, and before you can say 'Elgin Avenue Breakdown' Joe pulls out a chequebook, and on the spot wrote me out a cheque for the £500. I was flabbergasted "What the fuck Joe?" is the only thing I could think to say. He'd obviously heard the conversation the day before, and taken it all in. I regained some composure, and as he handed me this kite I said "To be honest Joe, I'm only buying this place so I can sell it on down the road apiece. I'll pay you back then." Then with a touch of class he said: "Don't worry about it Ray, that one's on the Clash." What a fucking diamond. To be sure I've had the odd booze up and many a chuckle with Joe, but I wouldn't have dreamt of asking him for a tenner let alone a monkey.

So the flat thingy is back on track. I take the cheque to the bank, and let all those involved know it's OK to carry on, and soon enough I'm the proud owner of a one-bedroom flat on Ladbroke Grove. My luck holds out for a little while longer, there were some geezers working around the back of our house, I didn't know what they were up to. I chatted to one of them, and it turns out they've just put a brand new roof on the building, so that's one cost I won't be getting caught up in. There will probably be other costs cropping up in the future, costs I wouldn't have had to pay as a council tenant, but let's worry about that when the time comes.

Getting some dodgy paperwork to show that you're employed isn't that tricky, if you're back and forth in front of the magistrates it goes hand in hand with the promises to alter your ways, tearful apologies and the forthcoming marriage plans that you and (fictional) girlfriend had made, or any other desperate manoeuvre that will keep you out of the nick. My dodgy credentials may have got me the mortgage, but if I'm to pay the bill every month, I'll have to get a real job. The dole won't be paying it, that's for sure. Where do you start? There are plenty in the pub who work for a living, so I concentrated my efforts around these fine fellows. I kept coming up empty, then out of the blue, Jock Scott said to me "I think I've found you a job." This from the one person in the pub who could possibly match me for years spent in dole and social security offices, came as a massive shock. It came as no surprise soon afterwards when I found out that Jock was offered the job first. He didn't fancy it, so he's passing it on to me. A date was arranged for me to meet my prospective employer later that week.

The guy I had to see was called Will Birch. He used to be in a band called the Kursal Flyers who were part of the Canvey Island scene, along with Dr. Feelgood, Eddie and the Hot Rods and Lew Lewis, to name but a few. Will was starting up a new enterprise; he had an idea for a tour bus taking in all the renowned musical landmarks in the Capital, it was to be called 'The Rock Tour of London Bus' and the job on offer was that of the tour guide. It sounded good to me; I mean how hard can it be? I went down to Piccadilly which was the starting point of this excursion, Will presented me with a script to follow and off we went for a dummy run. This is what I remember about it. Bus, complete with video TV and PA system, enters Glasshouse Street to the sight and sound of Nancy Whisky singing 'Freight Train' a popular song from the 1950's. This marks our entrance into Soho, up past Denmark Street, which is the London equivalent of 'Tin Pan Alley' and also the location of the 'Two I's' coffee bar where Cliff Richard and other singers of that generation used to hang out before they became famous. Up past Capitol Radio to the strains of, guess what? 'Capitol Radio' by the Clash. Then we were off to Camden to talk about Madness and the Pogues, taking in 'Rehearsal Rehearsal' go on, have a guess, yes you've got it, it's a rehearsal space that was used by the Clash. Rumour has it that police were called one time when the Clash were in attendance. The story goes that Paul Simenon had upset the boys in blue, for shooting at pigeons from the window. I don't know how true it is, but Will had it in the script, and I had to stick to it, or else.

On to Abbey Road studios where the customers were allowed off the bus to take pictures of one another on the famous zebra crossing and to read all the Beatles-related graffiti around there. Past a hotel in Swiss Cottage, where if you looked quickly, you might just catch a glimpse of a swimming pool inside. The very thin story here was about Dylan staying there, where he was spotted splashing around. On to more familiar ground now, down to Portobello, along Ladbroke Grove, (I go blank here) along Notting Hill, past Kensington Gardens, (I'm back on it now) up on the on-board TV screen The Who appear performing 'I Can't Explain' alongside the Serpentine. Then a clip of The Stones from their famous Hyde Park gig, past Marble Arch and on to Oxford Street. The story runs a bit thin here. 'Glitterbest' was down there someplace, which gave me a chance to let the punters know about the Pistols, a long pause then until the 100 Club, which just about marked the end of the story. OK, there was more to it than I've reported here, but after the first few trips I was finding it difficult to keep the enthusiasm going.

I was doing this during a hot summer. Oxford Street was always packed with traffic and consequently very slow moving. On this particular day I was still suffering from the effects of last night's debauchery, when, yet again we got stuck in Oxford Street. With very little to say, I went into semi-comatose, self-evaluation mode, which quickly turned to fear when I realised I couldn't just up and leave this vehicle like I might if it were a Routemaster. I began to sweat and freak out, I didn't realise it then, but this was my first ever panic attack. It was terrifying. I kept trying to think of something else, but I couldn't escape the feeling of being trapped. I even went downstairs to ask the driver to let me out, which he must have found odd, but just said "Hang about, we're almost there." So I gritted my teeth, took some deep breaths and waited.

After what seemed days we arrived back in Piccadilly, there were to be no niceties here, I was off that bus before the punters, and ran as fast as I could to the nearest boozer in Soho. I ordered up a triple Vodka, which is not a normal drink for me, but I thought anything less would not take the edge off my horrors. I was still a great advocate of the healing power of alcohol back then. Of course, it was the drink that got you there in the first place. So the supposed cure was just 'the hair of the dog' nothing new in that. My old mate

Bernie Walther for instance swore by his hangover cure, no raw eggs, tomato juice, or Tabasco here. His idea was a Port and Brandy. That just goes to prove how stupid heavy drinkers are, you sit there with a drink as potent as a Port and Brandy, and act as if it has some magical medicinal properties, when all you're doing is getting yourself pissed in double quick time.

The panic attack episode shrunk any enthusiasm I might have had for the job. Then Will got the hump with me for not pulling my weight. There was a kid downstairs on the bus, among whose jobs, I thought anyway, was to operate the on-board video equipment, and make sure it all ran smoothly. I got a big resentment towards him when I realised he'd gone to Will and said that I should have been doing it but wasn't. I know nothing of machines, couple this with me having to run up and down the stairs to change the fucking thing every five minutes, when the kid was there anyway, was plenty reason for me having the right hump. This youngster could have operated the machine with his eyes closed, whereas I on the other hand would take much longer to do it, and, in the process, shit bricks at the prospect of getting it wrong. Anyway, the die was cast.

My day of destiny arrived soon afterwards. Will had said to me that if I ever had any ideas as regards adding to the script, to let him know, and he'd decide whether or not we'd use it. I kept my eyes and ears open, but apart from a few snippets about Portobello, there wasn't much I could add. Jimi Hendrix took his fatal dose in the Samarkand Hotel which was just off Ladbroke Grove. The bus passed by the opening to the street, but by the time you would have got the words out, the bus would have breezed by, with the punters craning their necks for nothing, so that was useless. Tom Jones used to drink in the Elgin on the Grove; I might have mentioned that a couple of times, but none of the tourists seemed impressed, so I dropped that too.

As I mentioned, pickings were very slim on the long, arduous home straight that is Oxford St. One afternoon, bored and boiling I spotted Ken Livingston strolling along. I started letting the customers know a little about Red Ken. This would have been out of order even if they could have understood what I was talking about. The Germans, Dutch and Japanese thought they were probably missing out on some Rock and Roll gold dust, and would be annoyed that they couldn't understand me, so this was a no no. Will had always told me to stick to the script, and apart from slight additions, I had, but this was as far away from the story as you can get. Also Will had been recording the proceedings, and after this, he'd had enough of me. He was right, I should have been doing a lot more to promote this fledgling enterprise, but I was only just hanging in there myself at that time, I was drinking like a fish, needed help myself, and was in no position to think about anyone else. Will pulled me aside a just said: "It's not working out." And that was the end of my career as a tour guide.

Relieved as I may have been not to have to go on the bus every day and risk further panic attacks, I was pretty much bolloxed. I was only a few weeks into this mortgage malarkey, and already I'll soon find myself unable to keep up the payments. I had to sign back on the 'old king cole' just to keep myself alive. Down the dole office I told them all my circumstances, and was pleasantly surprised when they said "We can only pay your mortgage interest." I didn't even know what that meant really, but hey, it's more than I expected. Later I came to realise that this meant there would be quite a shortfall on the repayments every month. Nothing new there, I've always come up short, all my life. If I need £50 I can usually get £35, if it's £100 I seem to be able to find £85 and so on. That'll probably be the way of it until the day I die. But for now I have to do all I can to hold on to the flat. The longer I wait, the more profit, I hope. At the moment I'm pretty pleased not to hold the world record for the shortest property owner in history.

24. Record

Back in 1985 The Live Aid concert and the record that went with it did get people talking. One half seemed to be saying how marvellous for these fabulous people to give up their precious time, to help others worse off than themselves. That might be true, but many others would say that it was a blatant attempt by past their sell by date acts trying to revamp ailing careers on the back of the starving millions. Most people I knew were in the latter camp and the target for most derision was Bob Geldof, who many thought never had a career in the first place. Cynical times indeed. This was emphasised, as far as the detractors of Ladbroke Grove were concerned, when word got out that they were recording 'Do they know it's Christmas' at Sarm West studio in Basing Street. This is just around the corner from the Warwick, so all day we'd be getting reports of yet another limousine pulling up outside Sarm. When I was passing by, Basing Street looked like a Park Lane luxury car showroom. When you get home that night you hear on the telly more stories of these people giving up their spare time to help with the record. OK it's all for a good cause, but they're making out these people are, like, working. Leave me out.

One of our greatest men Ben Young had a studio in Brixton, and during a drunken session in the Warwick he said it would be OK for us to use the facility to record a track, which we would then, hopefully, turn it into a single, sell it, and donate all the money to Paul McCartney. Childish? Yeah, why not, who are you going to upset? No one you respect, that's for sure. We put the word out for volunteers to contribute, and by the positive reaction from all and sundry, it seemed to us that we weren't alone in our scepticism. So one sunny afternoon, thirty souls set off for Cold Storage recording studio in Brixton for, if nothing else, a good laugh.

I picked out a song that I'd remembered from years before. It was called 'Sympathy' and was originally recorded by a group called Rare Bird. It's a bit corny but it did boast a decent verse that was quite apt bearing in mind that the Live Aid campaign was about feeding the hungry people of Africa. Off the top of my head:

Half the world hates the other half
And half the world has all the food
And half the world lays down and quietly starves
'cos there's not enough love to go round

Not bad for a 1970s pop music business, that was about as close to altruism, as I was to a career in medicine.

With mostly boozers from the pub, and a person who could actually play, Gareth Sager, we managed to do a version of the song. The hoped for single never materialised, so it could be classed as a waste of time, but it was another good bonding exercise for the malcontents of W11. It also led to a friendship with Ben Young. From time to time he'd let Latif and me nick a bit of studio time to record a couple of tracks of ours down there. Latif had his own band 'Mystery Slang' and had been signed, and had a couple of albums out, but my singing career would never get anywhere, mainly because it was all over the place. I'd record a cowboy song with Mario, maybe a love song somewhere else, then one of Bone's anarchic anthems in Cold Storage recording studio followed up with a song which I thought people might like to dance to. There was absolutely no continuity involved whatsoever, and the 'act' never really had a name. If I ever did manage to present my efforts to a record company geezer, I didn't exactly do myself any favours either, the second my voice came booming through the speakers I'd drown it out by talking about something else, or worse still pointing out the shortcomings of the recording. No, presenting myself in a positive way was definitely not my forte. If I walked into one of those places with the equivalent of ' Like a Rolling Stone' on tape, and the next person up had an inferior version of the 'Birdy Song' to present, and one of us was going to get signed, my complete lack of self-belief would ensure a record deal for the avian artiste.

But I did have a few songs knocking about, so in 1988 I thought I'd try and get a few others to give me one of their songs and turn it into a Roughler compilation album. I got a good response, a lot of the musicians I knew were keen to help out, but some of these were tied in with record companies and publishing deals, and as much as they'd like to give something, they couldn't. Well I believed them anyway.

I went to see a guy named Rob Collins, an A&R guy who used to drink in the pub, I think Rob signed Culture Club, so why the fuck he'd have anything to do with this project is beyond me, but he was good about it. I had to bring him the master and the artwork, and he'd take care of the rest. I guess there was a financial agreement, we shook on that, but I didn't think we'd sell any, so I didn't give a toss. Ben Young was the producer, he had the unenviable task of getting the balance right, which wasn't easy, as all the demos collected were of, let's say, varying quality. Ben had another idea; he wanted it to sound as if all the acts were actually performing live in the Warwick, so we there with the old tape recorder to capture the absolute bollocks that's constantly talked down there. Then there was Davy Duke, an artist mate of Jock's, who from a position opposite drew the pub in charcoal, the result of which became the cover. I took this drawing, and many scraps of paper containing the relevant info to Nigel Coke at AD/CO, he did a good job. So we had an album cover, which although would win no prizes, was in keeping with the normal Roughler editorial standards i.e. as rough as a badger's arse.

The acts who very kindly bunged me a track were:

Jock Scott	*Ode to the Warwick*
Head	*Spank Spank*
Sex Boots Dread	*Pentel*
Green House of Terror	*Third Class Heaven*
The Rave	*City Buildings*
Paul Stewart	*Kiki and Pepe*
Vivian Stanshall	*Holiday Homes (intro)*
Ray Jones	*It's her Money I'm After (Not Love)*
World Domination Ent.	*Asbestos Lead Asbestos*
Keith Allen	*Groucho Club*
The Singing Sikh	*Rocking with the Sikh*
Band Wagon	*Trouble on the North Bank*
Bambi Slam	*I'm Left Wondering*

Jock penned his brand-new composition 'Ode to the Warwick' if anyone asks me what it was like in the pub I tell them to listen to this. Blind Bob, a well-known busker on Portobello was dragged down to Duncan's studio opposite the pub to provide accordion accompaniment on this one. Gareth Sager wrote the song 'Spank Spank' which describes the drying out period of a famous footballer. One of Keith's many alter egos 'Sex Boots Dread' tells the story of a Rastafarians love for his boyfriend 'Pentel'. James, a pub regular slipped me a tape of his group Green House of Terror singing of a 'Third Class Heaven. Old Roughian Sean Rogers and the lads from The Rave stepped up to the crease with 'City Buildings'. Paul Stewart, veteran of all sorts of Roughler shenanigans came up with 'Kiki and Pepe' there's love and crocodile wrestling on this one. To answer my critics who thought I spent too much time cavorting with Toff women, I sang 'Its Her Money I'm After (Not Love)' one of the tracks we recorded at Cold Storage. Joe Strummer came to the studio when we were doing this song. You could say he was the producer, but in truth he came down there for a day out. His production expertise stretched only to telling me how shite my vocal was. Recently 'Asbestos Lead Asbestos' by World Domination Enterprises was voted in some prestigious poll as being one of the top 100 records ever, fucking right, classic stuff. Ex Bonzo frontman Vivian Stanshall was doing something with Keith at the All Saints studio, Jock had written the 'Holiday Home' poem as an intro for the Page Three classic of the same name. Mario Tavares very kindly miked up Viv, who gave us a fab rendition. Keith must have been in a good mood, he gave me another song. It was untitled, after listening to it, it sounded to me like a conversation you might easily hear in the 'Groucho Club' so I named it thus. Paul Durden, the manager and songwriter of The Singing Sikh sent me the single 'Rocking with the Sikh' which is still Pete Singh's greatest moment. Seeing as we were now in Swansea mode, why not 'Trouble on the North Bank' my homage to the long suffering 'Jack Army' of Swans supporters.

That was meant to be the end of the record, then Rob Collins, or was it Pete at Rough Trade said a soon to be 'massive' band called The Bambi Slam wanted to be on it. They sent this song called 'I'm Left Wondering' good song, even in demo form. They had a pucka version at their disposal, but preferred the less polished effort for our record. Ben Young set about putting it all together, fitting conversation in between tracks. He's not so keen on it now, says he wishes he'd done it differently, but I liked it, but more to the point I'd managed to see something through from start to finish. If this book is ever published, it will only be the second time I've ever done that. We sold the thousand copies of what ended up as 'The Warwick Sessions' volume one. Out of the profit I bought a typewriter, about two weeks later, typewriters had become almost obsolete, and were being replaced with computery things. I'd managed to produce the paper for many years without one, now I'd modernised my approach to publishing, I was still out of sync. I don't think it mattered much though. I've written 75 per cent of this story on other people's computers, so where there's a will… Last word on the Roughler album, I haven't got a copy myself, I had to run around the place to get a copy. In the process I looked on the internet to see if I could pick one up on the cheap, I found out I can buy one off a Chinaman for a fiver, but apart from that, nothing.

25. Snagging Strummer

'You know what they say; well some of it was true'

One thing that I always looked forward to was when a Bash the Rich event was organised in W11. I wouldn't call myself an activist as regard the anarchist movement, but I would always lend my 'expertise' to the lads when they came over to Ladbroke Grove. I remember organising a gig at the Elgin boozer one time, so we could put on a bit of a show for the marchers to help them wind down after a day of hurling bottles and abuse at all and sundry in and around the Royal Borough.

I got myself fixed up with a little beat combo of my own this night. The only memory I have of our set is the lead guitarist (Dean from the Warwick) refusing to play on when, pissed, he'd dropped his plectrum, and couldn't find it in the darkness. We made a rare discovery that night though, in the shape of a West Indian calypso singer called Janno Janno. His songs really shook the crowd up: 'If station burn down, don't water it' was almost taken by the Class Warrior as a clarion call to take off that very moment and burn down Notting Hill nick. The other top song was 'Trouble in Brixton' (utter confusion, they burn down de land). Janno must have been in his seventies at the time, but he could rattle out a protest song. Where are all the protest singers gone, the ones who can supercharge the activist elements in our midst? Singing about recycling and trees, and how hot the weather is getting I guess. And trying to stop me from having a fag in the pub, FUCK OFF!

Janno Janno had been introduced to us by no less a person than the admirable Maxwell. Max was a standard dish around Ladbroke Grove for all the time I'd been in London, but his history goes further back than that. He knew all about the Mangrove set up, and had spent much time with Michael X. He'd had many sorties into the music business as well, I'm not sure how successful they were, but it showed that he was a 'trier'. When a Class War contingent came over the Grove to join the protest against the gentrification of the market, Maxwell, had somehow got himself onto the Council.

The protest, got up by market traders and residents, was, in the case of the traders one of outrage at the council's plans, plans which would seriously damage their earning potential. The residents' complaint was one of aesthetics, they liked what the Market looked like and stood for, and were up in arms over the idiotic proposals being foisted on the area by daft Tory councillors. In their wisdom these twerps had already started their makeover by cobbling part of the street underneath the Westway on Portobello. Instead of using traditional cobblestones, the workers had used what seemed to be concrete bricks, placed into the ground on their side. I don't know the proper jargon for this type of roadwork, but take it from me, it was fucking horrible. The bricks were constantly coming loose of the cement, these might make for useful weapons for any future riots in the area, but as a road surface, they were useless.

So a protest was planned, this would entail attending a council meeting at the Town Hall, where. In front of the 'high ups' of the council, the objectors could vent their spleen. I mentioned it to Bone, and he got a couple of like-minded people together, so along with costermonger and complainer we headed for the meeting. The meeting started as they all do with these council leaders sitting on high like the Politburo, you know they are only going to pay lip service to the public, and are never going to take into account any of their concerns. So as the chairperson rambled on Class War attendees just started heckling, calling all before them Toffs, Wankers and Yuppies, all bang on the money from where I'm sitting. Of course, these people who don't like being called anything except marvellous, took umbrage at this interruption. "Any more of this and the meeting will be cancelled!" This was met with "Fuck off home then". At this point the Politburo started gathering up their paperwork and started to leave the arena. As they were exiting Maxwell, from the council floor, was heard to comment to them "Meet the real opposition."

With the stage now vacated, a contingent led by Bone, myself and Piers Thompson decided to occupy the seats vacated by the high and mighty. Labour councillor Bob Pandy came over and complained about our behaviour adding: "I had it all under control" meaning he had a solution he was about to present to the committee when we started our shenanigans, but of course Bob is the type who still believes in democracy, even when the Tories are in power, bless him. So we managed to take over the chamber, with Bone (or was it Piers?) occupying the Mayoral chair. It was all a good laugh. The genuine protestors seemed bemused by all the goings on, Paul Simenon and the gorgeous Trish found it funny, but weren't too sure whether anything was achieved, maybe it wasn't, but you can't just let these people steamroller all over you. Maybe the demonstration didn't go the way the people from the market might have liked, but within weeks the 'cobbles were removed, and all talk of gentrification had gone away.

Around this time I was doing the usual pursuits – talking bollocks and sorting out my bets when an excited Ian Bone greets me in the Warwick one Saturday afternoon, he had a plan for taking the Class War message nationwide. A musical tour, to all the working class strongholds of our island was what he had in mind; he even had an idea of who he wanted to headline the thing, ex-Clash frontman Joe Strummer. He'd only just thought of it though because he'd just seen the geezer through in the other bar. "Go on Ray, you ask him." I wasn't having that. I knew Joe alrightish, but I didn't think he'd do it in a million years. "Look," said I "I'll introduce you, but you'll have to ask him yourself." I fucked off to the other side of the bar to watch the racing. Well that's my excuse. Really I was just hiding from a possible embarrassing situation.Don't get me wrong, you can't fault Joe. He talks to all and sundry, has time for everyone, and on more than one occasion has whacked the beer in for the boys, and had been outrageously generous to yours truly. He'd even turned up one night at the Warwick and sang a few tunes at an Old Roughians fundraiser; the disbelief on people's faces was the highlight of that night. But the difference between 'Junco Partner' in the boozer and fronting a Class War tour of the country was enormous in my eyes, and, don't forget, at that time, Joe was considered by many to be one of the biggest star frontmen in the fucking world.

I was in the process of throwing yet another losing betting slip to the floor, when Ian and Matt came over and told me Joe had agreed to do it. Joe had got a new band together, namely 'Latino Rockabilly War' and was keen to find out what they were made of I guess. So what better than a tour to find out if him and the boys could hack it in the burghs? So on reflection it was probably good for all concerned. Saying that though, he knew Class War had no money, and none was ever asked for. Bear in mind Joe's band were all from America, and he had to finance their staying alive in this country off his own back. So the Bash the Rich tour was on. Bone gave me a choice. I could either be Class War's parliamentary candidate at the upcoming election, or I could compere the tour. This would include introducing the acts, spouting anti-social poetry and prose, and being gobbed on in Sheffield. I chose the latter. Lapsed socialist John Duignan became the Class War candidate for Kensington and Chelsea.

26. The Tour

With thoughts of American author Ken (One Flew Over The Cuckoo's Nest) Kesey and the Merry Pranksters to the fore, we boarded the bus of discovery outside the Percy pub in Ladbroke Grove and we were off. Can't recall where the first gig outside London was, (The tour had opened to great ovation at the Lyceum) but it might have been Merthyr Tydfil. It soon became apparent to me that this was not going to be a leisurely tour of the country, boozing, shagging and taking drugs. Due to my 'status' I had access all areas, but try as I might I, and bearing in mind I've been a thief all my life, I found it virtually impossible to beat the road crew to the 'rider' of a night-time So it was a job in itself just to get rat arsed after every show. I must have managed OK though, because trying to remember the events right now is proving very tricky. Drugs? Don't remember any, and as for the shagging, there was probably more action at a Communards gig.

I had to pull a bit of rank early on. When the bus arrived at a town, the bands were dropped off at their respected hotels or b&b, and the rest of the crew were ferried straight to the gig to set up. They expected me to hump the equipment. I thought: "I've never worked in my life, so I ain't starting now." I'm not built for it. Matt, the tour manager thought I should muck in. Well, I'd certainly muck in when it came to vibing up the lads, having a laugh and lifting morale, but lifting bass bins and amps, not on your fucking life. I took it up with Joe. I asked him up front if he considered what I was doing could be considered an act. Very diplomatically Joe came down on my side, I think. Not out of any great conviction, but just to get us two tossers out of the dressing room.

God must have been punishing me for this when it was decided that my roommate was going to be a young Australian bloke named Darren. He is possibly the only Australian person I've met who actually made me laugh (Barrie Humphries doesn't count, he's been over here too long) but boy could he bunny. Non-stop questions, to which he wanted answers, hair-brained schemes which included going around some of the hardest housing estates in the country, knocking on doors, spreading the Class War word, and, more annoyingly, not letting me get any kip. Early on I saved him in a dodgy boozer in Merthyr. I think he was arguing the toss with some feral pool sharks, I noticed the atmosphere turn nasty, the kind of nasty that doesn't come from anger, more the kind that comes out of 'right I'm bored now, let's have a punch-up' that was enough for me to get us out of there. Couldn't help but like Darren though. There's always talk of him revisiting these shores. But there are visa problems I believe.

Joe's band were tight enough. There was Zander Schloss from the Circle Jerks on guitar, Willie McNeil from LA on the drums, Jim Donica, a Texan or was it a Mormon on bass, and the brilliant Roberto Plas on percussion. Joe had to be finding it hard though. He is a great frontman, but when he was in the Clash, the whole band was easy on the eye. Now he's the centre of attention, and all the punters want to see the Clash, so I thought he was on a hiding to nothing really. But having said that this band could fucking play man, and the crowd were never sold short.

Matt had secured a London reggae band as support for the tour. They were a great bunch called 'One Style' and the plan was to have a local band from each town to make up the show. As the compere I'd go backstage every night introduce myself to the bands, you know, ask them if there was something poignant they wanted me to say when I introduced them. But for the life of me, there are only two I can remember, Danak, a traditional Indian band, who played in Bradford, And the La's.

The La's were the only group who refused to go on first (i.e. before One Style) I had a chat with them backstage. There was something about them, clothes? Attitude? I don't know, but something. I called them up onto the stage, and then went into the audience to watch. The venue, The Civic Centre in Liverpool, seemed tailor-made for these songsters. They would have been good in any era. The songs were great, the look was great, and the punters loved it. I want to say right now, whoever managed to stop this band going Universal needs shagging by a Rhino horn. You hear all these rumours that the singer with the La's, Lee Mavers was an awkward fucker, and wasn't all that happy with the albums production, and had massive rows with the powers that be, well that's as may be. But they're all awkward fuckers in that game aren't they; at least Mavers had talent, and the tunes. So what went wrong?

I shot backstage and told Joe how fucking good the support were. I definitely noticed a change in his demeanour right then. Joe came up to the challenge, he worked his bollocks off, the band was hot, and they went down a fucking thunderstorm. Best gig of the tour by a street.

Along the way we'd been picking up waifs and strays from all over. Who gave a fuck, empty seats, why not? There were two cute Japanese girls who hopped on the bus early on; I had to save the prettier one from one of the roadies who was trying to make out with her. After Darren disappeared I even had her staying in my room. No sex. Dammit. I saw these two risking their lives one night, hanging over a balcony to try and get hold of Joe's set list. When I retrieved it and gave it her later she was over the moon. Still no sex though. This is bollocks, I didn't even try. Honestly. One of the funnier incidents on the bus concerned, a couple of Sheffield lads who were on board, they had with them a brew local to where they were from. It's called 'Roger and Out'. Never mind 'Reader I married him,' my message is 'Reader avoid like the fucking plague' this is a mother of a swallow. I couldn't resist the old: "You Americans think you know how to drink" routine to Zander and the rest. Couple of them fell for it literally. I'm not a great one for 'you're from so-and-so you can't drink' malarkey. In America I met some of the thirstiest bastards ever to lift a glass, but this brew would floor Rick Flare, Tyson and Jonah Lomu. Sure enough, it had the desired effect. It was rest day thank God. No gig that night.

The lariest place we played though, was, surprisingly Poole in Dorset. I was looking forward to a bit of peace and quiet down on the coast, after Manchester, Birmingham and Sheffield, but the locals weren't having any of that; they smashed all the windows on the front of the building. Maybe they couldn't get in. If that's the case they're twats. They only had to ask, and would have got in for free.

I'd stuck to the task, and now my tenure as compere was coming to an end. I had to get back to London to sign on. My last gig was at the Barrowlands in Glasgow. My more than adequate replacement, the poet Jock Scott had been ferried from London by a girlfriend of mine, the lovely Catherine, still affectionately known as Barmy. She was taking me back to London the next day. Nice. Big stage at the 'Barrers' Jock thought it a good idea for me to introduce him to the crowd that night, so he could ease himself into the tour. When we hit the stage, during the long walk to the microphone stand, with crowd noise lifting appreciably, Jock bottled "Not tonight Ray" Can't blame him, hostile crowds in these here parts. I hit the mic and delivered 'Tory Funerals' to cries of "Fook of yer cunt". It was a thankless task, it was meant to be a political tour, someone was picked to deliver the message, and it was 'muggins' here. No one wanted to hear me telling tales of killing Tories or burning down holiday homes, they wanted to know if Strummer could still hack it. All in all I think he did well.

Me, I'm on my way back to London to find out how the election campaign is progressing.

Political frenzy had hit the Warwick Castle, Portobello Road W11. With the market being a grade 'A' location for a photo opportunity, movers and shakers from all parties were to be seen schmoozing with barrow boys and the locals. At every turn these poor souls were being hounded by John Duignan and his loud hailer. He had very little time for any of the opposition, but he came into his own when he spotted a Conservative. 'The only good Tory is a lavatory' was his put down to them. John even became adept(ish) at talking to the press, even blasé. On spotting a journo by the bar he'd say: "There's another one, what rag is he from? Paul Durden answered in a flash "He's a big hitter John; he's the political editor of Exchange and Mart".

Of course the election result didn't go as well as hoped. I don't think John got as many votes as Monster Raving. I think Bone went down the Town Hall demanding a recount, and shouting 'fix' but that particular plan had gone awry. But it was a fucking good laugh.

I was looking forward to getting back into my own flat. I'd rented it out to a guy named Andy Ferguson. He was a pal of Peter Hamilton, Gordon Geddes and that. So it was cool. In fact, the flat looked a lot better than when I left. Andy hit me with a surprise though; he reckoned I'd agreed for him to stay another four weeks. I didn't remember agreeing to this, but this Andy is a manipulative sort, used to getting his own way, so he went straight for my weakest point. He showed me £500. That was me swayed anyway. Armenian Joe, a mate from Swansea via Christian Tehran said he'd put me up. This was very handy considering he lived right across the street. Then I had this idea that a holiday would sort me out. I should have just gone to Greece, where, at least, I had some idea of the comings and goings. That's too easy though. I decided on Spain. The only place I could find to go at such short notice though was Portugal. I didn't have a plan, so I went down the Star for some advice. John the Hat was there. He said he'd had the time of his life in a place called Monchique. He told me to fly to Faro, then a train to Portimao. From there you can get a bus to Monchique.

I followed his advice. When I arrived in Portugal, I was so pissed that no cab would take me into Faro town. I walked for ages. This must have sobered me up somewhat, because eventually a cab stopped and dropped me at a hotel. The next morning on walkabout I bumped into this guy. He was up to something, but nothing you hadn't seen in Ladbroke Grove. I never thought it possible, but this guy actually brought 'Bobbee Sharlton' into the conversation. He's more off his head than I am, so I decide to give him the swerve. Somehow we managed to arrange to meet later that evening, where he was going to buy me a meal "in a special restaurant." Yeah, sure. I had a look around that afternoon, and I have to admit I felt a bit old. This Faro was certainly a party town of sorts, but I didn't think I was going to fit in, so perhaps the 'Hat' had come up with the goods.

That evening I have to get something to eat, so I'm wandering about aimlessly, when I hear someone calling after me, it's the guy from this afternoon. What the fuck, my luck is poxed, Faro isn't London, but it's quite big, big enough you'd think, not to be bumping into nuisances, but here he is. We go into his special place, how special I don't know. No one seemed to know him there. We ordered some food. There's no way on earth that this guy is going to pay, so I order small, He can get what he wants. I won't be paying for his, that's a fucking nailed on certainty. He decides to visit the men's room. He's gone a long time. He hasn't finished his grub, or his drink, so if his angle was to sneak out a back door or something and leave me with the bill, you'd think he'd get his fill first. Wouldn't you?

All right I've been had. I do a quick calculation, and realise it's not going to kill me if I have to foot the bill. One off the waiters approaches me. "Come, come, your amigo". I try to explain that this is not my amigo not by a long chalk, but he insists that I go with him to the men's room. I get in there, this guy has passed out, and has wedged himself in there so tight, and they can't open the cubicle door to get the dumb fuck out .All the time their gesturing and saying "amigo". I peek into the cubicle and notice a works on the floor, now this is bad news. The waiters are pissed off, and they won't have it that I don't know this twat. I go back to the restaurant, pick up the bill, match it with money, and fuck off out of there, quick time.

The next day I get the train to Portimao. I always think that railway stations and bus stations are close together, are they fuck, not here anyway. I'm walking in circles I guess. Every now and then I'd stop a citizen and ask "Autocarross, Monchique?" I got the blank from everyone I approached. Autocarros is bus, I know that from the phrasebook, and Monchique is a place right, it's the equivalent of someone saying to me "bus, Slough?" I'd maybe have to think about it a little bit, but I'm sure I'd understand what they were after, and be able to help. Without any help whatsoever I lucked upon the bus station, and believe it or not, found my way to Monchique. Fucking quiet here folks, too quiet for me anyway. I get some digs, and soon realise by the cost, that it's not going to be cheap here.

Well I've made my bed etc, so I have to make do. This is not going to be a holiday, more a survival course. I wouldn't be able to drink and eat during the day, so I had to eat at night only. The Hat was right, it is a beautiful spot for the sightseer, but if any form of shenanigans is your glass of Raki, this ain't the place to be. I quickly ran out of dosh, I was going to do a runner from the digs, but the geezer was all right, so I had to explain to him my situation. He wasn't too happy, I said I'd send him some dough from London, but we both knew that would never happen. So I left under a cloud. I managed to get myself back to Faro. I had enough cash to find a bed in the worst doss house in town, but at least it was a kip. I had on my person ten £1 coins, I wandered around, hoping some British tourist would change it up to a note for me, so I could weigh it in for some Escudo's. Not a fucking one would help me out.

I arrived at Faro airport the next day. I had my ticket home, and the ten coins would get me from Gatwick to the Grove, so things could be worse. Wrong. When I got to the check-in, the girl said, "This ticket is for yesterday." What the fuck. She went on to explain that for X amount of money I could transfer to today's plane. I went through the lot, dying relations, job on the line, all the old fanny, but she was adamant. There was a bloke standing beside me, he piped up "I'll pay for his ticket." I was astounded. I thanked this guy with such sincerity it became embarrassing. What a sport. Funnily enough, if I'd had to go around the airport cap in hand, begging for money to get home, this guy would have been the last person I would have asked. So as Chuck Berry says "It goes to show you never can tell.

I made it back to London, Andy and his girlfriend had left the flat in immaculate condition, with a few improvements might I add. It's good to be home. So feet up, re-group and wait for the next setback, which is never far away.

27. Covers

The Roughler had been doing OK. From its slim, humble beginnings the latest issue had reached the monumental landmark of thirty six pages. I'm happy about that, but the construction of the thing is down to me, and I'm not very good at that part of things I'm sad to say. Year's later people would tell me that the mistakes and poor editorial components that made it up were part of its charm. Cheers. If I'd thought that then I would have cobbled it together between betting shop and pub, with a black-lead and a couple of empty fag packets. What I'd hoped was that some bright spark would show up in the pub, see some worth in the paper, and take over that side of things. Because although I was very laissez faire about it, I thought with the right people involved it might have a shot. Especially if these 'others' did the (what was for me anyway) hard stuff. This would allow me more time to run around parties, clubs etc with camera and notebook at the ready. This never happened. So for the most part I was flying solo. Don't get me wrong, lots of people were involved, but that final piece of work was down to me, and that trip to Ravenscourt Park was dreaded.

It was looking good though, especially the covers. We had a particularly good run of images on the front page. In five issues we had Joe Strummer, Neneh Cherry, Wendy James, Shane McGowan and Keith Allen beaming out below the Roughler masthead. Joe liked the paper, and often offered to do something for it. I could never think what though. Joe had probably been asked every conceivable music question by far better hacks than me, and if you think I'm going to question him about political stuff you're mad. So I let any form of interview go by the wayside. Now I realise I should have talked to him about living around the Grove, and kept away from the Clash stuff, that everyone already knew, but I never did. But with Joe offering assistance I'd be daft not to take him up on it. I had this idea to put Joe to work as a journo. Nothing too tricky. In fact I asked him to go from one side of the pub to the other to interview our old mate Kate Bernard. I gave him the Dictaphone and he was away.

They had a right old chat the pair of them. The tapes around somewhere, and I've still got the photos.

The obvious reasons for having Joe on the cover were, he's famous, he's local and more importantly he was a good bloke, who liked getting involved in local stuff. By some freak I had a cracking photo of Strummer taken at a party around at his house in Lancaster Road. Strummer had a liking for this rough Spanish brandy, and at this gathering there was plenty of it about, so we all filled our boots. So the fact that I was even able to point the camera in his direction was remarkable, so imagine my surprise when I eventually picked up the photos a few days later, to find a crisp good image of Joe. Doing the cover was the last job to do, and was normally last minute. So I had to think of a headline to go with his photo. I couldn't come up with anything, then I said to myself" What would the Sun do?" make something up obviously, so I did. STRUMMER QUITS W11 that'll do. A week after that issue came out, I was looking at one of the tabloids, I think it was the 'Bizarre' column in the Mirror, and there was the story we'd made up. Lazy Twats.

Neneh Cherry becoming a star was easier to predict than Shergar winning the Derby. She had it all, voice, class, fashion sense, she could dance, had the tunes and was gorgeous to boot. She'd been in Rip Rig and Panic with Gar Sager, Sean and Andrea Oliver. They all hung out around Portobello so obviously you get to see Neneh around and about the place, and a very pleasant sight it was. Neneh was feisty alright, but she was always nice to me. I'd often bump into her and Andrea on excursions into the West End. I was down the Wag one night when they walked in with another female vision. This turned out to be Neneh's beautiful sister, who was not without her admirers. They had the beauty genes in that family. I'd taken a nice snap of Neneh some time previous at a party up in Trellick Tower, so when the word went round that her record was soon to be released I shoved the picture on the cover, and called it The Roughler tip for the top. I wish I could pick horses like that. As I said she was a star in waiting. It would have taken some really bad management to hold her back. Of course nothing like that happened and soon enough Neneh is known all over the world. At the time she was streets ahead of everyone, including the Americans. A lot of what she recorded still holds up today. So in two issues, we managed to put two icons on the front of the paper. Not bad.

A blonde bombshell had been spotted of late in the Warwick. It was Wendy James. Wendy had come up to London from Brighton to try out for the part of Crepe Suzette in the movie Absolute Beginners. She didn't get the part but through it bumped into Steve O'Rourke the manager of Pink Floyd. Not a bad connection you'll agree. He asked Wendy to come up with some demos. Our very own Glen 'Career ending' Colson was working for O'Rourke at the time, and was asked to 'look after' Wendy during the recording sessions. The studio of choice was run by a guy called Duncan, and was situated in a basement across the street from the Warwick, so her and her band soon became regulars in the pub. The studio was housed behind what was to become the most famous front door ever. It's the one all the Japanese tourists take photos of, the one that appears in the film Notting Hill. (Tex Axile, who would go on to become drummer in T. Vamp, and also lived in that building, told me once that the reason he left Portobello and moved to America was that the 'door' had become more famous than him). But that was to come. For now Transvision Vamp were in there recording.

I always got on well with Wendy, and she liked everything about the pub, including The Roughler, so it made sense to nab her for an interview. Even if Transvision didn't take off, we'd still have an interview with a sexy recording artist who drank Guinness with us at the bar. Kevin Allen became Welsh rock reporter Luke Llanelli to conduct the interview. It all went very well. From a quiet corner of the pub, Kev found out that Wendy liked Patti Smith, The Flower Pot Men, and watching the boys play pool. (What the fuck you want? Rolling Stone?). Transvision Vamp were ready for the big launch when our 'Wendy' edition came out. She wasn't gonna let me loose with some dodgy snap I'd taken whilst half cut, so she presented me with a blonde bombshell picture, which we used. Very nice too, the headline ran 'The Roughler tip for the top'.

Very quickly Transvision Vamp became famous. 'I Want your Love' sold bucket loads, and the album was expected to do the same. Wendy became the darling of the press. Her every movement was catalogued in detail in the tabloids. She was bound to mention Portobello wasn't she? So fans of hers started turning up at the Warwick to catch a glimpse of the newest star. I was at the bar one evening when I get to chatting to this geezer that I recognised from the telly. It was Roland Rivron. He was sharply dressed this night, and had made this pilgrimage to West London on the back of info that he'd picked up in the press, that Wendy James did her drinking here. He casually asked me if that was the truth of it, I told him "Yeah, she's in here most nights when she's not busy". Rivron did eventually meet up with Wendy. I have no idea what went on there, but I tell you one thing, fair play to him for making the effort to try and track down someone he fancied in a strange environment.

Transvision Vamp was short lived really. But they shifted a ton of records. Wendy had a go at solo projects, but I don't think very much happened there. But hey, she bought a house on Chesterton Road out of it. Not too shoddy. I was in contact with Wendy the other day. She's in New York. She's recording still.

You often hear about the exploits of intrepid journalists risking life and limb in war-torn corners of the globe, dodging bullet and grenade just to bring you the story. The names of Simpson, Adie and Pilger spring to mind. They're all household names. We had our writers as well who would put their lives on the line for the paper. Being in Bosnia, Beirut and the like has got to be lairy, but what Jock Scott had to do to secure an interview for the Roughler has to be classed as perilous too. Jock had to go out drinking, for three days and nights with Shane McGowan. Rather him than me. You may think 'piece of piss', swapping yarns and guzzling away with the Pogues frontman. How hard can it be? The reality though is somewhat different. Shane never stops, and if you're with him, you're in for the long haul. For instance, at that time Shane would drink quite often in a Guinness and oyster bar just off Soho Square called The Toucan. When I was guzzling, it was one of my favourite watering holes in the West End. Go in there with Shane, as Jock did on many occasions, and you're asking for trouble. Shane is automatically recognised by everyone, and everyone likes the Pogues, he brings the 'Oirish' out in people, so the minute they spot him in a place like the Toucan, they feel the need to buy him a drink. "What're you having Shane?" they'd shout.

Now, in the Toucan they have a selection of whiskies, some so expensive, that the bottles have padlocks on them. Shane knows the names of them, and quite happily orders one up. You're not going to buy this poetic figure a single are you? You don't want to appear cheap do you? No. So doubles become the order of the day. "And how about your friend there Shane?" That's when the trouble starts. They've got some vicious whiskey in the Toucan. Eventually, after many a mishap and crashing falls Scott reports back with the news that an interview with McGowan has been arranged. He was living at the time right beside Highbury Stadium, and we were to report there post haste.

Scott and myself thought we were well prepared for our trip to Shane's house. We had notepads, pens, camera and a whole host of ideas for the upcoming interview. Well things rarely if ever go to plan and as we boarded the train at Notting Hill tube station, deep down we knew that this was probably not going to be the scoop of the year, the interview that gets to the heart and soul of the Celtic crooners psyche. The odds are that it would turn into yet another midweek, mid afternoon piss up. We'll see.

First thing that sticks out as we enter Shane's abode is the amount of medicinals that are on display on his coffee table. Oddly enough though, none of them are illegal. On closer inspection you soon realise that these potions, tablets etc, are nothing you haven't taken yourself to get rid of a hangover. Whereas you might have one or possibly two of these cures in your cabinet, Shane had every one known to man, just to be on the safe side. The minute we arrived, the drink started flowing and it was plentiful. So any plans of an in depth interview were scuppered before we even started. Instead we watched telly and swapped yarns. Of course not a single memo was taken, so the only ones that were remembered are sketchy.

The first contained a story concerning the actress Faye Dunaway and one of the Pogues' road crew. There's no way in the world I'm going to repeat that here, it would only shatter the illusions of about one million males of my age group, let it lie. Then Shane told us a tale about his first encounter with the hallucinogenic properties of the Australian Kane Toad. Shane had been offered this delicacy at a barbecue in Melbourne, and swears by its groove-inducing effect, but added, the toads, once captured, must be frozen alive to make it easier to peel them, prior to skinning one up. You'd think this was like hard work, but thinking back, ever since I became conscious of drug culture in the sixties, there have always been those types, who would bust their balls to achieve an alternative high.

Shane had to step out. Before he left he told us there was plenty of drink in the cupboards in the kitchen. We'd been doing all right up to now on the lager, but a change is always as good as a rest, especially after ten cans of gassy Stella. Investigating said cupboard, it soon became apparent that food wasn't high on the agenda. The cupboards were full of bottles of gin. Apart from Roadent, no one likes gin. But hey, I don't particularly like the taste of any alcohol, so it's gin with any mixture you can find. Odd drink to find in such copious amounts in someone's house though, I can't believe for one minute that Shane had bought the stuff. Perhaps it was a gift. We fell out of his house later that evening, with no copy. Luckily, I had the sense to get the camera out. So at least we had some snaps of Shane. The one we used was one of him reading the Beano.

Keith had moved on. No more seeing him every other day around Portobello. His star was on the rise too. He'd got into the film business, and was making movies with Peter Richardson and was in loads of the 'Comic Strip presents' series. His name was out there, so it was obvious that we had to do a feature on him, he was infamous. Keith was still a member and player for the Old Roughians, and still came to games. He was a fair medium pacer, and was keen enough, but he could also have a disruptive effect on proceedings. This was illustrated in spades the day he turned up at Boston Manor with his new toy, namely, a bottle of Amyl Nitrate. His behaviour that day would have raised eyebrows amongst the members at Lords, and would have been frowned upon wherever cricket is played, but the sight of the Old Roughian slip cordon off their tits on poppers was a treat. He even slipped it under the nose of some unsuspecting batsman at some point, which although hilarious, was also dangerous, I guess. He was also the ultimate piss taker, and was continually surrounded by players up for the laugh.

I guess we caught Keith at the right time. In the piece he didn't have a good word to say about anyone, which was great. If you're in the pub with your Roughler and a pint, there's nothing better than reading about so-called celebrities' shortcomings, and Keith didn't disappoint on that front. Keith was always willing to contribute for the paper; it was always a matter of pinning him down. In a previous issue we'd asked the question 'Whatever happened to the Greys?' This was a reference to this group of lads who were in evidence around the art gallery/book scene back then, but had recently fallen off the radar. Tim Burke was involved, and his mate Dan, I didn't really know them at the time, so couldn't answer my own question, so we waited to see if there would be any response. Then a letter arrived, and whichever way he'd dressed it up, it was obviously from Keith. This is how it went:

Dear Editor,

Re: The Grey Organization

The fall from grace of the Grey brothers can most definitely be attributed to the preference for colour publications of the Style/Art aficionados of the 'Standing Room Only' London scene. Dig?

What were once interesting and sometimes menacing facial tones were now recognised as the spots, boils and whiteheads of unrequited attention seeking.

For a brief spell the Brothers hawked themselves around the West End and many and various warehouse parties as exponents of a new art movement, namely 'Spotism'. But apart from a couple of gay wine waiters in Old Compton Street (well we liked their haircuts really), there were no takers.

Unable to stump up enough money to afford some No.2 pancake, they deserted the West End scene to concentrate their activities in the field of popular music. They formed themselves into an acapella-style quartet called the Lenny Bennett Critique, and their stock-in trade was making light industrial humming noises. Their only record to date 'Hoochy Coochy I'm Fucking Useless' was withdrawn from circulation, when it was discovered that their naive cover of 'Baggy Trousers' had been put on the 'b' side, without the permission of Madness.

Good luck,

A. Reader.

So we at least had the front of the magazine looking good. It was still full of mistakes, but the first thing anyone sees is the front, and at least that was eye-catching. I was quite proud of the front, people might think it not such a big deal, but all the people featured there were people we liked, and knew, and for the most part, were my very own photographs. No big deal might be right, but you try getting those bits together if you live somewhere like Redcar. Nothing wrong with Redcar, but if you doing a magazine up there, you probably wouldn't bump into the sort of folk you would in the Warwick.

28. Cricket

Some of the best times Kirsty and I had together were when we went on holiday to Greece. Holidays never entered the picture when I was a kid, and apart from my disastrous trip over the channel with Steve Northampton, I'd never been abroad apart from my quick Avignon punt in the army. Kirsty on the other hand came from a place where holidays were part of the curriculum. She came up with a plan for a Mediterranean vacation. I was nicking a regular few quid of late on the back of my speed sales, so she took a few quid off me whenever she got the chance, and the trip was sorted. We were off on a cheapie to Corfu, this may not sound that exotic, but when we got there I thought I was in Paradise. We stayed in a self-catering apartment in a place called Ipsos, I don't know what it's like now, but back then it seemed that we had the place to ourselves. The self-catering wasn't a problem for two reasons, Kirsty was a fabulous cook, and everything was so cheap, that you could eat out all the time if you wished. The weather was great all the time, swimming and sunbathing don't cost a cent anyway, and that took up huge chunks of the day. I hadn't had as much fun for years. I was born on the coast, so was happy enough on the beach, but if I ever got bored, I could retire to one of the bars nearby, and still be in contact with Kirsty, who liked nothing more than lying in the sun all day. So there you have it, everybody happy, and virtually impossible to go skint.

We liked it so much that we went back there for the next few years. On the last trip Kirsty had worked out a more complicated roster for our trip. On this one we had to travel for at least another day even after we landed in Greece. The destination was the island of Karpathos. It was a long haul, but this place was top drawer, and on top of that, this time we were staying for a month, so had plenty of time to take in everything. Kirsty had an itinerary worked out, and I would never object to any of it, simply because wherever you went there would be a tavern, to keep me happy, and because these places never seem to close their doors, there wasn't the desperate rush to get tanked up like there is in Britain. I have to say, that on these breaks, I actually felt relaxed, something that never happened to me before, as I'm always living on my nerves back home. What's nice about the longer time spent in one place is you get to know some of the locals. One guy befriended us, and took us off to some far-flung parts of the Island to see beautiful waterfalls, hidden caves and to some spooky mountaintop to hear the local musical hero perform his songs. I've thought long and hard, but I can't bring this friends name to mind. He had a job with, well I'd like to say the government, but the Brit equivalent, would probably be more like the council, who knows, he worked in an office anyway. One morning while sitting outside having breakfast, we spotted this guy, and he was in his Sunday best, we thought he would join us, but he simply waved and, at a rapid pace, headed toward the quayside. This wasn't like him at all, intrigued we finished off our grub, and followed him.

At the harbour quite a crowd had formed people we'd seen in various places during our stay, all in their best bib and tucker. A boat had pulled in, and we assumed they were awaiting the arrival of some dignitary from the mainland. Then a box is unloaded, smiles and a hint of anticipation follow, Kirsty and I were perplexed by now, and couldn't control our curiosity any longer, so asked one of the throng what was going on. It turned out that the people had come to witness the delivery of the first photocopying machine to the island, and this was to be placed in our friend's office. Wonderful. I don't tell you this for you to think this place was in any way behind the times. If it were left to the likes of me, we still wouldn't have a wheel, I tell it to emphasise how good the community spirit was on this beautiful island. If the delivery of this machine led to a technological invasion on Karpathos, I know not. But I certainly hope not, that's for sure.

On our last trip to Greece we had to stay in Corfu for a couple of days before moving on. We were in a cafe in the centre of town when it soon became apparent that some chaps were setting up a pitch for a cricket match. This'll do, couple of hours in the Corfu sunshine watching a game being played in what was, up until a couple of hours ago, the main car park. During the course of the match I strolled over to where the teams were congregated, and found a guy who not only spoke English, but seemed to know what I was saying to him.

I asked what the chances were of our team coming out and giving them a game. He was very receptive to the idea and handed me his card. I thought this would just be another 'We must keep in touch' moment, and nothing would come off it, but you never know.

Soon after getting back I went to Rough Trade to check in, and told Pete about the cricket thing in Greece. We left it at that, and said we'd bring it up at the next Old Roughian meeting. Over the last few seasons the interest in the Swansea games had diminished somewhat and certain members were always keen to try new ground. I can't understand this myself, one of the reasons given for abandoning the Swansea fixture was "we were thinking it would be good to take on a stronger class of opponent." What cobblers, if we ever did manage to beat the Badminton it was a hard-fought victory. In fact, they usually got the better of our meetings, and, I think they still hold the urn with the ashes. So for a couple of seasons the club had been to places like Alderney and Jersey on tour, and had been absolutely slaughtered on the cricket pitch. What does that do for the confidence? Don't ask me. These trips were out of the reach of a lot of the members financially. Pete works for gawd sake, but he had three kids, he couldn't even afford some of these trips. So that's two founder members not representing the club for a start. So a pattern emerges, it happened at Panto, and now it's reared its head in the cricket club, latecomers taking control, and not necessarily for the best.

Pete got in contact with the Corfu Cricket Club, and the guy I'd met was very positive about the prospect of taking us on, so it could be possible. On his way to work one day he spotted a Greek travel agent in Turnpike Lane. The girl who dealt with his enquiries was unbelievably helpful, and couldn't see a problem at all. All this positivity was brought to the next meeting. It was soon obvious to all that this would be a crackerjack idea. Now we had to drum up some other people as well as the cricket team. If we could manage this the costs of flights and accommodation would drop dramatically. We posted a sign on the notice board, and the response was immediate, so we set about getting deposits off those who'd showed interest, this would make them less likely to pull out later. Checking the list a week later we had sixty names on it. Don't know what Seamus would make of this, but if all those people did travel to Greece the pub would be empty. So the Old Roughians Cricket Club is going International. We've come quite a distance from those early encounters with the barrow boys.

Departure day arrived, and all sixty of us were told to congregate at Gatwick airport for the flight to Corfu. We took up half the plane, and by the time we took off more than half were half cut, and by half way, the other half, but that's not the half of it, when we landed there was some problem with the expected transport, which caused us to divide our number into two camps. So the first lot hopped on to one bus and they were off, while the rest of us waited impatiently for our bus. Everything got sorted out eventually and we too were on our way to our destination, which was in the north of the island, and considering how small Corfu is, fucking miles from its centre. Whatever happened, I know not, but it took us hours to get to base camp. The first news that we heard when we got there was the thirty people on the first bus had managed to get themselves banned from the likeliest looking bar in the vicinity. This was 'Nikos' bar, which was literally on the beach. On that first bus were Jock Scott, Luke Coke, Bernie Walther and Gordon Geddes, all pissed, and all capable of saying the wrong thing. Far be it from me to cast the first stone, but my money is on one or two of these as the likely culprits. Some say it was the diplomatic efforts of club president Terry Rogers that put this backward step behind us; others reckon that Nikos the owner on seeing sixty potential customers possibly finding somewhere else to spend their Drachmas reversed the ban quick time. Whatever happened 'Nikos' became our base for the duration, in fact by the second day, one of our number had come up with a sign 'The Warwick Annexe' so it was soon home from home.

It must have been the best decision that this taverna owner had ever made. Not only were most of us drinking in there, we were also eating his food and using all the marine equipment he had to hire out, all this revenue coming in when the place wasn't really ready for occupation yet. He may have thought us mad to actually want to spend time in his half-completed bar. How would he know the way these people's brains work, he'd never drunk in the Warwick, so why would he? Yes he was a happy man; it was early in the season, so our presence kick-started what would now probably be a very profitable summer. Nikos turned out to be a good lad. He always seemed happy to see me anyway; he'd greet me by bellowing out "Stavrides my friend!" Yeah, why not? "Yassas Nikos!" I'd shout back. Didn't know what Stavrides meant, until an English speaking Greek told me that 'Stavrides' was a famous Greek comedian to whom I had an uncanny resemblance. Whilst most holiday makers tend to take in the sights, try out many of the local hostelries and do most of the usual seaside holiday things, an element of our troupe never left the bar until it closed. The likes of Luke, Jock, Simple Simon and others had started up a card school, this proved very popular indeed for many, me included. I arose on our first morning and drank in our surroundings. We were in an apartment complex that wasn't quite finished. Pete Donne compared it to something out of 'Carry on Abroad' but for what we were paying it was luxurious. When all had risen and discussed the pros and cons of their kip conditions, the general consensus was a big thumbs up.

Right, everyone accounted for, everybody happy, breakfast over, time for a pint and a game of cards. This would have been my regime for most of the stay, me and all the other singletons. But hang about; I'm not completely single am I? When the idea of this trip was first mooted Catherine Holy-Hasted and I were still in the throes of a passionate affair, this was to fizzle out somewhat, but back then she was keen to go on this trip, and had paid up front. Our fling was almost over as the departure date approached and she wasn't going to come. That would have been a waste of money I talked her into changing her mind. So to all intents and purposes we were a couple, for this trip anyway. I'd hardly taken my seat at the card table when a hired moped pulls up outside, it's Catherine, she enters and announces in true Barmy style: "Look Ray, you can't sit around here all day drinking, let's go. I want to go up into the mountains to sketch." It was as if Tommy Cooper had entered the room judging by the hoots of laughter echoing around the place. But I had promised to be good, so I hopped on the back of the 50cc machine, and to much derision and guffaws, we were off. When people come up with ideas which mean you have to leave the pub you obviously aren't too fond of them, for a while anyway, then it becomes clear that there is more to life than the man/pub thing. Well there's one anyway, sex. I don't remember much art going on when we reached the foothills of Corfu but amore certainly surfaced. I vividly remember a Grade 'A' leg over taking place in full view of the Gods. If I'd planned all this it would have been genius, I hadn't of course, but when we got back to the bar I was invigorated by the day's exertions. The Dodgies (as they were now known) had been guzzling for hours by now, so their card playing decisions had deteriorated greatly by the time I sat down to play. I couldn't go wrong; I was winning Drachmas hand over fist. Good old Barmy.

We are all having a high old time of it, even Steve Underground who seems to have been wearing that three-piece worsted suit since we arrived. But of course when everything is going so smoothly, something arrives to put the kybosh on the jollity. And as sure as you're born, it arrives, it's the cricket. That's the reason we're here, but on the morning of our first game, enthusiasm wasn't a word that sprang to mind. Everyone is hung-over for a start, and the journey to Corfu Town is arduous in the sweltering heat. We meet up with extra keen Corfu boys, and soon enough it's game on. If there is ever such a thing as home advantage this was it in spades. We batted first on this 22-metre rubber strip, the extra length didn't help our sunstroked batsmen's co-ordination any, and we were bowled out pretty quickly. When we took the field to bowl, it soon became clear that there had been rain recently, and the soaring temperature had baked the tyre marks into craters, so fielding would be difficult. First thing you notice is the Corfu batsmen's stance. To compensate for the extra length of the batting strip, they took guard like halfway down the pitch, a trick they must have learnt over the years, and quite rightly, didn't pass on to us. They could bat all right too, and when they connected they would always pick up runs because as the ball approached a fielder, it would invariably find a pot hole and bunny hop over one's shoulder. When they were in the field they adopted a goalkeeper style, another thing that never caught on with our lads. We've heard of the old après ski and the nineteenth hole, so whatever the cricket equivalent is, it was never more appreciated. Some of our lot resembled Partisans after a battle. The opposition looked like they could go again.

We thought revenge was on the cards for our second encounter in Corfu town. This time we were to take on the older generation, the men who taught Prince Phillip to play, when he was a boy. Don't let the age thing fool you, we did. They hammered us too. To rub salt into our sunburned wounds, after the game they announced that this was the first game the senior team had won against tourists in thirty years. How bad is that? So over the two matches, crap would be the first word that springs to mind when summing up our performance, but unlike a drizzly Sunday fixture down Boston Manor, with another defeat on the cards and the sun going down, we had the Corfu Town hostelries in which to drown our sorrows, and of course the sun is shining.

The sun and the drink had done for all the players and the spectators hadn't fared much better. Trying to drink Portobello style out here is madness, and by the end of the trip, as beautiful as it was there, most of the party were urgently in need of a rest. So on departure day we said our goodbyes, packed up our troubles in the Old Roughians kit bag, and headed for the airport. We must have had a late afternoon flight, because there was plenty of time for everyone to do a bit of duty free shopping, and too much time for others to get pissed. Just before boarding Bernie Walther and Gordon Geddes were completely off their heads, one or both had been spotted by the local officials crawling around the floor in the airport lounge. They refused to let them board the plane, and all attempts of diplomacy fell on deaf ears. The rest of us had by now had already taken our seats on the aircraft, apart, that is, from two of our party, trying one last time to get Bernie and Gordon onto the flight. They just weren't having it at all. One of our lot, Dick, tried to start up a solidarity movement. "Either they let them on, or we should all get off." This sort of rhetoric is first-class in the right circumstances, but it wasn't cutting much ice here. The touring party was definitely a divided entity for most of the stay here. There were those who did all the sensible things, sightseeing, trying out different foods and even took to the water on occasions. They'd had a good time, and were now looking forward to getting home to families and jobs. No votes for Dick from that quarter. Then there were the 'Dodgies' who did nothing all week but drink and play cards. Several of these had made the trip on a giro and were now skint. So Dick fell well short of the required number of votes. So we headed back to Blighty, with two of our number missing in action.

Bernie and Gordon were put on a plane the next day, and rolled into the pub that evening. They had to kip rough the night before, and hang around the airport for hours waiting for the flight, and all the time skint, not even enough for a drink. Thank Fuck.

29. The Panto

Evelyn Doggart was a regular in the Warwick. She was gorgeous, feisty and a good all round sport. She drank and played pool with the best the pub had to offer, and held her own. Her father Herbert had played cricket for England, which also added to her appeal, especially to the useless Herbert's of the Old Roughians C.C. She was also an actress. From what I can recall Evelyn and Dennis Smilley had knocked around the idea of staging a pantomime in the locale. Their working title was 'Drinkerella'. I don't know how far the project had progressed by the time Jock Scott had suggested to his girlfriend Anna Chancellor that she get involved, but by the time I was asked to join in Evie and Anna were in the driving seat.

Anna had some experience of putting on theatrical thingies. She'd staged Oscar Wildes 'Birthday of the Infanta' at the Tabernacle. This was memorable for many things. Key among them though was a sterling performance by Warwick sage and runaway winner of The Roughler Man of Year contest, John Gordon, and the shapes thrown by one Genevieve Monastesse, the Trapeze artist who kept many a males interest during the show, Especially Jock Scott and yours truly sitting underneath the swing in the front row.

Anna then set about staging a 'Nativity Play' at Caroline Younger's house in Notting Hill. Anna was in it, Laura De La Mare, Jock, Kevin Allen, and Henry Tennant. Kate Chancellor and Catherine Holy-Hasted were a double act, they were dressed in costume, but fuck knows what parts they were playing, many others were involved on and off stage, and all in all it was a success. But this was played to a select crowd of mainly friends. How would it present itself on a Friday night to a crowd of unquenchables from the Warwick and surrounding hostelries? We'll see.

By the time we'd found a rehearsal space at the British Oak boozer on Westbourne Park Rd, The title of the show had changed to a more traditional 'Cinderella', but that was about it. There was no script, so it was written as we went along. I'd got myself the plum role as Buttons so I knocked out a few sentences which I thought were apt, so that was my part taken care of. Anna, Evelyn and Kevin Allen, who'd been talked into joining the cast, took on the rest. Eddie Cain from the fruit and veg stall metamorphisised into Baron Hangover, Andrea Oliver would be the Fairy Godmother, road sweeper and former Class War candidate John Duignan teamed up with Dennis Smilley as the Ugly sisters. Katherine Donaldson, who I didn't know then, was roped in to play the Baroness. So there you have it, the first knockings of the Portobello Pantomime, which is still going on today.

I suppose the obvious place to stage this production would have been the Tabernacle, but for some reason the venue would be The Cobden Club on Kensal Rd. This was before the Cobden was taken over by the 'money' and was still very much a working class establishment. So although the locals were a bit bewildered by the comings and goings of the cast and helpers, they couldn't have been more helpful as we decamped there for rehearsals and start setting up the show.

As well as playing Prince Charming, Anna was now the director, if she wanted this gig or not, I didn't know, but someone had to be in charge. Rosie Johnson was on the firm as assistant. Then we had a cross section of backstage help, from toff costumiers to bricklayers and plasterers from the pub, building and painting the set, and as Showtime approached I was amazed at how much talent could be assembled on such short notice for no money.

There were probably rows and fallouts during the set up and rehearsals, as there always will be, but on the 16th of September 1992 the Portobello Piss Artists production of Cinderella hit the stage. It's mostly a blur now, but I did alright, I was remembering my words, and I nailed my song 'Shall we dance?' then I had to deliver a line to Cinders, "lets run away from all this, I've saved up a bit of money….." as I hit the word money, someone in the audience (Pete Hamilton I'd guess) shouted out "Well where's that twenty quid you owe me then?" I knew plenty of people in the audience that night, most of whom knew what my financial structure consisted of, so it brought the house down. It didn't faze me though. In fact I realised right then how many mates I had in the area.

The show was a roaring success, everyone was brilliant, and if anyone in the audience had any qualms about the performance I'd say the sight of violinist Sara Sarhandis' legs were worth the entrance fee alone. In the bar later the compliments were flying, one ex of mine was trying to organise a threesome with me, her and another ex of mine. That never came off, but it's the thought that counts. The North Kensington Women's aid project were stoked about the money we'd raised for them, the Cobden were happy about the bar sales. What more can you ask for?

The next year saw a promotion for me. I'd been raised from the ranks, and was given the role of Prince Charming in "Sleeping Beauty". Don't know if I had more lines to learn, but hey, I'm an actor. I didn't really matter if the likes of me forgot words anyway, the audience loved to see vulnerability, especially when it came from guzzlers they'd seen in the pub. I got two songs this time. One of which was 'Dream a little dream of me'. Sleeping Beauty was Lucy Fawcett, who I fancied like mad. She was also the choreographer, which only added to her appeal in my book. Bit like fancying the teacher. She was lovely, but truth be told I don't think I had any hope there. Even when I had to deliver the magic kiss I didn't think her heart was in it. But I did awaken Beauty. I never saw her arise from her slumber though. I was engaged in one of those brilliant 'behind you' moments with the audience at the time. Ben Young and Billy Mac made their debuts in this show. I had to sing and dance with them. No big deal you'd think, but you try keeping a straight face singing to a pantomime horse, for that was the part they had, Ben the head and Billy bringing up the rear. You had to start at the bottom of the bill, as loads of people were trying to get into it show now.

What I noticed about this production was the scale of the project. There seemed to be bodies all over the gaff. Painters, scene builders, stage managers the works. And of course there were the bleeding kids. Most of who were bored shitless most of the time, and up to no good. And of course with the new 'theatrical' regime, these urchins had to be constantly fed. Don't ask me why. They wanted to be in it, or their parents wanted them to be in it, so why couldn't they wait until they got home? I started getting a bit irritated about the outgoings and I'm sure some people were getting paid too. So I think there was a divided camp. One side talking about unprofessionalism, (no more drinking at rehearsal) the other claiming that the 'peoples' panto was being taken over by luvvies and toffs who many thought were using this as an opportunity to up their profiles, and use it to showcase their 'talents'. The 'you never know who might be out there' credo was never truer than at the Panto. I still believe that certain members of the cast thought they might possibly nick a job on the back of their performance, and consequently weren't that keen to be seen on stage with, let's say, the less professional in our ranks. These were the seeds that grew into what came to be known as the 'Panto Wars' around at the Warwick.

But through all the cobblers, the shows that week were a smash. Packed every night, with compliments flying round like coke in the Groucho Club, it was a hoot. Kevin had dug out his address book and called on some of his celeb mates to come and do a turn too. I remember Stephen Fry being on stage. Rick or Ade, or the both of them. Martin Clunes and Neil Morrissey, and in the audience the great and the good of Ladbroke Grove, names too numerous to list here.

Everyone must have felt like a star on the final night. And why not? They had all worked hard, and the punters went home happy. But what happened next done my brain in. The producer (yes there was one of them too) had decided to present all the girl members of the cast with huge bouquets of flowers, and not the type you get at the 'Flowered Corner' shop either, and all the boys with massive bottles of Champagne. If this wasn't bad enough when I went to get my slurp the thirsties had beaten me to it. There was not but a thimbleful left. Worse was to come though...

The Powys Square/ Colville area of W11 is not without its opportunist criminal element, and on this night some of them were active. Now without pointing any fingers here, someone who shall remain nameless had naively left the takings for the show hanging about unguarded somewhere in the Tab. You guessed it, the lot was nicked. I don't know how much went missing, but the place was packed to the rafters that night so I'd say a pretty penny. Too many chiefs for my liking.

Peter Pan was next on the agenda, with Kevin as Captain Hook and our old mate Cheyne Pride, the American country and western singer, playing Tinkerbelle. I'd lost my way dramatically speaking by now. I'd been cast as Schmee one of Hooks shipmates, a definite demotion, but at least I got to sing the great Nick Lowe song 'The Beast in me' which remains one of my all time favs. Backstage this time looked like a Wimpy building site. They even had a contraption there that made people fly. I wasn't one of them, thank fuck. There were problems with this piece of equipment though, and after all expense and manpower I'm not sure if any one flew at all.

Throughout all this Anna, Kevin, Evie, Eddie Cain, Ben Young and Andrea Oliver shone. We all had our ups and downs, but if it had been left to the complainers (like me) fuck all would have been done probably. The people who I've failed to mention know who they are, but special mention to Roadent aka Stephen Connolly WHUFC, MCC and bar. Every year he turns up with the PA, Lighting etc, blagged from his days in the show business, works the mixing desk and adds all round support, and all he gets is a bottle of Gin.

Peter Pan was my last panto of note for a while. In fact there was a total regime change. Peter Hamilton, in my mind, the funniest geezer you'd hope to meet in the Warwick, and Chick McLaughlin had taken over the writing mantle, and our old mate Dodge Pomphrey was now the director. Peter has this great knack of making comparisons between Portobello locals and some of the less salubrious characters from Victorian novels. So with Chick, another who could spot the oddities in his surrounds, to help with local colour and 'what was happening' around the area, you couldn't see how they could fail. And by all accounts they didn't.

Panto is still ongoing. I've been called up of late to add my undoubted talent to the proceedings. As ever I'm useless at rehearsals, can't remember my lines, then I turn up on the night, and hope for the best. I can still hold a song though, so I have no worries there. I finish my performance, and bring the house down. Some of my fellows seem bemused by my ovation. What they don't realise is, these people have seen me poncing around the Portobello for nigh on thirty years. They're just applauding my staying power, not my talent. People like to see familiar faces in Panto, they like people forgetting their lines. It's part of it. There's talk of it becoming 'more professional' Bollocks to that. ALL THOSE IN FAVOUR SAY AYE. Saying that though, they've done well with the old 'celeb' cameos of late; I've seen Ray Winstone, Danny Dyer, James Corden, Lily Allen, Aneka Rice, Dominic West, Noel Clarke, a few others that even panto historian Piers Thompson can't recall, and of course David Guest, who was the best of the lot. You'd think he would be a first class twat wouldn't you? Not a bit of it, he was as good as gold, cracking gags, sharing gossip, giving encouragement, posing for photos with anyone who asked and signing autographs. His companion at one of the shows was none other than Petula Clark, now there's a legend. I didn't get the chance to chat to her though. Gary Dempsey told me a story he'd heard about Sean Connery and Petula Clark. Ask him nicely, he might tell you too.

Underwater poet and Roughler Gallery partner
Lord Patrick Conyngham

Mushy Peas was never the same after the sheriff
took his guns away

Alfie Allen transfixed by the author's performance in Sleeping Beauty

Two of my all-time favourites. Catherine H.H (left) and Kate Chancellor in the original panto at Caroline Younger's house

Evie, who started the Notting Hill Panto
takes the breeze with our old mate Jo

Jock Scott, Pete Mullins, Bernie Walther,
Gary Dempsey and Stitcher in the Cornwall

Gary Dempsey and Gordon Geddes feel the effects of the first day of all-day drinking in the Warwick.

"Get the beers in, Joe"
Ray Roughler-Jones and Joe Strummer.

Strummer sings 'Junco Partner' in front of the
'Old Roughian' notice board in the Warwick

The beautiful Neneh Cherry plays music for our pleasure

Panto regular and Powys Terrace diva Andrea Oliver

Gareth Sager and Jock Scott

My fabulous girlfriend Kirsty
taking tea at the Ritz on her birthday

30. End of an Era

Be honest, we had a good run in The Warwick. But alas, all good things...When the pub was buzzing I remember standing outside one sunny day when three roughnecks, who I knew, stopped for a chat. "Why do you use this place Ray, it's full of old men?" And that was the attitude of most folk who never drank in there. And I remember thinking "Yeah, full of old men" as 'The Green fields of France', 'Fields of Athenry' or some other paddy anthem drifted out through the door. Someone must have got the message though, for all of a sudden it's Dodge City in there. So the quest for another local would be on quite soon. I had a bit of unfinished business to attend to before the mass exodus. Lofty O'Reilly phoned me to say he was coming to the Warwick this very night with John Lydon. It was Roughler publication time very soon, and what could be better than an interview with the Pistol's frontman accompanied by a photo of him drinking in our pub.

O'Reilly told me he'd squared it with John, so when they arrived and with Lofty away at the bar, I approached Lydon "All right John, is it OK to have a few words?" Vague, yes, but if Lofty had already sorted it out, Lydon would have known what I was on about. He turned around and said to me: " Fuck off you cunt, who the fuck are you?" and the rest. I mentioned Lofty and the OK he'd given me, but he still wasn't having it. "Fuck, cunt, bollocks!" He left me in no doubt that wherever I was coming from, I had no chance. I'm no fighter, but as a rule I wouldn't take this abuse from someone, especially in my local boozer, I would have at least given a bit of verbal back as retaliation, but this is Rotten so I wasn't completely surprised. In fact, if he was ripping into someone else in there I'd have been laughing my cods off. So I turned on O'Reilly instead. He just gave me a shrug of the shoulders, which I read as 'you know what he's like'.

Although my journalistic approaches had been greeted with derision, I was still welcome at their table. John was all right to me then, he said: "Fuck all this interview bollocks, let's have a drink." During the course of this session, a call comes from behind the bar. "Is there a John Lydon in the bar?" Now I know bar staff and regulars in there didn't bat an eyelid when famous faces wandered through the door, and in many cases, didn't even recognise them, but Rotten, come on. He was easily on a par with Shane McGowan when it came to being recognised; especially with his orange hair and Rupert Bear suit, anyway he was wanted on the phone. Glancing in his direction as he was taking this call, he had that look on his face that says 'grief from 'er indoors', well that's his business. He came back to the table, but in his absence the geographic had changed, in fact someone had nicked his chair. "Oi you cunt!" he started "That's my seat, fuck off out of it!" The bloke sitting in said chair, far from being disconcerted just glanced up and said: "The last time I saw you I had to give up my fuckin bed for you." Lydon was taken aback by this, the grimace on his face slowly, but definitely turned into a smile. These two then started bear hugging, Oi Oiying, and giving it the big up, turns out that this fellow was John's first cousin. So in less than an hour I'd witnessed the terrifying Godfather of Punk, go from the scourge of all journalists, the bloke to hide your children from, to an ordinary geezer down the pub.

Couple of days later I'm at Heavenly Management, Keith asked me to go in the cab with Lydon and this other mush to show them the way to the pub. I thought I'd get another chance of a story, but when we got to the pub it soon became apparent that the other geezer was there to do exactly that. Turns out he was called John Savage, and he was working on the book 'England's Dreaming' which is all about the Punk days. Well he'd be fucked without an interview with 'Johnny Rotten' then, wouldn't he? So I let him get on with it.

Just before the end we did have one cause for celebration. In that month's Roughler I described it as 'the greatest day in the history of the world'; it was the first day of all-day pub opening in England. Much more reason to celebrate this than say, St. David's or St. Paddy's, they come every year. This thing was quite new to every drinker in the land, unless of course they were born before the First World War. This was how it was reported at the time:

Anarchy in the Warwick

'Whilst you were away one of the greatest events in the history of the world took place, all day opening of the pubs in England and Wales. To celebrate this monumental moment in guzzling history, Warwick regulars had turned up by the score to celebrate and get steamed up in their and everybody else's favourite supping spot. It was a jolly atmosphere, with bollocks and banter flying around like twenty pound notes in a coke dealers front room. Then at about 4:15 pm like some recurring nightmare a voice above the pub noise shouted "Time gentlemen please". This cannot be true. "Bollocks" was the response that went up from the unquenchables. "Come on lads, let's have those glasses," says Seamus. So it's not a wind-up. "We shall not, we shall not be moved!" was the cry that answered him from our section in the corner, which by the way consisted of legendary swallowers Peter Hamilton, Gary Dempsey and Gordon Geddes, The Roughler's number one contributor Steve Underground, Old Roughian cricket secretary Terry Rogers, yours truly and W11's finest Joe Strummer. Joe had a couple of mates with him, an American called Josh and Dan Donovan out of B.A.D. I don't think the last two mentioned knew what was going on, but when the cry went up, they were as vociferous as the rest.

Seamus soon gauged the seriousness of the situation. " Well," he said," I don't know who's going to serve you," to which two of our number said "We'll do it" and promptly vaulted the bar and started pulling pints for all and sundry. Seamus, back onside by this time, and never one to spoil a party said "I'll get these lads" which was answered by a mighty cheer. There was singing after that, with Terry kicking things off with 'The Old Alarm Clock', Peter followed that with ' Dancing on the Kyle', then the Taff slaughtered 'Delilah' and the Page Three classic ' John Bindon,' many other long-forgotten songs were ruined, and just as the singing was about to abate, who should walk through the door, none other than Mole, one time bass guitarist with the mighty 101ers. He was met by the Scottish contingent breaking into 'Stay Free' and 'The Keys to Your Heart', which was a big song for the 101ers way back when, and on this afternoon, featuring Joe Strummer on backing vocals. Not a day for the fainthearted, but a day to remember.'

Moving on from the Warwick would be a bummer. Where else

will you see drunken people crashing to the floor after tumbling over Dog Woman's pets, or Pete the Murderer, on being asked to leave yet again, punching a hole through the partitioned wall that held the dart board, and where are you ever going to see the like of Mushy Peas again? I asked him how he came by his unusual name. "They call me Mushy Peas cos I fooking luv 'em" he replied in his Lancashire accent. I believe he was on the dust, a road sweeper, but got fired for parking up his barrow, and going into the pub once too often. So now he was a man of leisure, living out his life as a six gun toting cowpoke. Dressed in shiny shirt with not one but two of those metal/boot string ties, hat covered in badges, drainpipe trousers and cowboy boots, he certainly didn't go unnoticed. He was also packing steel, he had two gun belts complete with bullets and housed in the holsters, two shiny pistols. Mushy would clank his way into the bar, order up a Guinness, then head for the pool table "Is anyone using this table" he'd enquire. He'd then spend the day shooting pool and getting pissed. He didn't go for the usual trail hand talk, he was too modern for that, instead he'd try and show his prowess at macho pub activity, with dart and coin tricks, at which he was useless, and as the drink took effect he insisted on displaying his talent for fast pint drinking. I know how this one goes, my next door neighbour in Colbourne Terrace was a bloke called Les Sargeant, now he *could* neck a pint. Les would tell you to put a matchbox and an unused match side by side on the bar, the bet was that he could finish a full pint before you could strike the match. It was one way traffic, by the time you got the match in your fingers; he'd be replacing his empty glass back on the bar.

Mushy couldn't hold a branding iron to Les Sargeant, in fact I'd take him on at it, he was hopeless. But of course he wouldn't give up on it, which led to much coughing and spluttering and would usually end up with him puking or on more than one occasion, shitting his pants. I've rarely seen a person descend from perky wrangler to town drunk quicker than Mushy. Then he'd become a nuisance to all and sundry, this included the bar staff. He manufactured a grievance with Dennis the barman one evening, and as with the pint drinking, he wouldn't let it go. "Outside you coont" he yelled at Dennis, this went on and on. In the end Dennis left his post behind the pumps.

This wasn't to have a fight; it was to throw the pea eater out. Mushy read it differently and proceeded to strip down for action. He took of his hat, belt and guns then his shirt and vest, interestingly underneath his vest he had a chain held together with a padlock. He couldn't find the key, so, much time was spent looking for this, all the time Dennis is standing in the doorway, holding it open. With Mushy now stripped to the waste, he was ready to fight; he walked past Dennis, and out into the street. Dennis was just about to close the door behind him, when Mushy made a grab for him, Dennis shrugged him off and threw a fresh air punch in Mushy's direction which missed his chin by at least six inches, Mushy went down as if he'd caught a bullet from the gun of Jesse James. He was on the floor for many minutes, crying for his Maw, and asking to be buried in Boot Hill, someone flung some water over him, then he got up. Dennis said "Now pick up your stuff, and fuck off out of it" Mushy, beaten by now, re entered the pub to retrieve his rig. All the stuff had been piled high on the pool table, and as Mushy started getting dressed, it soon became clear that someone had made off with both his gun belts and guns. Despite his protestations, he still had to leave, especially now that Seamus had surfaced. So Mushy was sent out to roam the mean streets of Portobello, in the cold, and without a firearm to protect himself.

Mushy was not seen around the homestead after this incident, one of his catchphrases was "Cancer, I'm fooking riddled with it" so many thought he might have died, or was at least in hospital. One night I was watching the telly, they were showing a programme about drunkenness on our city streets. The cops arrive at a scene, much noise and scuffling, and then a person is apprehended and escorted to the van, and in the process, heading straight into shot of the camera which had been following the action. A bloke draped in what can only be described as a Poncho raises his head, sees the camera, smiles and says "They must be going for the Fooking world record these coonts, this the ninetieth time I've been nicked for drunk and disorderedly" It was Mushy, he'd managed to get this statement out before the old bill flung him into the van.

With the Warwick becoming less than fun, it was time to move

Roughler, Roughian and all other operations to the Portobello Star. This is a tiny pub on Portobello, with no nooks and crannies, so shenanigans were rendered obsolete, Ray Lisi, the landlord wouldn't put up with it anyway. It was to be our base until Bernie took over at the Cornwall pub, where normal service was resumed, in spades.

31. Bores, Barbours and Brilliance

Good old Kevin Allen. He's come up trumps again. He'd done a couple of documentaries of a sporting nature, most notably the one about the 1990 World Cup in Italy. He did it on a shoestring and had to stay in a tent in the same field as many of England's finest football firms. His nightly reports under cover of darkness from his tent were hilarious, but must have been a bottle job for him 'cos these lads weren't all that keen on being filmed and of course they were mostly fired up on whatever the Italian is for Lager.

He got through that O.K. now he'd been asked to try his hand to the 1991 Rugby World Cup, which were being held around the British Isles and France. For some reason he asked me to accompany him, as, I suppose, the token spectator. I was made up. My first love was football, at which I was shite, so I'd never make the team playing that. So when I got the chance I took up Rugby. I made the team at that, but I wouldn't describe myself as exactly brave when it came down to the 'getting stuck in' side of it. We had a bloke in our team called Mike Gange, He's 6' 2" at least, and the fastest runner in the fucking school. He was so good at about twelve or thirteen that he sometimes played for the under 16 side. They were not good days for me, because playing in the same side as him was just a dangerous as playing against him. He'd be everywhere, ruck, maul, scrum on the wing in midfield, he was amazing, and God help any poor 2nd former (like me) that got in his way.

I believe Mike Gange went on to play for the All Whites (Swansea R.F.C.) and I used to attend matches at St.Helens quite regularly. The Swans were always hovering around div 2 or div 3 at that time, so you wouldn't get the same calibre of footballer visiting the Vetch that you'd get at the rugby. All the touring sides went through there. All Blacks, Springbuck, Aussie were all given a good game by the All Whites. And of course a lot of the local teams boasted players who would become household names. It cost next too sod all to get to watch the rugby, and all people involved seemed friendly enough, even the players were approachable back then. I'm not all that keen on them now though.

Kevin had got hold of a camper van and Graham the cameraman, and we were off. Things didn't start out that clever. The first game of significance, for Kev and me anyway, was the Oct 6th clash between Wales and Western Samoa. Like everyone else we thought Wales were a shoo-in against one of the 'minnows' WRONG. Tough bastards these Samoans, and through their sheer will to win, they upset the odds and broke 50,000 hearts in the process. Sections of the crowd were shouting "How can they beat us at rugby, they haven't learnt how to dress yet even" Which was a reference to their colourful supporters who were in National costume I suppose you'd call it, complete with spears. It was the first big scalp for the Samoans, and you could tell they were made up. When we bumped into them after the crowds had gone off to drown their sorrows, they were doing this clicky finger little dance of theirs, and were truly over the moon Harry.

So, a bad start for the taffs, dark days indeed. All we could hope for now was a disastrous run from the English team. And with the likes of the All Blacks, Springboks and Aussies around the gaff, it was thought only a matter of time before they got theirs. WRONG. They were destined to go all the way as we'll find out later.

Can't remember too much of the pool games. A bit like watching the early rounds at Wimbledon I guess, although I remember a magical trip to Grenoble, to watch France hammer Fiji. What a fucking setting for a stadium, slap bang at the foot of the Alps. During that game Kevin sent me off with the smaller camera, to see what footage I could get. It wasn't as bad as all that, but of course when the film was finally cut and everything, it had been edited to make me look absolutely useless as a lensman. I've got no career ambitions in that direction, so didn't give a toss, and it turned out to be funny. We must have taken in some other matches, but if anything monumental happened at any of them I've forgotten. Research? Whatever. I do remember going to visit Robbie Coltrane in Scotland. Kevin and Robbie go back a bit so Robbie showed us hospitality; he also showed us his ever-growing collection of vintage cars. I know bugger all about cars, but even I was impressed. Car mad is Robbie; I remember Pete Hamilton and me bumping into him one afternoon in Dean St, he took us to the Colony Rooms. Peter's a top end motor mechanic, so I just sat there guzzling lager while they spent hours talking cars.

I'd told Kevin I wouldn't have a drink on the tour until we got to Ireland. No disrespect to the blarney stone or all the other places of beauty which are in abundance over there, but whenever I'd thought about being in Ireland, drink had been the main priority. Call it clichéd, call it what you fucking like, there was no way I was going to stay sober in Ireland. When we arrived in Dublin we headed for the Shelbourne hotel where the Aussies were staying. You couldn't have failed to be impressed by the Aussies by now. They'd assembled a good pack, and the backs, Nick Farr – Jones, Lynagh, Horan and especially match winning winger David Campese, were all top drawer.

Couldn't get to talk to any of the combatants before they left the hotel, but watching them board the bus you were left in no doubt they were well up for this semi final against the mighty All Blacks.

Lansdowne Rd was electric that day. That's even taking into account the presence of the All Black supporters, who, on the whole, resembled a group at a Billy Graham gig. All dressed alike and not adding too much to the party.

We got great seats at the game. Then this Aussie mush comes to sit next to us. Noisy bastard, calling the N.Z. team 'black bastards' and the like, it couldn't have been racist, the N.Z. team were mainly white, bit like us calling Cardiff fans 'scum' I guess. Anyway this noisy fuck wouldn't ease up, and when Tim Horan was floored early on he went ballistic. "Ease up" or words to that effect were uttered in his direction. He didn't "Fuck off" he said "that's my brother" Well in that second everything altered for me. Can you imagine watching a sibling playing for his country, against the biggest side in the world in the semi-final for the biggest prize of all? I was with him all the way after that. Horan actually scored a try, along with the unbelievable David Campese, and Australia were in the final after this 16–6 victory, where their opponents would be England.

Kevin's sister–in–law Alison had arranged for us to stop off at Marina Guinness's house so that we could top up the water supply and recharge something or other on the mobile home. She lived in a cracking house called 'Pickering' in county Kildare. When we arrived she Okayed our requests and invited us in for a cuppa. Glancing around the kitchen I noticed a photo on the mantel piece of our old mate Simon Miller – Mundy. When Marina realised we knew Simon and other mutual acquaintances from Ladbroke Grove we were like mates. Before you can say, "if you're Irish, come into the parlour" we were told we could stay in this fab pad. We even had our own rooms.

We had a few days to kill before the final, so we decided to take in a bit of Irish scenery. I guess Kev might have been wanting some exterior shots for the film. Marina lent us a car; which might have been a Citroen DS. Now Gaz Mayall had used this car to tour round the whole of the Emerald Isle some time previous. We managed the trip from Marinas to the Wicklow hills when the fucking thing blew up and caught fire. Firemen Kev and Graham started trying to deal with it; I kept my distance, and took in the surrounding scenario. All the talk of Leprechauns and Fairies came to mind, this is a scary location, wouldn't want to be stuck up here on my own, for sure, for sure.

Don't ask me how, but Red Adair Allen and his sidekick The Salamander Kid had quelled the flames, but I don't know how we got back to base. Were we towed? Did we free wheel? Gawd only knows. But we made it back to Marinas. She might have been mad, but didn't show it. In fact she'd organised a night out for us. Julian Lloyd had told anyone who was listening about this drag act called Miss Pussy who was playing this very night hereabouts. With my limited knowledge of what's what on the Irish entertainment circuit, I wouldn't have thought there would be much call for a drag act in rural Ireland but you never know.

So off we set. Marina said "We must pick up Marianne on the way" That's cool, the more the merrier. So we arrived at what I know now to be The Shell Cottage. When we got inside it soon became clear that this Marianne was in fact Marianne Faithful. If you don't know who she is, gawd help you. She's the thing of adolescent fantasies, the virgin with the voice and Mick Jagger's ex bird. We were invited inside.

We all sat around a table, Marina struck up a conversation with Marianne "Van knew you were in when he called the other day", Marianne theatrically replied "I just couldn't face Van right then" or words to that effect. It didn't take a genius to realise they were talking about Van Morrison. So it's not just the likes of me that get the "Bums rush' It also happens to people with amazing song writing talents, great voices, and I guess, a few bob in the bank. Van Morrison used to live up Notting Hill, and I used to see him breakfasting regularly in the Galleon café of a morning. He didn't seem to be the type of bloke you could go on to though, in fact he seemed a right miserable sod. But oh, oh, oh, listen to the music.

We got to the venue eventually. I don't remember much of the Puss's act apart from a few gags about hookers. This was a reference to rugby hookers by the way, and was for our benefit. There was an open mike vibe going on in there too. I gave a song. After I'd ruined another one of the classics I returned to the table whereupon Marianne said to me in that sexy, twenty embassy voice "That was brave of you" I said "aren't you having a go?" she declined. Marianne Faithful was not the young, virginal, sexy chick of her youth, but there was plenty left to admire, and with her history, the mystery aspect came into play. I was sat next to this iconic woman, I was merrily pissed and I thought 'Tonight Ray you're going to try it on with Marianne Faithful.

For the return journey, I'd manoeuvred my way into the same car as her, on the way to the car park I'm trying to be witty and charming, and then the sky fell in. Some thieving Irish toe rags have smashed their way into the car and stolen whatever. Talk about throwing a bucket of water over a randy dog, any thoughts of 'amore' were scuppered in that instant. The journey back was uncomfortable to say the least. So I'll never know which way it would have gone. Don't forget even a knock back from her would have made a good yarn. So in the car I sat and watched as tears rolled by.

The Irish leg of the journey ended on a bum note though. We were off to this nightclub in Dublin. Someone said it was owned by Bono. Didn't see him there, and they weren't playing his records either, thank fuck. There were a few familiar faces around the place, some young girls who knew me, and thought of me like they would a distant uncle. I'd met them on their visits to Lad Grove etc. I was having a right old chuckle, bevvying and dancing with these bright young things when Kev came over and joined in. All of a sudden one of the girls empties a pint over Kevs head. Instead of him taking her to task, he rails on me. Yeah, I was laughing. Well it was hilarious for anyone who wasn't the victim. He said "Do you think that's funny?" and proceeds to sling a slap at my head. I retaliated, and before you know it we were 'kicking and a gouging in the mud and the blood and the beer' well not really. The bouncers came over and stood they're laughing at what was probably the most useless fight they'd ever seen. I don't think we were even kicked out. But Kev was furious. I was out of the van, out of the team and on my own as far as he was concerned. I stayed that night with the Lloyds in Leixlip, thinking that by morn everything would be ok, but he wasn't having it, and I could find my own way back to London. I didn't have a shilling so I thought I was fucked. With much negotiation he eventually relented, but the journey back to England was not a pleasant one. We got there though. The only thing left now was the big final, England v Australia at Twickenham.

You might have thought that I hadn't been paying much attention to the goings on with the rugby, but I'd quietly been monitoring England's progress to the final. The Aussies had a monumental struggle against NZ, couple this with the idea that they probably thought they'd already won the cup, got me to thinking that England had a chance of the upset. In fact I put my money where my mouth was. I bet Alan off the fruit and veg stall in Portobello £50, that England would nick it with a six point start.

Final day arrives, and we've got these corporate tickets, meal, drink, good seats, the works. I'd heard I could have got £500 for mine. For some reason I didn't flog it. I didn't need to go inside the Stadium as Kev only needed to film me arriving at the game and walking around the place. But still I didn't sell it. To make matters worse Australia held a 12 – 6 lead deep into the second half. Very late on England were awarded a penalty kick that Long John Silver would have popped over, but England had to run the ball, they had to go for the try, this was the WORLD CUP FINAL. The Aussies held out and I lost my £50 to 'orrible Allen Williams. It was a good jaunt though, I watched the documentary in the Portobello Star with the lads, and everyone thought Kev had done a good job. So did I.

I'd been seeing a girl of late, so I had someone to bore with my tales from the road. She was an agony aunt. How good at that caper can she be if she's hanging about with me? It was Charlotte, who quickly became known as 'git face' by me anyway. She took this new name in her stride, which makes me think she's probably been called a lot worse. I was drinking like a lunatic by now, and like all my other partners, this one had a lot to put up with. She had her own problems right then, and I became yet another. I felt pretty friendless at that time, and when she gave me my cards, I didn't take it on the chin. In fact for a couple of weeks I drove her mad. As with just about all my relationships I'm still big mates with her. Here's another trick for all you girls out there, courtesy of 'git face', keep your geezer laughing. Charlotte was the funniest chick I ever had a grapple with, in or out of the kip. She's married with kids now.

32. Stocks

The Old Roughians Cricket Club were nothing if they weren't social and self sufficient. If we needed to raise some money, it didn't turn out difficult. We'd put on gigs, sell raffle tickets, punt out 'spot the ball' tickets, have fund raising darts competitions, there were many avenues to follow to ensure the clubs finances were usually in a decent state. On the social side I'd like to think we created a hospital atmosphere down at Boston Manor, and were good fun opposition when we travelled. That said, I don't think we ever managed to achieve on the pitch what we did off it. Granted we did have a few players who knew what they were doing, but for the most part we were rubbish. As I wrote that last sentence, I had no qualms, most would agree with it. Those who wouldn't probably think they are among the 'few'. Yeah, sure. But getting back to the fund raising and being 'hail fellows well met' side of things, it was this that got us our most 'glamorous' fixture to date.

The Rainforest Cup offered us the opportunity to enter a competition where the first prize was a chance to play against a celebrity team at a place called Stocks. Stocks used to be the Playboy Mansion, England style. I didn't know much about it, but there was high excitement at the special meeting convened to talk over our strategy. The plans we were making weren't cricketing ones, these concerned how we would go about selling shed loads of tickets for this honourable cause. Not even the most optimistic among us could possibly have thought we'd win our way through to this match with bat and ball, as there some decent amateur teams entered up. So we decided on the ticket selling route, simply because the club selling the most would also be granted a game against the celebs. I don't know how far we got in the playing stakes, but we waltzed away with the other prize, so its game on.

I did my fair share of selling, and expected that to guarantee my presence on the day. My cricket life seemed to be over by this time, so I didn't expect to play, but as a founder member, and devoted servant to the club, I didn't want to miss out on this free drink, free grub beano at, by all accounts, a country house in a beautiful part of England. High excitement reigned on the day itself, I was full of the posh stuff, so I can't for instance, wax lyrical about the journey, but when we arrived there I got my second wind, and started to drink in the atmosphere, and drink. I found Pam Brogan our scorer so I could check out who the opposition had in their team. First name I noticed was Roy Virgin, ex opening batsman with Somerset C.C., I'd seen him play, he didn't quite make it to the top table international wise, but he'd been facing the new ball from the best England and the rest of the world had to offer for twenty years or more, most of those years he also passed the benchmark for a county batsman, and scored more than a thousand runs in a season, usually with ease.

At the bottom of the oppo's list two other names leapt out, Emburey and Edmonds, no chance of being ignored by the selectors here, in fact these two were the current England spin attack, it didn't come much better anywhere in the World. Well, I thought, it'll be something for our players to tell their grandkids, and perhaps these three hardened pros might go easy on our lads. Then I see another side of things, one of the organizers had popped into our dressing room, and subtly mentioned that Gary Lineker, the current England centre forward, who had given up his time for this event, and, I would have thought put plenty of bums on seats, would be batting at No.3 or 4, all this guy asked was that if Lineker skied one early on in his innings, could we not break our necks trying to catch it. I'd read about Lineker's prowess with the bat, I believe he'd scored a hundred for Leicester seconds, so I didn't think our attack would cause him the slightest problem anyway, and as for holding a catch, the guy should have said "try and catch him out", that would have ensured Linekers longevity at the crease. There were paying customers at this gig, and I thought it was spot on what this guy had said, after all no one had come to watch us, but what he said caused consternation among the Roughian ranks. Many were up in arms, there were mumblings about giving the other team an unfair advantage and talk about well if he hits it to me I'm going to catch it. Are these people mad? Yes is the answer to that. Their worst player was, I'll wager, far superior to our best. That was the end of me and the Old Roughians, instead of being grateful for this great day out, some, not all, of our boys were still under the illusion that they were good players. Don't they remember that we got here through being charitable, not by being any good at cricket?

This minor incident didn't spoil the day one bit. Pam took her place beside Bill Frindall at the scorers and commentary table, and we were off. I found myself sat beside David Essex of all people, poor bastard, he'd come to add his weight to the cause, and he got me reminiscing about great gigs I'd been to, he took it well, for a while anyway. As for the cricket, I didn't take much notice, I'd glance up from time to time, the Lineker thing didn't happen, and as far as I could see, the Celebs were scoring whenever they needed to, and would then retire to let someone else have a knock. Some among us must have taken a wicket or two, something they could talk about down the pub in years to come, but I don't remember any earth shattering analysis being talked about. When it was our turn to bat wickets were falling with the same regularity they would at Boston Manor or any other venue, I watched Kevin Evans batting, mainly because he was facing Phil Edmonds, Evans played what looked like a decent shot, and scored a couple of runs, next ball, without much effort Edmonds put a little something extra on it, and clean bowled him, middle stump. Needless to say we lost the match.

I was completely off my nut by the end of the game, but with the help of a female friend, I found myself in the Jacuzzi room. I seem to recall a snog with her, which might have become something more substantial if it hadn't been for the shock to the system caused by a body surfacing to my right, it was Nicholas Parsons, he was in there splashing about with a friend, this knocked me out of my stride, as drunk and stoned as I was, I couldn't imagine having a bunk up in the same bath as Nicholas Parsons. Could you? There was plenty of it going on though, over the following weeks, from what I can gather, I must have been one of the few who didn't get any.

33. The Long and the Short of it

Lofty O'Reilly was in a right state. He'd lost his job with Siouxie and the Banshees, he'd also lost his girlfriend by the looks of things, but the worst of it is he's fucked up on coke. I don't know the whys and whats regarding the Banshees gig, but he seemed to be cruising along nicely in his previous job at Heavenly Management. The main act on their books at the time was P.I.L. There was then a falling out of some description between John Lydon and Lofty's boss Keith, which culminated in the onetime Sex Pistols frontman taking his business elsewhere. Normally this might spell disaster for a small operator like I believed Heavenly to be, but as it turned out it freed up their time to concentrate on another act they had on their books. It was a case of "The fans are upset, Dean Windass has gone down injured, he can't carry on, he'll have to be replaced, and the sub is warming up. Let me see. What's his name? I've got it here somewhere, yes I think you pronounce it Lionel Messi" that's not as ridiculous as it sounds, because the next band on the rota at Heavenly were Soul II Soul. Not my cup of tea, and I'm sure they lost a lot of sleep over that, but as everyone knows, they went on to conquer the globe. I knew one of them from way back. Nelly Hooper used to get down the Warwick. He was a good Bristol lad, who back then was involved with the 'Wild Bunch' He was pally with all the Bristol kiddies who got in there, Gareth Sager and Sean Oliver from Rip Rig and Panic, Mark Stewart, Andy Viney, Simon Roberts and the like. He was a quiet enough guy, who had a knack with the music. Once the group took off, and Nelly was called in by all sorts to mix their records, he began to go clear. They tell me he was having a great time of it. It was all Gold Amex and Supermodels after that. Good luck to him. (All those in favour say Aye). So as you can imagine things appeared to be rosy at Heavenly, your guess is as good as mine as to why Lofty left. Perhaps he couldn't pass up the chance of being the manager of a name band in his own right.

He found himself a job in a managerial position at a Pizza outfit on Walm Lane. When he finishes his shift he borrows one of the firms' ridiculously undersized mopeds, and heads for the pub. He's six foot six if he's an inch, he looks stupid on this mode of transport, and he knows it. To many this was a vast improvement to his previous job. This was a driving job at the Grunwick plant. That job was nothing short of scab labour, so we're all glad that he didn't stay there long. 'But you have to earn a crust' he says. But Lofty had lost his twinkle; in fact if I wasn't so fucked up myself I might have noticed that his self worth was evaporating before our eyes. He's got a plan though. There is no way in the world that the Pizza job can sustain him and his habit, so he gets to plotting as to how to rob some money from this shop. The way he figures it is if money goes missing it would be a choice between the three shift managers as to which one of them has nicked it. Unluckily for him, he wasn't the first employee to think along these lines, and the bosses had something in place for this eventuality. So Lofty nicked the dough, and he's collared in next to no time. He's now got a date with beak, and he's totally fucked.

I've got my own problems right now. I'm drinking like a fish, and doing too much of the posh stuff myself. I'm finding it hard to keep up the arrears on the mortgage, and I've got the added pressure of trying to find the money for the dope that's gone missing. I call over to Bernie Walther and Pam's for a bit of peace and quiet. Unusual as a rule, but its midweek, everyone's knackered, so there wouldn't be any shenanigans going on there. Then the phone rings, Bernie answers, and I don't know why. I just knew it was bad news. When he sat back down, he was white. Then he tells us that Lofty is dead. If that's not bad enough he goes on to say that he's killed himself. Bollocks! We'd already finished all the drink that was available that night, and it was too late for the shops, but fuck did we need a drink right then. Bernie dug out some cooking sherry or the like, that'll do.

It turns out that Paul 'Lofty' O'Reilly had it all planned in advance. He'd built up a stash of prescription drugs, made his way to where the Cutty Sark is situated washed all the drugs down with various brands of alcohol, sat down, fell asleep and died. At the time he obviously thought his problems were insurmountable. If he'd opened up a bit he might have got help and beaten them, but he didn't think so., he'd just had enough. And that help would have been there if the number of people at his funeral was a yardstick, it was packed. John Lydon turned up. He told me that Lofty had often said to anyone who was listening, that if he hadn't made something of himself by a certain age, he would end it all. So it seems his mind was made up. Lofty was a good lad all right, great on the wind up, and the football arguing. He had his opinions on every conceivable subject, and was great company. Who knows what sends people over the edge? He's still missed today.

34. Mel, More Hell, Time to Sell

Jock Scott and I were in a very similar situation in the love, financial, career and never betting winners department. We'd have a good old moan about our lot. So the evening when we were sat at the bar in Ma's Café on the All Saints the conversation between us was more than likely, less than optimistic. A girl approached us; she must have overheard the doomy dialogue because she said to me "You could do anything you wanted". This girl was about twenty-five, blonde, very attractive and six feet tall, she reminded me of a Germanic Tri-athlete. I had spoken to her in passing before, she would get in the Warwick and the Portobello Star, but I wouldn't have dreamt of it being more than a friendly hello. She'd probably seen me talk to just about every customer in both boozers, and through that probably thought I was approachable, and more importantly, safe. Much as I admired her youth and athleticism I'd be a bigger Welsh twat than I already am, if I thought I'd make any inroads in the 'LOVE" department.

But I'd had a few pints this night so I said, "If that's the case, I want your telephone number". To my surprise, she gave it to me. Perhaps she was pissed; maybe she wanted me as a mate. Who knows? I kept her number, but I never got up the nerve to call her. On a sunny afternoon on Ladbroke Grove a vision approaches. It's her. She stops and says hello. "I've still got your number," I say." But you haven't rung me yet have you?" I was flummoxed, but managed "I will, I will" At that, she took off at a licking clip. Cor blimey!

Bernie Walther and I had been putting on a night of entertainment lately at Paradise, which is on Chamberlain Road. Bernie had come on the scene at the end of our time in the Warwick. He was a builder, and as lively a drinking partner as you could wish for. He was a plumber by trade, and when he had to do some work around at Joe's house on Lancaster Rd, he quickly became known as; yes you've guessed it, 'Strummers plumber'. We'd earn a few quid once a week putting on a show in the upstairs bar. This coming week I was actually going to play there myself with my occasional band, which featured my mate Latiffe Gardez and a couple of others. We'd been getting a decent crowd of late, so I figured that if this girl saw me as a promoter, and the singer with a decentish group, she might think there was more to me than just a bloke who props up bars in Portobello and surrounding areas. I invited her along.

The night went well. When it became obvious that I was with this girl, I got the usual "What the fuck is she doing with you?' queries. But I've had that with most of the girls I've been involved with, so I took no notice. After the show I walked her home. As we neared her place it soon became clear that she lived right opposite me on the Grove. (I later discovered that from my window I could see straight into her flat) She invited me in. Her name was Melanie, and she was a nurse. We started chatting about this and that, had a drink of something or other, then I started to die. I'm rarely ill, always been lucky on that front, now here I am on a first date, doubled up in pain, and throwing up like a student.

Mel just switched into work mode. She put me to bed, found some legal drugs, and then jumped in beside me to administer comfort. I was ill for four days. Mel went on with what she had to do, at the same time making sure that I had all my wants taken care of. What a champion.

I'd been missing from the pub for a lot more than twenty-four hours, so by this time, search parties were being arranged. When I eventually came around I contacted Bernie Walther who had news. An Australian bloke he'd met in the Star had asked him if he'd like to take over the Duke of Cornwall pub on Ledbury Road. He put it to me that, perhaps, he and I could run it. My first question to him was "How much is it gonna cost us?" He said "Nothing". Well what have we got to lose? The joint arrangement that was talked about soon went out the window as takeover day approached. Bernie was now to be the landlord, and I was to be head barman, whatever that means. But hey, this could be an adventure. We spent all our time in one pub or another anyway, this way we might earn a few quid as well.

The Cornwall had seen better days. But Bernie was insistent that money for renovation would be forthcoming, so for now we'd have to make the best we could of it. Carole Key and Dennis Smilley did what they could, on no budget, to make the place look a little bit easier on the eye, from the outside anyway. They painted murals on all the windows of the pub. This looked good. But the furniture and carpet were beyond help I'm afraid. There was an opening party, which was well attended by the right sort of people, which boded well, but after a few days it became clear, that our lunchtime trade would consist mainly of people who had been barred from every other boozer on the manor.

There were a couple of plus points. There was a stage in there, so instead of us having to take our night to Paradise, we could do it right here. We'd get acts on in there. Nothing fancy, but a change from the jukebox. Unbelievably, the Cornwall had a licence that allowed the place to be open after eleven, the time that most other pubs closed back then, so Bernie hit on a plan. He decided to charge anyone who arrived after that time. He got a couple of Hells Angel mates, Brian Downey and Tiffin, to hang around the front door in case of trouble. It was half a good idea. The crowds did materialise and the tills were singing. Just after midnight a posse of locals showed up. They were told to cough up, but they weren't having it. So they were told they couldn't come in. Five minutes later there was an almighty bang, and all the windows in the front of the pub were going through. There was glass flying everywhere, and people were diving for cover. This went on for what seemed like a long time. All of a sudden, a local, Paul the Painter, who had armed himself with a bottle and a chair leg shouted "Let me out" He then ran headlong into the attackers all the while howling what sounded like some Viking war chant. Seeing this maniac on the rampage put off the other lot, and they scarpered.

It was a long old night. I said to Bernie "I don't want to work the late shift anymore" He was in a right mood, and said "You can't pick and choose your shifts" so for the moment, I was out. He'd forgotten all about it a couple of days later, and let me work the afternoon shifts. He had this routine, he'd say "I'm off to the bank." Well he was. But how long does that take? What it meant was he was off to the

Star, to talk landlord bollocks with Ray Lisi, who was the governor down there. I didn't mind. I could cope. And I don't give a monkeys what anyone says; I was good behind the bar. But as always my luck never holds out for long. One afternoon about forty people pile in, they seemed to be of an Irish persuasion. It soon became clear that this was the pub landlord's worst nightmare, a gypsy funeral. These people had loads of money to spend. And it's as if it's a mortal sin too them if they don't get seriously pissed. I was out of my depth. During the course of this session fights would break out between fellows who five minutes before, and five minutes after, were the best of friends. On more than one occasion I was asked to soak a bar towel in cold water. This would then be administered to any person who appeared the worse for wear through the drink. Remarkably, it seemed to work, for a minute later the recipient would be back at the bar ordering more drink.

I must have had about three or four hours of this. I'd sent out many an SOS to Bernie, but I couldn't get him back. Then as they'd entered, the gypsy's left en masse. On cue, with the pub emptying, Bernie strolls in. He's half cut. Not a word of apology, not even a question about how the till got so full. He just looked around, saw the mess, and said to me: "Keep on top off those ashtrays." I hadn't had a chance to empty my bleeding bladder all afternoon, let alone clean the fucking ashtrays, so I went ape." Shove this place up your arse," I shouted, and off I went.

Mel and I were having a good time. The sex thing was a bit lopsided though, she could shag like a porn star, problem is, I couldn't, but I gave it my best shot. She got me to cut down on the drink. We went swimming, I started eating, I cleaned my flat, and I even turned my hand to a bit of cooking. I wasn't doing my bollocks in the bookies at this time either, so I had a few quid. I dusted down the Delia, worked out what I was going to make, dived up to Sainsbury's, bought the gear, then I'd cook up a supper for me and Mel, which we'd have of an evening in my place or hers. I'd never done this once in all the time I was with Kirsty. But she was a great cook, so it never came up. Mel was quite impressed with my culinary prowess, so much so, that she volunteered the pair of us to cook up the scran at her mothers' birthday party. I was off the drink completely then, and I needed to be. This had nothing to do with health issues, or guilt or blackmail; it was more a case of enjoying Mel's company. We had a good time together, and she'd all but convinced me that there was more to life than hanging around betting shops and boozers, Mel's mum lived in what's called a 'Gated Community" in Isleworth. Nice gaff. We used to spend quite a bit of time down there, away from the distractions of Portobello. But I needed a small earner, so I came up with a plan. Bernie and I were O.K. by now so I talked him into letting me do sandwiches in the pub. He said all right, so I'd go off to Sainsbury's in the morning, get all the 'doings' and knock out my doorstep sandwiches at lunchtime. This worked out fine. I always sold out, made my few quid, and because I'd told them I was 'on the dry', I could shoot off right after without having to spend my hard earned over the bar.

Bernie was always having trouble with what he affectionately described as his 'Farmers'. (Haemorrhoids)He would sometimes be too ill to do anything. At long last he decided to visit the doctor. I don't know if the Aussie had stumped up the money or what, but he was going to see a Harley Street doctor. He duly attended. When he got back he had all sorts of medication. For a few weeks he religiously took the doses prescribed, and, looked a lot better. The doctor had told him to quit the drink too. And fair play, he hadn't had a drop in this period. I went in there one day, and Bernie's having a slurp of something. "I thought you were off it" His reply was "I'm alright, as long as I keep off the Jack Daniels." Fuck sake. Yeah Bern. What a story that is. So he's back on it. At least he's had a rest.

I can't talk. I've had a good few weeks off it myself. I feel great, my flat is clean, I'm fittish. I can put on a full set of clean clothes at a moment's notice; I'm the governor, sure. I'll find out years later this is the most dangerous time for a drunk; it's called a pink cloud period, but now I'm going to act like I just came out of prison, go on a bender and fuck everything up, AGAIN. First piss-up, Harry from Swansea is meeting up with Clive Hadley, a Merthyr mate who lives in Paris. I can't miss that. I don't. Strike one. Theresa, a Swansea girl who was everything except a girlfriend of mine turns up in London.

I meet her, and get pissed. Strike Two. I'm back on it big time, I don't even remember the incursion now, but Melanie said to me: "If you go it's all over." I went. Strike three. Mel was as good as her word. She told me later that on that night she'd gone to Tesco's to get some bits and pieces, some geezer approached her. She was pissed off with me, so they swapped numbers. Next thing you know they're a couple. Turns out this bloke is a banker of some shape or size, and spends most of his life in Zurich. When I think about it Mel was probably the best girl I've known as a friend. She was gorgeous as well, but I didn't miss that side of it as much as I missed her friendship. Good luck to her, every time.

Mick Pallent was known to all and sundry as Mick the Busker back then, he had another act which he presented to the audience at Mr. Saucy's Blind Date, but for my money he was at his best singing Jam songs with his acoustic guitar. Now I know that Mick is always up for trying out something new, so I approached him with the idea of putting on a poetry night in W10/11, he was up for it, so we went off to find a venue. We find the ideal venue at Camelot Studios on Kensal Road. The guy up there was on our side, so we got a good deal on the room, and were soon to be up and running.

Poetry is a hard sell, irrespective of what the entertainment press might say. About every few months they come up with something that's going to become the new rock n roll, and poetry had been mentioned thus on more than occasion. This is cobblers of course, but nevertheless we attacked this new project with gusto. First of all we needed a catchy name for the night, after countless crap attempts at this Paul Stewart, Bristolian poet and Roughler stalwart, offered 'Pull My Daisy'. This sounded catchy enough, and gained legs when Paul went on to explain that 'Pull My Daisy' was a film written by Jack Kerouac and was directed by Robert Frank. This little known flick boasted performances by 'Beat' poets Allen Ginsberg, Gregory Corso and Orlovsky, and purports to tell the story of no less than 'Beat' icon Neal Cassidy and his wife Carolyn. So we've got a venue and a name, now we have to find some acts. Knowing next to nothing of the poetry scene Mick and I set about checking it out. Someone mentioned a night in Soho that would prove helpful.

The gig we chose to attend proved fortuitous, mainly because Carolyn Cassidy was performing there that very night. When she'd done her bit, Mick and I approached her and told her all about our night, you can imagine how disinterested she was in our pitch, after all, she must have been cornered by hundreds of people like us, trying to get an 'in' with 'Beat' Royalty. She could care less. Funnily enough though, her interest perked up a bit when we mentioned the name of the club. A smile came across her face, and she said "Pull My Daisy, I haven't heard that in years". So now we've got her attention, we thought a chat would follow. I didn't know where any conversation with her would lead, but here we are starting up a poetry night, and we have an opportunity to nail down our reputation by spending time with a leading figure from the top drawer of the American Beat movement. Not only that, but if you believe what you read about that time, this girl had not only been the wife of the hero of 'On The Road' but had had a fling with the writer of the story, and who knows, we might even get her to play at our gig.

The reason for her attendance at this gig was part of her doing the rounds promoting a new book, so she wouldn't be in London when we planned our opening, so that was a non starter, to make matters worse, just when we thought we had her in our company, some guy came over to the table and told her it was time to leave. She wished us good luck with the project, and off she went. Bumping into her definitely made me and Mick think we were on the right track anyway. It was like an omen.

Poetry is a hard sell, the main reason being the crowd. These are Cocaine days, and many of our audience were not averse to participating in this practice. When you're on that gear you think you know more than Stephen Fry, and of course you want to share this knowledge with anyone within earshot. These people have paid to come through the door so you can't outright tell them to shut up, and if you politely ask them to keep it down while the acts are on, you're wasting your time. We didn't have a bad line up at our shows, but the better poets, if there's such a thing, were used to better order than they were getting here, so they were pissed off. The more rumbustiuos acts were more acceptable, but was the quality there, I don't know. 'Pull my Daisy' was short lived for me, Mick and I had a small falling out over nothing, and I left. He kept it going afterwards. Poetry was not going to be the new Rock n' Roll, that's for sure, but on one of the nights I thought it might have a chance. Murray Lachlan Young was a poet creating a stir, Mick booked him to appear, and when he showed up he was accompanied by a dozen or so attractive women. He cut a Wildean dash, had some good verse and a great delivery. If anyone was going to make the grade at this game it was him, he went down a storm. The record companies must have been reading the same papers as us, and bought into the idea of poetry becoming massive, because one of them put pen to paper, and signed Murray to a massive (some say a £1,000,000) deal. Good luck to him.

Two mates from Swansea arrive. They've just got back from Amsterdam, and they've got a few kilos of hash. It wasn't their intention to sell it in London, but if I knew of anyone, it would save them of having to take a risk, however small, of taking it to Wales, where they are well known. I knew a few puff dealers around and about, so I made a few quick enquiries. These Scottish boys, who had been busy of late, found that they had money, but no dope to buy with it. Perfect. I was miles behind on the mortgage by this time. The dole might have been paying the interest, but my arrears were more than worrying. If I could sort this little transaction, I could at least buy a bit of time with the Bradford and Bingley. They left the dope with me. I did the business with the Jocks and handed over the cash for what they'd bought. That was the best ploy. This way I can get my money off the last transaction in a lump sum. I gave the remainder to this guy; he'll be back later on with the dough. You guessed it. He did a runner. Now I'm in trouble. The biggest problem I've got is that the Swansea boys, one of them anyway, thinks I've nicked it. So I have to try and locate this dirty bastard somehow.

I make a few enquiries. It turns out he lives up around Scrubs Lane. I don't want to walk back and forth up there all day, so I try to borrow a pushbike. Chick lends me his. I wasn't having great success on my quest, and then it gets even worse. I woke up one morning to find not only the bike missing, but also the fucking lamppost it was locked to. I'd had bikes nicked in the past, but this is unbelievable, the work involved in nicking this bike was formidable. How skint do you have to be? I'd lose a bike when I was in San Francisco. Well not quite. I left it really securely locked out side our apartment block. It was the weekend that I went up to L.A. When I got back, my first thought was that the bike had gone. On closer inspection it was still there, but, by now resembled the bones of a Kentucky fried chicken, which had been devoured by a Saturday night drunk in Skewen. Every nut bolt, gear, wheel, brake, wire, seat, handle bar, everything was gone bar the frame. It happens a lot around the Mission. Right now I propose that Ladbroke Grove be twinned with 24 Th and Mission streets

When your luck is this poxed, you tend to swear off anything with the slightest bit of chance involved. You probably shouldn't. Because how can your luck get any worse? I had to face Chick, and the Welsh fellas. I was hiding from creditors. Nothing big, but worrying, I'd had a guts full. I don't have any option as far as I'm concerned, there is going to be no miracle here. The only asset I have now is the roof over my head. I won't be able to put the mortgage people off much longer either, and the TV and newspapers were awash with stories of repossession. It was happening all over the country, and not just to chancers like me, straight goers were finding it tough, so I made the decision to sell up.

The common consensus is that "It's a bad time to sell", that's all well and good, but come on, I need to get out of this mess. If you're holding something stolen in a carrier bag for instance, and you know it's worth X amount, tight bollocks, who keeps on knocking down the price knows what it's worth, and you know you can get that price tomorrow, but you think of your Mother Hubbard and fridge crying out for company, you're gagging on a pint and a fag and your gas is about to run out. What do you do? Take what's on offer of course. There's a recession on. I need to get everyone off my back, so the flats going. I inform the estate agent to put it on the market.

The female agent was all doom and gloom. "We'll try our best, but you might have to come down in price" She suggested I make a few improvements e.g. a lick of paint, a good clean and a de-clutter. I did all this, but I still didn't seem to be getting that many people calling around to 'view'. Then one day she calls "I think I've got you a buyer" I think she knocked me down a few quid, but I said yes. I still wanted to sell.

When things weren't going as fast as I'd hoped I'd pop into the office for an update. During these visits I learned, by reading between the lines, that the guy who was buying it was not only an estate agent, but also a pal of the woman representing me. I pulled her about it. She assured me that the price was right. I wasn't pulling out now, so I went along with it, but I wonder. The deal went through, and I must say I was sad. If I could have kept the place going it would have made me look slightly more eligible I guess. Kirsty had made these beautiful curtains years before, they were made to fit the massive window on the stairs. I didn't want to leave them there, because I would have enjoyed the thought of the new incumbent buying everything new, but I left them anyway. On reflection I wish I had left a time bomb under the floorboards as well. I'll tell you now., I sold that flat at the worst second of the worst period to sell property, but what the hell, if I hadn't I might still be drinking, or dead.

It didn't take that long to get the money. I had somewhere to stay, so I wasn't paying Grove rental prices. I didn't go as mad as I thought either. Everyone was convinced I'd be skint in the blink of an eye, so I was a little careful. I'd have a few pints, and low and behold I didn't go nuts in the bookies. And of course what happens? I can't stop betting winners.

I didn't really have a plan, but it was great to be not under pressure. As I mentioned earlier, my panto parts had been getting smaller and smaller. Just because Peter Hamilton and Chick McLaughlin were my mates, it didn't cut any ice as regards my part in their debut panto "Robin Hood'. They had to find something for me, so I became the narrator, a job normally reserved for the Legendary Jock Scott. At the dress rehearsal I did my bit quite well, I thought anyway. Chick came over and said "Well done Ray, by the way I couldn't understand a word you were saying" Nothing new in that then.

The Panto was yet another smash hit. I didn't quite know what I was going to do for Christmas. Should I go to Wales or what? Simon Millar – Munday came on to me at Panto and asked if I'd like to go to Ireland for the holiday. Not Half! Simon had a new girlfriend. Her name was Belinda; she was a sculptor, but much more importantly a good sport. En route to Ireland, Belinda, who was doing the driving, wanted to stop off in Tenby. She used to holiday there as a child. We used to have the odd trip there back in the day too. I can't remember if they were school trips or trips arranged by the Royal and Ancient Order of Buffaloes, which my father and all my uncles were members of. As a kid Tenby didn't hold a candle to Barry Island or Porthcawl, because it didn't boast a funfair, and seemed a bit quiet to us kids. But now I realise how lovely it is. In fact I'll take this opportunity if I may, to sing the praises of all coastal resorts in South and West Wales. If ever you fancy a holiday in this country get down the Gower or over the Pembroke coast. Fabulous.

After many a stop, we arrived in Ireland. We were headed to Corries in County Carlow. This house used to be owned by Denny Cordell. Denny was a well-known figure in the music and horseracing world. I'd met him a few times around the place, but didn't know him well, which is a pity, because he'd obviously had a very interesting life, and it was hard to find anyone to say a bad word about him. Denny, sadly, died young. The house was now in the stewardship of his son Tarka. I'd met him a few times, he's not a mate but he made me feel like a long lost friend. He had a few guests around the place apart from us. This guy called Mim Scala was there, he was the writer of the 'Diary of a Teddy Boy' book about his life in Soho, and he knew everybody in the World. Starts out he's an ice cream man in the sixties. Then he's in every other fun thing imaginable. Gambling, music, and films you name it. He was a good boy. John Hurt was there too. Everybody in the World knew him; I don't know what he's like when he's away from these places, but I have to say whenever I went for a pint with him in Bagnelstown, he was top drawer.

I've only ever seen two ghosts in my life, both times in Ireland. The first was at Marinas, when Kevin and I stayed there. Something rushed across the landing right in front of me. I told the girl who helped out around the place what had happened, she said "That'll be the ghost" A day or so later I saw an object fly across the room. There was no one else about. Spooky. Now in Corries, I was aware of someone sitting on the sofa. I asked Tarka quietly, if his dad used to use this sofa. I told him I thought I saw him, he said "It doesn't surprise me; he used to spend hours in that chair.'

I was having a fabulous time of it. For the first time in ages I didn't feel under pressure. I might not have been looking forward to returning to the Grove, but for the first time ever I was going back there without WORRY. Christmas day arrived at Corries. Lots of good food, and booze, stories told by professionals. Not me. The thing that'll stay with me is our rendition of 'Danny Boy' changed for this occasion to 'Denny Boy' for obvious reasons. It wasn't sad at all; all these people loved Denny Cordell, and loved singing to his memory. And of course I can say I've performed with John Hurt.

Back to London; I'd had a fabulous time thanks to Tarka. Just recently I heard he'd died. He was years younger than me, and seemed to have plenty going for him too. It's a crying shame, and a fucking waste.

Rival cricket skippers me and Laurence Toole (skipper of the Badminton in Swansea) with the famous ashes

The great Ian Bone rabble-rousing at the launch of his book 'Bash the Rich' in Notting Hill

TV and film director Roger Pomphrey in the office of Roughler Mansions aka the Warwick

Hank from Swansea. A survivor who outlived them all

Roughler Gallery partners Orlando Campbell (left)
and Piers Thompson at the Globe, 1989

'Keep that Welsh git out of my studio.'
Ben Young, producer of the Roughler album

Lofty O'Reilly on the trail of a Roughler scoop

Sean Oliver: "I'm half asleep, man. I've been up all night with that Terence Trent-Darby"

Latif and Bernie

Lily Allen (left) and Maquita Oliver in Peter Pan

Capt Kevin Allen (left) with Simon Roberts and Glenn Coulson (front) on the maiden voyage of 'The One Brow'

Thomas Rees on Portobello Road

Spider Stacey: penny-whistle player with The Pogues

Me and Gary Dempsey at the Wag club

35. San Francisco

I met Elvis in the Cal-Food store on South Van Ness
He'd lost a lot of weight, and his hair was in a mess

With the help of Peter Rickenberg, a local estate agent, Thomas Rees had managed to get the finance to set up a new local magazine called The Portobello Review. Rees is a good mate of mine who did have a fair amount experience in the publishing game, and seemed to know what he was doing. He asked me to get involved, doing much the same thing I did at The Roughler. Why not? It survived a few issues until lack of advertising revenue did for it. It was good though. It had good contributors, photos and investigative stories. One of the best stories, written by Thomas, concerned Hungarian Frank, an émigré, who in a bout of madness had shot dead a customer in the Pelican on the All Saints Rd. I knew Frank of old; he drank in The Warwick and used the same betting shop as me. Whenever he needed any D.H.S.S forms filling in I was the one he came to do it. He'd buy me a pint or whatever. I found Frank to be a passive guy, and can't imagine what went wrong.

Apparently he'd been in the Pelican earlier on the fateful day and said to a guy sitting at the bar "Do you want to die?" The guy said "Not today Frank" and Frank left. It was a different story later though when he actually pulled the fucking trigger on some poor sod in there. All sorts around the market were shocked. Who knows what sends people over the edge? Thomas tried to get to the bottom of it by tracking down Franks' countrymen, but most of them were very tight lipped. Frank got life.

During his quest for advertisers Thomas had approached all the usual suspects, which included Virgin. They declined but sent us a lovely letter wishing us luck, and all that cauliflower. Very cleverly Rees got back on to them, quoting the letter, and asking if they could provide us with a return ticket to San Francisco, so I could shoot over there and interview the cast and crew of a travelling freak show. This idea had come courtesy of Titch and Clive Hadley, who had spent time with the Bearded lady and Elastic Man and the rest, unbelievably; Virgin said OK. and sent over a business class ticket to the Promised Land. So this was to be my first taste of America. I couldn't wait.

I had mates over there. Titch from Merthyr had been there for years. So had Ratso and Vinny (who we used to call Enzo) so I wasn't walking into a trap. On the day of my flight I arrived at check-in only to find that I'd been upgraded further, so here I am on my first transatlantic flight in the best seats available. I was very excited about the prospect of swapping yarns with the rich and famous, and telling a few lies. It was very luxurious in the nob end of the plane, but apart from a miserable fat French bird, I was alone. Drinks were a bit on the thin side too, I've swallowed more on a National Express coach than I was getting here, I had to keep on asking the steward when I wanted a drink, all the time worrying if I was stronging it (that'll tell you how sober I was) I've got to be the biggest goon in the history of aviation, because as I found out later (too late) there was a free bar underneath where I was sitting. The steward must have thought I was a right twat, not being able to fetch my own drinks. I vowed to make up for it on my return journey, *in spades.*

I had a few quid for a change, so I was expecting a good time. Titch picked me up at the airport and took me back to his place in the Mission. Ratso was about and so was Cedric Bowen, who also hailed from Merthyr, where he had been a steady Eddy, working in the same butchers shop for the best part of thirty years, until one day he decided to up sticks, and head for S.F. They seemed to have a scene going on out there, with plenty of mates around and about. I was to stay with Ratso and Brenda who had a flat on Courtland St., which was at the arse end of Mission, but even out there, there was plenty going on. On one of our first evenings out we landed in the 3300 club a poetry dive on Mission St. I got up and read a few of my own, which must have attracted the attention of a woman sitting at the bar, because asked me to write my poem down for her. She had a bit of the Faye Dunaway about her (no kidding) so I did what she asked, and I also got her phone number. This was Linda, she lived up on Bernal Heights and was such a gentle soul, so much so that I couldn't gauge whether it would be appropriate to pounce or not. She had a nice house and car, but didn't seem to work, so I'd go to her place. It had a nice garden, so while she would be doing whatever indoors, I'd lay in a hammock she had set up outside, drinking beer in the sunshine. We spent a bit of time together later, but something wasn't right, and when she mentioned that she sometimes had to 'take to her bed' I took a backward step, just to be on the safe side.

There were quite a few bars on Courtland, and I visited all of them. 'Charlie's' had an English saturated juke box, and he knew more about British music than I did, by a country mile. Further down the street another neighbourhood bar. I fell in there alone one afternoon and got chatting with the barmaid, nothing flirty, just the usual cobblers. She didn't mind gossiping away with me, which was lucky. I found out the next day that she was the ex and still good friend of Sonny Barger, and this was an Angels hangout. I never went back in that watering hole again. Just opposite the flat, another bar, this time a lesbian establishment with some sort of cowgirl name I can't recall. In there playing pool with Ratso, he takes his shot, the ball hits about six cushions and goes in the pocket "you jammy cunt" I called out, the place fell silent. Now you have to bear in mind that I still had my London head on, and calling someone the 'C' word around Portobello was almost a term of endearment, so I thought nothing of it, the clientele did though, and I was asked to leave, I thought they were having me on, but then two or three of the bigger girls stepped forward, and I knew they were serious.

Titchy wanted to show me something, so we arranged to meet at a bar called 'Donnington Park' I know what you're thinking, with a name like that, yes, yes, the guy who ran it Dave was a massive car race fan, he may have even done it competitively at one time, and they used to show all the grand prix races in there. During the course of the evening Titch mentioned that the place was up for sale. He said he and Clive Hadley, also from Merthyr, who used to live hereabouts, could come up with some money and did I want in. I liked the feel of the place; it was a nice manageable neighbourhood bar. It was a fair hop from the main drag of Mission St., if truth be told it was within spitting distance of the Barrio, but he thought that it was an up and coming area (which we now know to be correct) and I thought with a few ideas and with Titchs' familiarity with the surrounds, we could make a go of it. So I was in. I had to go back to London, so I told Titch to keep in constant touch, and if any money were needed (which it would) I'd send some over there. If we were going to get a pub, I'd shift over there full time. Everyone in London thought I'd 'spunk' my windfall in no time. I thought this was a good opportunity to put my few quid to work.

So I headed back to London to bide my time, until I heard more from Titch. My sister Linda had moved to London to try her luck in the teaching profession, and she'd got herself a flat just off the Harrow Road., I stayed there with her, which was cool, come and go as I please, she even gave me the best kipping place. I was doing the usual pub crawling around Portobello. On my way along Westbourne Park Rd one evening I was approached by what was obviously a brass. "You want business?" she enquired. She was a bit rough, but she did boast those hard Slavic looks I find quite appealing so I said "what's on offer?" Quick as a flash she said "I have hard neeples and a tight pussy" She was obviously wasting her talents out here on the cold street, with a pitch like that she'd be a shoo-in winner on that Apprentice programme. I was intrigued. I don't usually entertain brass action, nothing moral, ethical or religious in that decision, it's just difficult. For a start the girl is never going to enjoy it. Then who do you pick? A girl who you think you'd be compatible with in real life to make it believable, or go for the girl you'd never ever be able to pull in the real world, all too tricky for my liking. My feeling is it's going to be disappointing whichever route you take. They're working girls and they're on the clock, you don't come into the equation. Page 3 had a song on this subject written by Jan Green, A nice sing-along ditty entitled 'Prostitutes World'

We are always pretty and smell nice just for you
High heels and stockings half an hour and we're through
Our days are a jumble of pretending that we've come
We've seen enough, enough of men, to make our hair curl
But we've got to keep on working; it's a prostitute's world.

So instead of diving up the nearest alleyway for the knee trembler I took her to 'Galicia' one of our favoured watering holes on Portobello. She was interesting. Her name was Eleanora and she hailed from Belgrade. Two things quickly became apparent (a) She had a drug problem of some description, and (b) she didn't like sex, which on reflection was a result for me, remember I was off my nut all the time back then, anything might have happened. She was a great girl though, we hung out some. One night she invited me to some of her Yugoslav friends' house, up Wembley way. I didn't know what to expect, but it was fun, great grub, plenty drink. What else do we need? I soon realised by the amount of respect Eleanor was getting from these people, that there was a lot more to her than you first think. She came from a good family, but had fucked up a bit in London. Who hasn't? She talked about getting off the drugs, I hope she has, there was a lot more to her than chippying around the Royal Borough. Who knows I might track her down some day.

As you can imagine I was awaiting every call from Titch with great excitement, And before you know it, the deal had been done. It was going to take time. The legals etc. would take weeks, and so would something called Escrow, but there's always something to be getting on with, so post haste I said my cheerios, and was off to America again, this time with a project.

Titchs original suggestion of a name for the bar was something like 'Taffy's Tavern', I soon nipped that in the bud. My thought was that we should hold our heads high here, and name it after one of our great Welsh heroes. Seeing as I come from Swansea, I suggested we name it after the poet Dylan Thomas, who, as well as being a legendary boozer, was also well known in America, and not just for dying there either. Dylan had toured extensively in the states; he'd even performed at Berkeley, which is just outside San Francisco. We both agreed it added a touch of class to our operation, so 'Dylan's' it was. Not that the 'Rimbaud of Cwmdonkin Drive' was universally hailed in his hometown. Not by Don Rosser, late of Covent Garden Opera House, "He'd drink all you had, and then try it on with your wife" nor by the lovely barmaid at the Mermaid in Mumbles, who used to serve the poet, "He was a bloody nuisance. I don't want to talk about him" She'd then go on to ask how our mate Viv Cory was doing. "A much nicer chap", and certainly not Sooky Davies , demolition man and regular around the tap rooms of Wind St. where Dylan used to drink when he worked at the Evening Post, he even went as far to say "He was a cunt that Dillwyn Thomas" when confronted by some Thomas enthusiasts. The bar was located on 19th and Folsom St. in the bowels of the Mission. Internally it had some age to it, especially by U.S. standards. There was a fine old solid wooden bar, which gleamed after years of polishing. One could easily do the old western slide a drink along the bar trick on it. The metal and wood stools, which were bolted to the floor, were authentic too. It was small, but it fitted snugly in this area. Titch might have nursed dreams of Dylan's expanding all over California, good luck to him, me, I was happy with this for now.

The takeover date was announced. On Dave's leaving night he had a big send off party. This was the first opportunity for Titch and I to familiarise ourselves with the mechanics of, well, serving customers. The place was packed, and we coped OK. The plan was that when we started working there properly, Titch and I would work the bar, draw no wages and live off the tips, on that nights performance I was more than happy with that arrangement. Sexist or not, girls shaking cocktails and pulling pints had an advantage when it came to drawing tips, but I was confident we'd manage.

Next day brought the start of the Welshifying of the pub. People had been sending all kinds of Welsh memorabilia over for us. Thomas Rees had even got in touch with Dylan Thomas aficionado Geoff Townes, who runs Dylan's bookstore in Swansea, and he'd sent a few pieces. Although Dylan's is no more, the new owners still retain what I think was the best thing in there. Above the actual bar there was a recess, just big enough for a sign writer to paint in the immortal 'Do not go gentle into that good night, rage, rage against the dying of the light' It's the first thing you'd notice when you entered from the street. Titchy had got an artist to paint a picture of Dylan in one of his more famous poses as a pub sign, and this fluttered back and forth in the wind on Folsom Street. We had pictures of the great and good of Wales covering the walls.

Not many of the locals new much about Wales so we would gladly take them on a tour. They came away none the wiser, but hey, it's called hospitality.

Opening night arrived, it was a big deal. All sorts turned up to wish Titch well. There was food I guess, and probably some kind of entertainment. How would I know I was flat out busy behind the bar? One thing I did notice, there was an antiquated glass washing thing behind there, you had to plunge the glasses down into it manually, shake them about a bit, then pull them out, then dry and shine them with a clean towel. Laborious was not the word. Titch didn't seem to get on with this contraption to well. After a couple of plunges I saw him applying hand cream. Fuck sake, what would have been like down the mines.

We got through that OK but I don't think Titch was in love with actually working the bar. My fears were realised the next time it was his turn to relieve me and start his shift. His missus turned up instead of him, so much for our earlier plans then. I was pissed off.

Shortly after wards the word came from home that my father had died. Although from what I've mentioned previously, it may appear that he and I didn't get on very well. But latterly we'd been getting on OK. We did have our problems, mostly when I was still a teenager that was to do with my lifestyle. When I was even younger than that I didn't like him very much at all. When he wanted me to stay in the Grammar school and the army, I hated him. But he was right. When Ossie Austin and all the bike boys hung about outside our front door, revving, swearing, spitting, and chatting up birds it was the closest thing around our area to anything cool (This was before the Mods took off) so when he had to fuck them off from outside our door I was embarrassed. He was right. When, as a cricket umpire, he had to no ball Terry Price, the new teenage Wunderkind of Welsh rugby, for overstepping the crease whilst bowling, I was mortified. He was right. Sometimes my mates would tell me how their dads had been booked or even sent off by my father when he was reffing the football; I didn't know where to look. But, again he was right, but at the time it just felt like he was in some enemy camp.

I suppose he wanted more out of me than I'd shown to date, but as his jobs became much more working class orientated, and he started drinking in proper pubs, he began to realise that I was up to the same 'strokes' as a lot of people he was playing darts and cards with. It was always difficult between us, but we got on OK. When Sunday league cricket started getting televised, I used to go down my folks' house to watch it with him. He'd be sitting there, curtains drawn, fire on (cricket is a summer game) watching the action. Almost invariably, after stumps had been drawn, there'd be a story on the news of some catastrophe concerning ordinary Joe's following their weekend pursuits. God help us if it turned out to be a potholer. "Leave them down there" he'd bellow. He had the same disregard for mountaineers stuck on glaciers, Yachtsmen drifting out to sea and Walkers lost on Snowdonia or somewhere up North. He'd be apoplectic. I wouldn't put this down to him being unfeeling. It was more a case of him loathing the idea that these 'fools' could be putting ordinary volunteers lives in jeopardy, while pursuing a stupid dream.

My dad was a Socialist at heart. He used to help people who were having difficulties receiving what was rightly theirs from the government. He'd sort out affairs for people when there'd been a death in the family, and, on occasion had been called upon to 'lay out' a dead body. So I guess we got off on the wrong foot, and it carried on. Him giving up on me as a lost cause, and me giving up on him, as I thought he was blaming me for his shortcomings. But to be fair, he always worked and provided. We just never got close. One particular time I was kinda heartbroken over a girl, I didn't think he'd take much notice, but one night he came to my room and said "You never forget them. But the hurt goes away" This of course is bog standard sympathy talk, but at least he said it. And he was right.

Titch was surprised when I said I wasn't going home for the funeral. But I'd seen my father before I left this last time. I don't think he expected to see me again. He looked pretty weak in the hospital bed, but I'd seen him look worse. I knew one thing, with his views on after life, burial services and all that stuff, the last thing he would have had me do, was travel 8,000 miles to see him be put in a hole in the ground.

I'd found somewhere to live by now, so I had a new independence I guess. Whenever I wasn't working, I'd be off exploring, bars mainly. Well what do you want me to do on my time off? Everybody who comes to S.F. wants to visit Alcatraz, I never went there. Who the fuck wants to spend an afternoon walking around a sodding nick? Not me. I'd be over Clooney's on Valencia St. playing killer dice, or at The Original McCarthy's on Mission, where, for a buck a beer you could watch the baseball on the telly. Mission was a lot like Ladbroke Grove, multicultural ,vibrant, and of course, dodgy. On 24th where I was staying, the BART (underground train) was on the doorstep, so I'd dive up to the town or over to North Beach to drink in the Beat vibe (which isn't there) at Vesuvios, and call in the City Lights bookstore, but with all the tourists around about it was hard to get any continuity going as regards talking bollucks, or as they say 'chewing the fat'. So I spent the most time around the Mission. My walk from 24th Street to our bar was quite colourful, I would walk down Capp St. home to some of the lowest end hookers imaginable, I'd chat to a couple of them, they thought my accent was 'cute' especially when I said "No sex I'm British" Further on you're in the Barrio, I'd stop off at a couple of Mexican bars just to watch the gorgeous barmaids in action, forever preening and bursting into song and dance mode whenever a lively Mexican number came through the speakers. I wouldn't dare talk to them, apart from ordering a drink, after all this is a gang area.

I was in a place one afternoon when I noticed a big poster for the Chavez/De La Hoya fight that was being broadcast that very night. I asked the guy if they had it on in there, he said, with a smile, "Don't come here to watch it" Later that night I realised he was doing me a favour, passing by, on the other side of the street I noticed four armed bouncers on the door. As for gang activity I didn't see that much. I saw youngsters spinning their Cadillac's through 180 degrees in the middle of Mission St. Not caring what the public or the cops thought about it. It must have got nasty though. There was a drive-by shooting one evening on Mission, this guy told me later that his pal was walking down there with his six year old daughter, she came up to his knee, when the shooting started, he scooped her up into his arms, almost at once a bullet hit him in the kneecap, so danger did lurk, maybe I was too drunk to notice. Titch started going on at me about my drinking. I was drinking a lot. But was I drunk at work? Don't think so. But I said I'd sort it out anyway. Then one night he's off to Reno or Tahoe to see Tom Jones 'live' this made sense, maybe he could do good promo work for the bar whilst there. He got to talk to Tom, told him about the bar, Tom showed an interest and said to Titch "Give the address to my manager (his son) and if we're ever in S.F. I'll call in." You never know.

I was in charge this night, and the pub was never busier. I was not officially working the bar, more of a host I guess. I thought I'd been charming throughout. I had girls phone numbers in every pocket, I was cracking gags, and getting laughs and the bar took loads of money. But when I saw him the next day he was full of it. "It's not going to work" he kept saying. Apparently I hadn't done enough to impress a mate of his. I don't want to remember this bloke's name, but he'd gone to Titch and painted a less than rosy picture of me. So now I can't work the bar any more. I said I'll clean the pub and work on promotion and the like. He replied, "You don't want to do that, what about the glory" what fucking glory he was talking about I don't know. Then I realised he was the 'glory hunter' who wanted the accolade of the masses, and this pub would be a step in the right direction by God. He wanted the pub for himself all along. No compromise was going to be reached here, so one night I just said "Give me my fucking money back then." He agreed.

On reflection what I should have said was "Well the pubs up and running now, it's got an identity, and money from the till has been spent on improvements, so I want more than I put in" But I never did that. I even agreed when he asked me to wait for the money, when all the time I'm paying my rent out of my dwindling stash, and his is coming out of the till. Fuck it. That was the end of my adventure as a Californian bar owner. But my life is full of reverses. Just have to get on with it. For the first time in a long time my luck with the women wasn't so bad, and people from London would pop up from time to time.

Kevin Allen had finished 'Twin Town" a film shot mainly in Swansea and written by him and Paul Durden. It centres on a pair of rapscallions played by brothers Llyr and Rhys Ifans who wreak havoc in the Welsh city. Their characters are loosely based on two real brothers who live there, Julian and Jeremy Roberts. These guys spent most of their time 'Bonging' whilst playing Subbuteo. They had it down pat. They'd discuss the merits of the various players and relive great moves and goals from past matches. Paul discovered this pair, he even put them out as an act to a paying audience, just them playing Subbuteo. I think he missed a trick here, if he'd put them out complete with bong, speed and cider as a work of art it would have won the Turner prize. Never mind he got a film out of it.

Kevin, Paul, Llyr and Rhys Ifans turned up in S.F. on their way to the Sundance film festival, to show the film. I don't know what the deal was, whether my obvious bad publicity had travelled across the Atlantic already, but when it came to who was going with them to Sundance it was Titch who got the nod, I wasn't asked. Paul is one of my oldest mates, Kevin lived beside me in Ladbroke Grove and we'd done shitloads together, I'd been the driver of the boat on the Norfolk Broads with them both when they were finishing off the script, and now here I am left behind on one of their biggest gigs. That was a right kick in the bollocks, I can tell you.

Sitting in Dylan's one day, who should happen in, but Trigger, a mate of Lofty O'Reilly's from London, who was involved in the Rock and Roll. He came up trumps. He was the tour manager with Oasis. "We're playing in the Civic Centre tonight, come down" I took Ratso and an American couple he knew. The band were great, I couldn't knock it ever, working class lads, lead, bass and rhythm guitars, drums and a singer, great songs and not a cello or violin in sight. After the show Trigger took us back. Didn't see Noel Gallagher but his brother and the rest were there. Liam was with Patsy Kensit, when she was going out with Dan Donovan out of B.A.D. I used to see them a lot seeing as Dan lived beside the Warwick, I mentioned this quietly to her as an 'in' Sitting there next to Liam he asked what I was doing in San Fran, told him about the boozer and that, then I mentioned Trigger had invited us along for the 'Lig'. Liam didn't like that, he turned on me a bit, "nobody ligs around here" he said. I made myself scarce and went over to chat to the boys out of Black Grape who were there. Good lads.

I suppose it was homesickness that dragged me to every Brit concert I could blag into, but one night I became intrigued when I got a call from this scalper (ticket tout) I'd gotten to know. He asked if I wanted to go to the Fillmore to see Donovan, my immediate Reaction was "I thought he was dead" but I went along anyway. The crowd played a big part in this experience. When we arrived I noticed all these really young 'chicks' dressed in hippy garb, they must have raided their grandparents wardrobes 'cos their parents would have been too young. It was a 'groovy' vibe Man. Donovan hits the stage, just him and his guitar. You forget how many hits this geezer has had, 'Mellow Yellow' Catch the Wind' Universal soldier' he kept banging them out left, right &centre, then disaster struck. Some twat passed me a joint. I've never got on with pot in any shape or form, but I have smoked it, what these fuckers over here were smoking was a different thing altogether. My fucking head caved in; swiftly followed by extreme paranoia, without a word to anyone I flew through the door and didn't stop 'til I was back in the safety of my room, Fucking hippies.

The Pogues are in town. No Shane McGowan in this time, he's either been sacked or maybe resting, But why not? It's sure to be a great knees up. I track down Spider Stacey who has taken over the singing duties. I knew Spider all right, he used to come over the Portobello for a drink with us lot quite often. I'd saved his arse one night too. On a boat trip on the Thames one night, my mate Viv was in the process of throwing him overboard. Viv said he saw Spider hitting the girl he was with. I calmed that one down. It could have been worse. So when I'm talking to Spider on the phone I expected a little more than "I suppose you want to be on the guest list" But I arranged to meet him in the bar next to the venue anyway. While I was hanging on for him I struck up a conversation with this guy.

We were just talking the usual bollocks when he hit me with a googly. "What're you doing tomorrow?" he asked. I told him I was around if he wanted a drink. He said "I'm going to rob a bank tomorrow, will you sit in the car?" This guy was smart, and I've met enough flannel merchants over the years, and I swear he didn't come across as one of them, but hey, Police, Guns, San Quentin, please. Thanks but no thanks. I haven't got that type of bottle. I wonder what happened to him. Two hours later dopey bollocks Spider turns up. No howdy doody. What are you up too? None of that, only, on seeing this guy "I suppose you want a plus one now" I went mad. He's the penny whistle player for fuck sake. I called him a cunt and went home.

Mick P. my old partner on the poetry venture 'Pull my Daisy' was in town. On one of the 'Daisy' nights he had discovered this singer/ songwriter called Noella who hailed from Derry. There wasn't much of her, but she was a tough one all right. She had about sixty original songs, and she could sing the shit out of all of them. Mick had got her a deal, part of which included Noella coming to America to cut an album. So she and Mick were staying in Sausalito, and recording just up the road apiece, the production was in the capable hands of Gerry Harrison from Talking Heads. Got to talking with him, and it turns out he's from Welsh stock. Mick had free days, he'd say, "Come over tomorrow we'll chill out here" this was no hardship for me in that, Mick was plotted up on a houseboat in Sausalito, it was beautiful. I was drinking like a fool by now, so a quiet time would have been great. So of a morning I'd jump on the ferry at Pier 49 and breathe in the fresh air, past Alcatraz and on to Sausalito. We'd usually last about 20 minutes when Mick would say, "Fuck this, let's go to town" meaning S.F. I didn't take any persuading; it was great to hang out in S.F. with Mick P., It had been a while since I'd hung out with someone who didn't think I was nuts. We had some time of it running around bars. One Sunday afternoon Mick even stopped me going off with a sex change. "You can't go off with someone with a beard" quite right too.

I don't know what happened with Noella's career. But Mick's still about, running nightclubs and turning out kids.

My uselessness with the women in London didn't seem to have followed me across the Atlantic. Can't say I was in a pick and choose situation, but it was all right. One night in particular sticks out. I'd spotted this girl working behind a bar on Valencia St. who I was taken by, but with my luck, didn't think I had more than a 25/75 chance of getting anywhere with her. These odds became 0/100 a couple of days later when I saw her in Dylan's with a boyfriend, who was English. I'd forgotten any amorous ideas by the time I saw her next, throwing blood stirring shapes, behind the less than roomy bar which was her work station. I was shooting pool when I get a tap on the shoulder from Miss Wonderful. "What are you doing later" Before I could even say "Washing your car" Ironing your curtains' or "painting your flat" we were on a 'date' I took her to this Mexican bar/ restaurant place on the corner of my street, and soon became clear we weren't here to talk about the weather, or her boyfriend. She was great company, but better was to come. At her place we dived into the most comfortable bed ever made I reckon. As it turned out she was a damn good kisser, and she wasn't all that strict as a Christian. It was a night to remember, for me anyway.

In the morning there was food and orange juice and coffee and one of those showers that hurts the top of your head taking with it any semblance of a hangover, then she said "I'm such a slut, I had orgasms last night, such a slut' Don't beat yourself up girl. Remorse, guilt, all these things must have been patrolling her head I guess, so I said my goodbyes, sadly, as I didn't think there'd be much hope of a rematch here. So imagine my delight, when the next day I get a call summoning me over to the scene of last night's shenanigans. I got there only to be told that she'd made a mistake and that her girlfriend was calling round and she'd forgotten about it. I was disappointed, but hey, I had some money and there was a great bar just around the corner. I hadn't gone but a hundred yards when I hear this whistle a Carmarthenshire shepherd would have been proud of, I turned, it was her calling me back. She'd put the other party off, "I'll take you for a drink" she said. Strangely we landed up in a bar in the Castro, the infamous gay district in San Francisco. There was a lot of homo erotic goings on going on, which you might think would be a lust buster, but no, we were making out just like everyone else. Then back to hers. Wow! Next day while walking her dog upon Twin Peaks, overlooking downtown San Francisco, she told me her boyfriend was coming back, and she didn't want to fuck it up with him. I thought they'd already broken up, but I was wrong. Perhaps she was a slut. Do I sound like I care? Better to have loved blah, blah, blah.

Yes, I had a few flings; the girls seem very forward to me. None of the ones I met wanted you to think of them of anything other than bi sexual for instance. One girl I had a grapple with sort of summed it up when she said "I'd never go with a married man, well I did once, but I did his wife as well, so that doesn't count" Spread that love around I say. I had a couple of girls around the flat who'd stripped completely naked whilst I was out of the room making tea or whatever. I wasn't exactly shocked, but it knocked me out of my stride a bit. I like a bit of a build up to the event, if you get my drift. In the Dubliner pub on 24th street one Sunday afternoon, talking cobblers with the Irish barmaid, drinking a real pint of Guinness, I'm joined by a very attractive Latino chick. We get talking about this and that, it's fun, I invite her to my favourite place of seduction, the Mex bar on the corner (again). My seductive powers didn't have time to surface, because before you know it she says "Bite my teets and I come, Bite my teets and I come" She wasn't exactly whispering this into my ear either. I don't know if the people working there could understand what was going on but I got some funny looks. It then dawned on me that she was half cut. I got her out of there and back to mine. All the time with the "bite my teets" mantra. "O.K. I'll fucking bite, but is there anything else on the menu?" We landed up having shite sex, and then she passed out. I let her sleep it off, and went for a pint. I thought when I get back, round two might go my way. She wasn't having any. In fact she said to me "I'm not looking for a boyfriend you know" Funny you should say that, thought I.

There were two special girls for me in San Francisco. Beth, who helped me through thick and thin, and Kathleen who I once believed was the reason my higher power sent me to S.F. Beth was a friend, she let me stay in her flat, she fed me and lent me money when I was out of the game. I phoned her from London after I had been sober for a year. She'd seen the worst of me so I thought she would have been pleased, well she did say she was pleased for me, she also said not to call her again. For the life of me I can't understand that one. Maybe I did something I've conveniently forgotten. Not to worry.

Kathleen was another being altogether. She was beautiful, for my eyes, she had a bit of the Natalie Wood about her; I saw her first when she worked a bar. She was friendly, funny, interested and she said yes when I asked her for a date. The date was a foursome; I guess she was being careful. We landed up in some club on the Bay. I must have had just the right mix of drink and drug in my system that night as I excelled on the dance floor and in conversation. We went home together and started dating a bit. I remember going to see 'Trainspotting' with her. She wouldn't believe anyone talked like that. So from the pub I phoned the Cornwall and summoned up Edinburgh's finest, Gary Dempsey to have a chat with her. We drank a lot, talked about giving it up together, but it wasn't my time yet, so that never happened. Then I noticed that her world was falling apart slightly. She didn't have that job anymore, she was having trouble with her car, her flat and her father was not well. Then we argued, and I never saw her for a while. Some money arrived. I contacted Kathleen and invited her out; I didn't want it to end on a sour note. We did have some fun for the short time we were together. Anyway I meet her in a nice bar on Valencia. We're not there two minutes when she's being hit on by a lesbian. She's playing it up for the audience (me) I'm furious, I approach the lesbian and say (like a twat) "where I come from if someone hits on your partner you have a fight" So here I am offering a girl outside for a punch up. That was the last time Kathleen ever talked to me. I saw her a few times, I think she would have chatted if I'd pushed it, but alas.

I'm still waiting to get weighed in by Titch, and I'm skint. Luckily Vinnie can find me some work with him. He's got plenty, so he brings me in. The day started normally enough, a bit of fetching and carrying from the timber yard, back to the job, some construction and then he'd have his first joint. It was basically down tools then because all he wanted to talk about was his less than successful love life. When I first arrived, there was an odd situation as Vinny's then girlfriend had left him for a bloke in a wheelchair "Where does that leave me" he'd lament. At a party one evening I saw this ex and said "Where's Vinny?" she pointed done this driveway, and there was Vinny pushing this guy in his wheelchair. I didn't get it nor did anyone else. Anyway Vinny overestimated his chances with any girl who'd spare him the time of day. He didn't seem to take into account whether they had boyfriends, were married or were gay even. If they'd been pleasant to him he thought he was in. Just behind Dylan's there was a climbing school. Once a week these two nice girls would pop in for a drink after practice. They were both attractive. But one of them had the best arse anyone has ever seen. It was perfect, accentuated even more by the skin tight trousers she wore for the climbing. Now there wasn't a human, man, woman, gay or lesbian who could honestly say they hadn't caught a glance or two of this wonderful bottom. Vinny of course took it a step further. He didn't just look at it; he followed it wherever it went. It was as if it had a life of its own to him. He was completely oblivious to the fact that it was part of a human body. Do you get the picture yet? Vinny was hopeless with women.

As well as keeping me alive with employment Vinny had access all areas to the best place I think I visited out there, The San Francisco Boat Club. This wasn't an elite establishment for toffs, this was for ordinary folk who liked messing around on the water. Vinny had done his yearly stint as the Commodore there and was well in. It was terrific, cheap drink, outside barbeques, all kinds of music. Jazz, Soul, Bluegrass. It was a good night out, situated right next to the ocean. One particular night we'd all had plenty. There was dancing. A woman was dancing away out on the floor, so I stepped up to join her. Before I'd hit my first pirouette someone has belted me hard in the chest, swiftly followed by an equally heavy blow in the same locale. In fact this guy pummelled my ribcage from the middle of the dance floor to the exit, where, luckily, he was restrained by someone on my side. Everyone thought it best for me to leave, which I did. The next day, I was in agony. I was convinced I had at least broken several ribs, and couldn't breathe properly. Not much chance of going to the Doctor out here, people who are residents can hardly afford it, let alone an illegal like me. So I had to suffer. Maybe a pint will help. In the pub later Vinny showed up. "What the fuck was all that about last night?" I asked. Vinny replied "I don't know. I've never seen him like that before". "Who is he then, a mate of yours?" "Well he's a regular down the club. He's a Homicide detective with S.F.P.D." Oh bollucks, Here I am thinking he's some pissed up catamaran cowboy, when all the time he's in a position to cause me unthinkable grief. Apart from the fact I'd already outstayed my welcome in America; this guy could take me for a 'ride' and lose me in the Mojave Desert. The time had come for me to eat great dollops of humble pie. I said to Vinny "Phone him up and tell him how sorry I am, for anything wrong I had done". As it turned out this guy was a bit nervous about his behaviour too, and the thing went no further. But hey, the Murder Squad.

Vinny was a good old stick though. One of his ambitions was to put a roof on the old Norman Castle in the centre of Swansea. Through copies of The Herald of Wales newspaper that he got sent over regularly, he was right up to date on any changes taking place in our old home town. He'd spend hours regaling Texan tourists, who had no idea where Europe was, never mind Swansea, about the marvellous improvements Swansea council were making on the banks of the River Tawe. Bless. But the wages I got off him kept me going when times were rough.

At long last Titch has come through with my money. Most welcome too. I've been living on fresh air for too long. Although things you need like food, fags and bottled beer are reasonable out there, I was finding it hard just to get hold of them now. So after Titch weighed in, I went on a bender, during which I agreed to finance this drug/ money making idea that Ratso had been bandying about for quite a while. He seemed to know these cats who were descendents of Owsley the great L.S.D. maker. I should have known better, I'd already given him a grand to do the groundwork for this scheme, and seen no hint of a return. But being the mug that I am I handed over the lion's share of my return from Titch to him. I've known Ratso since the sixties, I also knew he was iffy around money (other peoples) yet, and I can't figure it out to this day, I still trusted him to do the decent thing.

These words are obviously not in his vocabulary. He bought the acid alright, I saw it. The process for getting this to England goes like this. You send the blotting paper with the motif on it through the post to the U.K. Then you take a hip flask size bottle of 100% rum, into this you pour the drug. In the days before they went weird on carrying liquid on to a plane, this was a sound idea. DON'T TRY IT NOW. And he got through no problem. When you get to the other side you pick up the paper, then, using an eye dropper thing, you simply cover the paper with the liquid and there you have it, strong Californian acid. In my experience I hadn't noticed much call for this where I'm coming from, but he assured me that he had bulk customers. I didn't think he'd leave me for dead in S.F.

He did though.

Weeks pass by without a word. I'm skint again. Worse than that, I'm about to be homeless too. Then one day $2,000 arrives, that was soon swallowed up by back rent etc. but at least I thought this thing was moving along at last. Wrong. I never heard another word. I'm now no use to man or beast, a broke, homeless drunk, in a foreign land. The only alternative now is to get back to Britain to see if I can't salvage something out of this sorry situation. I didn't have enough for a ticket even, and my credit had run out. Luckily this guy called Lichen, who was a throwback to the sixties in dress sense, ideology and drug consumption paid my fare. It's funny to think, of all the people I met out there, he was the last person I would have asked. God, or whoever he worships, bless him. Lichen was all 'Burning Man' and the world famous San Francisco Gay Pride Parade, and was the type I would have expected to see a lot more of over there, but alas Lichen was a dying breed. So my time in San Francisco is almost up. I had some laughs and made a few mates, but all in all I was disappointed. I expected more of the hippy, anti social type behaviour we'd seen and read so much about. The cars weren't even 'Americana' The Mission was good, but not as good as Ladbroke Grove. But what fucks me up the most, is going all that way just to fall out with my mates. So it's back to the U.K. Got nowhere to live in London now. I'm a very worried man.

I can't leave America, on these pages anyway, without clearing up my thoughts about Titch. I'm changing nothing about our time together in the pub, but I'd like to say that Titch Jones is one of the most honest helpful people I've ever come across. When the Miners strike broke out, Titch gave up his comfortable life in S.F. and went back to Wales, where he could be seen on the picket line for the duration. I well remember going for a drink with Titch in The El Salvadorian club one time. We were on a quest to find footballers of Latin American descent to pose as Welshmen for an upcoming four nation's competition. We played those games without one Welshman and nine El Salvadorians in the team, and did OK. Titch kept in touch with these guys long after I'd left town, and through a lot of fund raising and hard graft Titch managed to somehow build a school for the underprivileged kids down in Latin America. So hats off to him. Just don't go into business with your mates.

36. Buried in the Graveyard of Ambition

I had a couple of days in London when I got back. I had a bit of a sun tan and some recently purchased clothes I'd bought over there, so I didn't feel like a complete tramp, I might even have given an impression of stability to those I bumped into, inside though I didn't have a clue which way to turn. Normal procedure when you've been robbed is to track down the person responsible, so I had to make an effort to find Ratso, even though I knew deep down I'd get little or no satisfaction. I should have just toughed it out in London I guess, I might have lucked into something and as a consequence missed out on the five years of Limbo I was heading towards.

I'd managed to travel the 8,000 miles to Heathrow, and the journey back to Ladbroke Grove, but now I'm skint. Kevin Allen stumped up the price of a ticket to Swansea, so here goes.

Initial enquiries point to the fact that Ratso has been having a fine time indeed. Everyone loved him. It turns out that one of his sales techniques comprises of laying a hundred or so 'tabs' on a potential customer as a sample. Why on earth would they come back? They'd just sell them and pocket the money. Who wouldn't? This place is not a hotbed of honour and gallantry for fucks sake; it's every man for himself. What annoyed me more was that he'd even been on a jolly to the Balearics. I wonder if this was when I was starving and sleeping on the floor in Dennis's passage in San Francisco. I find out he's at his mother's home. When I get there I bump into him. He lied about knowing I was in town, and how he was on his way to look for me, yeah, sure. He assures me that although everything hasn't gone to plan there is some clear sky on the horizon. He goes off to get a few pounds to tide me over for now, with a lot more to come tomorrow.

That was his chance to be a man right there, he never took it. And I hate him for that more than anything else the sly fucker has done. Next day and there's no sign of him. I'm trying to keep on top of it/

him, but my days of walking the length and breadth of Swansea for fun are over, it's hard graft now. Let's hope I can get something back before he pulls his next conjuring trick. I can't find him anywhere. Three days go by without a word. Then out of the blue I hear that he's been spotted walking along Valencia St. in S.F. He's done a runner on me. A flight back to America couldn't have come cheap at such short notice. It would have at least given me a grub stake to try and get started in Swansea. But he's gone. Now I'm totally fucked.

In the Tenby pub everyone is cool with me. But the last thing they want to hear are my problems. They've got enough of their own. Badminton cricketer and my soon to be roommate Paul Balzer found me somewhere to stay, and, fair play subbed me a few quid if he had it, he'd also let me know of anything social that was going on, if I fancied going out. By now, if I had money, I was generally pissed by tea time. I'd spend the rest of the time stewed in self pity, back on Constitution Hill, on the dole, and very unhappy. I still had some mates around the place, but my demeanour wasn't conducive to anything remotely approaching what you would call 'good vibes. Durden was cool, but he'd be going on about my drinking all the time. He was right of course, but the last thing on my mind right then was packing that in, the first thing on my mind was finding a way to get money to get pissed. Long time ally Paul Grey gave me some work here and there, which was good. He didn't have to, there a plenty of people down there more capable of an honest day's toil than me. Chris Bennet, a guy I'd met through the betting shop was a good lad too. He'd call around with a bottle of wine and some fags when he had it. Basically my life reverted to what it would have been like if I'd never left Swansea in the first place. And of course I felt like I was a disappointment to the people who might have been bigging me up when I was in London and S.F. Of course certain people who hadn't seen me in years tracked me down initially, but when it became clear that I wasn't saying much, their enthusiasm cooled somewhat.

Before you know it I'm back out 'hoisting' this is a dangerous occupation in Swansea. There are so many at it. I tried to offset this a bit by always being up very early, and, hopefully beating all the other rapscallions to the shops. This worked, I'd make my few shillings, but I was trying to gamble my way out of misery. As anyone will tell you my luck is poxed, so I'd soon lose my little bit, which meant I'd soon be doing the afternoon shift as well. This obviously increases your odds of being nabbed appreciably, so now it's only a matter of time before I revisit the Magistrates Court.

I was lucky to be reunited with old mates Dougie and Cathy, who I've known forever. They even lived beside us in Brynmelyn Flats. We were close, so much so they even named their daughter Kirsty after my girlfriend. They'd improved their lot considerably, and were now living a middle class comfortable life in the smart area of Tycoch. Nice house, conservatory, full fridge and always a drink to be had. I may have to had to keep my mouth shut about London life in the pubs etc. in case of being accused of name-dropping, but at Doug and Cath's as they seemed to like them. Not that there was anything earth shatteringly original in my yarns, but I guess it was a nice change to hear my bullshit, after years of the Swansea equivalent. They looked after me well.

Latif Gardez who is a song-writing partner of mine, and was going through his own 'nightmare', came to visit. We were on a similar downward spiral right then. He had to leave London and take up residence in Bristol. He was about as happy as me. I thought that maybe we could get some musical thingy up and running, and that he could spend a lot of time in Swansea. He impressed a few guys around my flat with his guitar playing, and had some good times with Doug and Cathy, but it was much like the gig he had in Bristol. So why bother?

My London outlet had all but gone now, I didn't even have a phone, so who could I keep in touch with anyway? I was watching Fifteen to One on the telly one afternoon, and standing in the number one spot was John Duignan, Class War candidate and barrier man at Ladbroke Grove tube station. John was a member of the all-conquering Warwick quiz team. Now don't quote me on it, but I think he won. A few weeks later he turns up in Swansea. He stayed with me; he went off on a pub-crawl. This was one of his habits. Years earlier Bernie and I sat John down with a 'British Pub Guide' and asked him to tick off the ones he'd been in. He's got no reason to lie. The number he'd been in was to put it mildly, staggering. He even had anecdotes from lots of them. Nothing short of heroic was his quest for the perfect piss up. On this particular night in Swansea, I let him in and showed him where he was going to sleep, and left him to it. There was plenty of banging during the night, but I took no notice. In the morning it soon became clear that the banging was him having a punch up with the ironing board I'd left standing in the front room. John looked like he'd come off second best.

Watching telly one morning, Johnny Vaughn is interviewing an old mate. Jake Arnott is on there talking about his new book 'The Long Firm' He's looking good, talking sense and seems comfortable in the hot seat. I had no idea he'd taken to writing. Last I'd heard he was a tumbler in the circus or some such. He's doing well. He's come a long way since his days as an embalmer in the mortuary. Jake used to hang out at the Warwick, he was a big mate of Pete at Rough Trade, and they both came from Wendover.

At least Kevin Allen hasn't forgotten me. He's about to get married and I'm invited. The problem is the ceremony is in Death Valley U.S.A. "No worry" says Kev "we'll sort something out". I couldn't see it happening though; I'd find it tough to get to Cardiff on my money at present. Salvation arrived in the form of Linda Richards, who has been one of our best girls for years. She'd heard about the trip and lent me a hundred quid. What a sport! I haven't paid her back yet, but I will. So I'm on. The plan is for me to get to Paddington and team up with Kevin's brother Keith, who had a plane ticket for me. I've got Linda's £100 and a giro, and I'm off to California again.

Up to Paddington on the train, Keith's there. On to Heathrow, to catch the plane to Los Angeles. Whether by luck or judgement, we have four seats between us in the middle aisle. I can't sleep on anything other than a bed; Keith doesn't have this problem, and stretched out over three of them, and slept most of the way. At

LAX it's straight into a hire car and we're heading for the desert. Keith loves to be in control, and is never wrong, so we were soon travelling in the wrong direction, but to be fair, with me doing the map reading it was inevitable that we'd get lost. It had to be three in the morning when we pulled into a hotel. I'd been up for hours by now and was probably looked a right state. Keith was in shorts and was unshaven, couple our appearance with the late hour and you'd expect the woman to be a bit iffy about letting us in, but she did eventually. I was hanging around the reception desk, while Keith went off to the bathroom. When he returned he was completely drenched from head to foot. The scene may have resembled something out of a David Lynch movie before this, now it took on the bizarre. The woman seemed disturbed until Keith described how, when using the washbasin, he had somehow dislodged the cistern off the wall and almost drowned himself. It was a relief to get to the room that night.

We didn't stay long at the hotel, not long enough for me to have a kip anyway, and we were soon on our way again. A few hours later after another bout of useless map reading and pathetic compass supposition, it was an SOS phone call that set us, at last, in the direction of the wedding site. It was a place named Panamint Springs; it's in Panamint Valley in Inyo County, California. When we arrived it was a site to behold. Most people had travelled there in Mobile homes. Let's see. There was Pete and Shell, Tom and Pam, Ben and Clare, Aaron, Simon Roberts all from Ladbroke Grove, Titch, Cedric and others from San Fran. Paul Durden, Rhys Ifans was about too. They'd circled the wagons and were settled in when we arrived. I was pointed in the direction of Tom's beer stash, sniffed out some coke, and that was it for me. They tell me my behaviour was completely out of order. Well I hadn't had a good time out like this for ages, have I, so I might as well do what comes naturally to me, i.e. ruin it for myself, and along the way no doubt, for others as well. They set up hay bales as pews, and the altar was a natural rock jutting out of the desert floor. Martin Ace from Man sang 'Teenage Wedding" Kevin had taught the American opera singer to sing 'Myfanwy' in phonetic Welsh. Tom from Merthyr was seen working an accordion. Yeah, a right good knees up.

I don't remember, but have been told on good authority that I told the beautiful bride to "shut up" which in itself is terrible, but I still cringe when I'm reminded that I also told her to "fuck off" People recall that part of things with a chuckle, but look, Kev's made a big effort to get me out here, and I pay him back like that, it's definitely not funny. I was in blackout by the early hours of the morning; I didn't get to sleep again. I managed to badly injure my shoulder though, a problem I still have now. Keith scraped me up the next day for the return journey. The last thing I remember is Aaron saying to me "I'm gonna 12 step you when we get back home" Keith and I set off for the airport. In the departure lounge we bump into Caroline Ahearn. Keith knows her a bit. He explains about the wedding, and the couple of harrowing days we've had, she says to him, "you look alright, but your mate looks like death warmed up" or words to that effect. Well it could have been worse, she's probably premier division when it comes to piss taking, so I got off lightly.

I was exhausted when I got back to Swansea. Thank God the wedding wasn't anywhere near here. I would have had to bury myself deeper than ever to escape the repercussions of the last few days. But as usual I was quickly back to normal. I'd been nicked a couple of times recently. The magistrates in Swansea are more heavy handed than there London counterparts when it comes to doling out punishment, which meant for two counts of petty discretion I'd been given probation. I had this young lad on my case, he wanted to see me all the time, checked up on my efforts to find work and all that stuff, which felt a bit like a parolee would feel. But I'd made my bed blah blah. Then I get nicked again. It would take all sorts of arse licking and manoeuvrability to keep me out of the nick now. I'm not having it. I get enough for a bus ticket, pick up a bag of clothes and fuck off to London. I don't know what reception I'm walking into, but what the hell, life's over anyway.

Bernie Walther and the boys aren't too hard to locate, they're drinking in the Pelican. I tell Bernie my plight and he's sympathetic. I stay a night or two with him, but there are others in residence so it was lucky that Thomas Rees and Eileen took me in. They have a young son now. They put up with me for longer than most would have done, and me rolling in at all times in worsening states is plain unfair. I manage to get some money together, and get myself set up sharing a flat with Irish Paul, he's a good lad, used to work behind the bar at the Cornwall, he's got a nice gaff, a room of my own and all that, but when it comes to tallying up for rent and the like I've blown most of the money on gambling and booze, so I won't be long around here. The bridges are burnt once again. I bump into a scallywag, who I've had criminal dealings with in the past; he offers me the chance of making some money by taking some drugs over to Ireland. This is not the perfect way of getting by, but what else can I do? We shop around for some photographic paper, which apparently disguises the dope from the X ray machine at customs, he gets me a ticket for the boat, and I'm off, putting my freedom on the line again. What the hell. I'm going to jail anyway, sooner or later.

37. Fed Up, Fucked Up and Far From Home

I'm sat in a pub in the coastal town of Dun Laoghaire in Southern Ireland. In my bag are fifteen kilos of Moroccan hash, in my pocket there is exactly fifty pence. Is this the rock bottom I've heard so much about? Not yet, but not far off. I'd taken on this smuggling gig in the hope that the wages earned would enable me to get a deposit for some sort of living accommodation in London. Getting here in the first place was not without its complications. As I was about to board the ferry, the girl on the check in desk took one look at my bag and said: "That will have to go in the hold." I shit it right then. If anyone was to lift that bag right now, they could only think one of two things, dope, or the head of Alfredo Garcia. It was a dead weight, concentrated in the middle of the bag. Self preservation kicked in. I stuttered out: "I can't do that, there's someone picking me up at the other end, and they're very impatient people. They'll just drive away if I'm not there waiting." Unbelievably she said: "Go on then." I must have an honest face I guess. I hurried to board the boat. Out of the corner of my eye I noticed two guys almost strip searching two student types so my luck was holding up so far. When we arrived at the Irish end there was no security in evidence, so I strolled off the boat. I was elated. So off I went in search of the nearest pub for a pint of the black stuff.

Now here I am in this pub, and I can't get through to any of the other parties on the phone. It's getting late now. What happens if something has gone the other way for the Irish boys? I'd be well snookered. I couldn't go to the authorities to ask for help. I can't get back on the boat without money or ticket. Maybe I could set up shop around here, and start punting out ten pound deals until I'd raised enough for the fare. Yeah. Sure. When you take on a gig like this, you haven't much choice in the matter. The other fella is only interested in two things, his money back, or the safe return of his merchandise. If you're unlucky enough to get nicked, he's not about to visit you with a consolatory bunch of flowers, no, what he wants to see is a charge sheet with your name on it and the right amount of dope written in block capitals below. So as much as you might like the idea, you can't just dump it. This isn't BIG time, nothing in my criminal life has been, but whether it's The French Connection or Howard Marks bringing tons of the stuff over from wherever, or me with my half a bag full, there is one constant, people want their fucking money.

I waited and waited. Six hours had passed. I had a choice. I could either use the fifty pence to try the Irish lads one more time, and if that came up blank, there was one last hope. Pam, who was Bernie's ex lived somewhere hereabouts, maybe she was the answer. When she and Berny were running the Cornwall there were problems galore that needed to be sorted out, and usually were. I got on really well with Pam, we always had a good laugh, but I would have hoped to have met up with her again without the burden of yet another shitstorm. But any port in a shitstorm hey?

But things picked up, more accurately the Irish boys picked up the phone, at last. Halleluiah! Apparently there'd been a breakdown in communication. I was meant to be on a later boat. The put me in the car, put the dope in the boot, and we set off at high speed to wherever they laid there heads. They gave me a room, and I slept like a smuggler. Next day, as usual, it was as if yesterday never happened. The lads were taking me to the airport later on, so I took the opportunity to sample the Guinness at the local boozer. Irish pubs are the best. It takes no time at all to strike up a conversation with anyone who's in them. Oddly enough though, the first person I got chatting to lived in Ladbroke Grove. I couldn't place her, or her me, but we knew a couple in common. The lads came to get me to take me to the airport. I thought they were a bit on the naughty side these lads. When they told me that they were actually banned from this boozer, it verified to me that they weren't averse to trouble. Getting barred from this place was on a par with getting barred from the Warwick i.e. virtually impossible. On the plane later I was a happy man. I had my money; I had the other fella's money, so I had a bevy and relaxed.

'Job done' would have been the sensible call, but not for me. When

I met up with the guy later, he asked if I'd like to parlay the money I'd just made, by turning it into cocaine. I should have thought long and hard about that one, but after a few samples, married to plenty of drink, I said yes. What a twat! We spent the rest of the afternoon sniffing and supping, so by the time I got back to the Pelican pub I was fucked. Apparently I've only gone and put the bag of nose on the bar while ordering a drink. Everyone noticed this daft manoeuvre, including the bar staff. Luckily for me, Bernie was in there. He retrieved my parcel, and pocketed it for safe keeping, as I was being flung out of the bar. When I got it back the next day I was shocked to see how much of it I had gone through. So now I have to cart this stuff down to Swansea, sell it, just to have the same amount of money I had yesterday. MUG!

In Swansea I stayed with some mates. I let it be known that I was holding some decent product, and waited for the rush of customers. What you're meant to do now of course is stay clear headed, you know, take care of business. What I did of course was spend the afternoon sniffing and swallowing away. So by nightfall, when some interested people arrived, I bought every hard luck story, ranging from "Come on Ray. I've sorted you out in the past" to "I'll pay you tomorrow". I've used similar tactics in the past. More than most I'd wager, but I still fell for it. So I was getting nowhere fast. For my part, I was off my fucking rocker that night. I even had to be put to bed. I definitely had some money on me when I retired, by morning I couldn't even find that, and if things couldn't get any worse, I'd managed to put my foot through my pal's glass cabinet, the one that housed all his very expensive model soldiers. I scarpered before I got flung out. Now here I am skint, homeless and friendless. This must be rock bottom. I couldn't stay in Swansea, I still had some unresolved with the law, so I had to make it back to London somehow. I didn't have a penny, so I resorted to old faithful. I had to dive into town to grab hold of something. I settled on two of those heavy French frying pans out of Debenhams. I suppose I could have gotten something a bit lighter, and a bit easier to disguise, but I'm coming down like a suicide off Golden Gate Bridge. I couldn't see straight, let alone think straight. I shuffled over to the George and found my old mate

Ivor the Cheese. Ivor likes a bargain, and he duly came up with the dosh. So I could at least get the bus.

Back in London I'm being swerved big time. And because of the guilt associated with my recent behaviour, I'm swerving plenty myself. The friends I'd been staying with had a young son, and me falling through their front door, at all hours, in terrible states, was not a good atmosphere for him. That's for sure, so quite rightly I had been shown the door. I had an outside chance of a kip if I could track down my mate Aaron. He was the guy who threatened to twelve step me when we were at Kev's wedding. He'd told me previously that he'd put me up for the weekend at his place, provided I didn't drink. Right now that sounded more like a birthday present than anything bad. That's just what the doctor ordered, the problem was I couldn't track down Aaron, and I needed somewhere to kip that night. I bumped into Dennis Smilley on the street, he offered me his couch for one night, which was great right then, and I can tell you. But right at the death, at last knockings Aaron answered the phone. That's when my life changed.

I stayed at his house for that long weekend. And for the first time in living memory I was sober. He'd sorted me out with some fags, food etc; but he'd also sorted me out with some meetings. At first I felt I had to go to keep the peace. But I was soon being approached by people at the meetings who actually wanted to help. No angles, not for there own devices, just plain, straightforward help. You couldn't help but be impressed. I was, I thought 'I'm gonna give this a go.' My time at Aaron's was up, so I'm still homeless. Then to my amazement, considering all my antics and shenanigans in the Pelican, Bernie stepped up to the plate, and said I could stay with him. I'm not talking luxury here, I had to kip in his passage, but I put up with it and still didn't drink. What made this all the more remarkable was this was Carnival weekend, and Bernie lives right in the middle of it.

Over the next couple of weeks, I kept up my sober regime. I attended AA meetings regularly; I then presented myself at the Alcohol Related Counselling office, to see if I might qualify for a place in rehab. Then I visited the doctor. When I was with Melanie, and I had that short rest from the drink, I went to the doctor then. The guy I had to see happened to be the Arsenal doctor. When I asked him for something to help me sleep, his response was "Do a lot of walking." He didn't offer me a prescription of any sort, so on this visit I wasn't expecting any different… What I needed was a letter of some kind, laying out my problem, which I could then present to ARC and the council, to see if I could get some help. They say 'when you do good things, good things happen' or something like that. It was certainly true on this occasion. When I saw the doc, it wasn't the miserable bugger from before; instead it was a young locum. He gave me a letter alright, Dickens couldn't have bettered it. It was full of hopelessness, destitution, unmanageability, homelessness and chronic self abuse. What a toff. Not something you want your nearest and dearest to read perhaps, but for the great march forward, it was magic.

Considering I'd sold my last council flat, I didn't hold out much hope of getting any help with accommodation down the Town Hall. Wrong. The geezer I saw couldn't have been more helpful. Before you can say 'Simon Le Bon can't dance' I'm back on the housing list, and by that very afternoon I've been found a place in a B&B in Kings Cross. It's not the Dorchester, but I'm not Elton John either. It was good just to be able to close a door behind me, and be on my own. My luck holds out. Two weeks later ARC has found me a place in a treatment centre. The place is called Sharp. It's a daytime recovery programme, situated down Chelsea way. By now I've been moved from Kings Cross to Earls Court. This gaff is within spitting distance of Sharp.

I have to admit, all this manoeuvring was just a plan to get re-housed. But after a while I started to get into it. This was mainly the result of being told by one of the counsellors that I wasn't taking it seriously. He said "If you don't want to do this, fuck off, there are plenty out there who would gladly take your place" That's the best way to act with the likes of me, someone with a short memory, someone with the knack of forgetting all the shit times the day after they happen. Of course that is not a solution, that way of thinking just invites the problems back, in spades. I knuckled down after that. I did what was expected. Step work, attending plenty of meetings, and generally stopped being a twat. After a few months in B&B I'm eventually offered a small studio flat in the not very posh end of Kensington and Chelsea. At the time I was a bit miffed because my mate at Sharp, Terry, had been given a very nice gaff in Chelsea. I went back to the stinking thinking, why not me. Then I thought it through and said to myself "Who the fuck do I know down Chelsea. The place I've got is not the best, but at least I'm back on the manor where I've lived since 1979.

38. End Game

All my life I've figured that money is the answer to all life's problems, odd that considering I've never had any. So how the fuck would I know? I read somewhere about the apprehension of some high-ranking member of the Medellin drugs cartel, it could even have been Escobar himself. Anyway when they found this guy he was attached to a drip and this contraption was used solely to rid him of a hangover. How good is that? If you have the money imagine it, up in the morning, into the steam room with a Bloody Mary, then maybe a massage, a power shower, a proper shave with a cut-throat razor performed by an expert. All this will put you in the mood to at least get some grub down your neck. Into the dressing room, kit yourself out in all lovely, clean, brand new clothes and shoes, call a cab, and get delivered to your favoured place of boozing. Compare this with waking up skint, no milk for a cup of tea, into the ashtray and dig out a dog end, which you smoke to ensure you get the full effect of guilt, remorse and uselessness. So it would have to be money every time wouldn't it?

Getting myself into AA soon changed my opinion on that subject. There you might bump into some fellas who, on the surface, seem to have life by the balls; they've got the nice clothes, flash cars, desirable addresses and hot girlfriends. Then you hear their stories and soon realise alcoholic misery is not confined to the people, I for one, would have thought to be the obvious candidates. Alcoholism is no respecter of class, creed, gender or upbringing, it can slip round your neck like a Dior tie and before you know it, turn into the hangman's slipknot. When I was younger I thought the geezers on the benches were the 'alkies' and the rest of us were just getting pissed and having a laugh. This theory, shared by all my drunken mates, was based on the fact that we had somewhere to live, and the bench dwellers didn't.

I know now that many a mansion is populated by people with this killer disease, all the wealth brings them is the chance to disguise their problem for a lot longer, and if they are lucky realise in time that enough is enough and do something about it. It's exactly the same for me and your bench dweller, money has nought to do with it, when you make a commitment to sobriety you start on a level playing field. So money can't buy you love, happiness or contentment. What's that thing they say at AA, be careful what you wish for, it might just come true. That's spot on, but I still wish, that just one time, I had some of the darn stuff.

As I write I am over eight years sober, this doesn't mean a lot if you're not actually working on the stuff that helps you to change your life. When I first got involved in AA I was keen to ingratiate myself with the programme, I volunteered for all the tasks that have to be taken care of to keep the meetings running smoothly. From tea person to secretary, I did the lot. So on that side of things I was doing my bit, but I certainly came up short where step work, helping others and 'giving it up' were concerned. I must have learnt something along the way though otherwise I wouldn't have got to eight years, but I have to admit through most of it I've been a dry drunk. In my case, what that means is, I just don't drink. But I don't advance myself either. Instead of (like many) enjoying my sobriety I tend to put up with it.

Giving up drinking re-opened many doors for me, people who had been giving me the mighty swerve, were now happy to see me, they invited me into their homes and in some cases, they even employed me. So things were looking up. Then because I hadn't been paying proper attention with my recovery I slipped back into another one of my addictions, this time gambling. When I think about it I've brought more grief upon myself with gambling, than I ever did with booze. As well as the drink you see, I was also addicted to the pub itself, so when that became a no- no, I was on a search for places where one could continue to talk bollocks and have some sort of a laugh. I started spending more and more time in the betting office. I've never been lucky in that sphere, so losing my money would make me miserable, and consequently I became less and less keen to haul my ass to a meeting.

The result of all this is I never get to do the things that I'd have like to. For instance I haven't managed to put myself into a loving relationship, or any other relationship for that matter, I haven't as I'd hoped put myself into a position to 'up' my eligibility by taking more pride in my appearance through fitness and wardrobe, and have put next to no effort into making my living surroundings more comfortable. One of the main aims of people in AA is to gain self worth and confidence, I've fallen down badly on this one because of my mule headedness and my failure to believe that things can be better for me if I bothered to try. Seeing things through to the end has always been a problem for me, which is why I've written this story. I didn't start doing it with the hope of becoming some literary lion; on the contrary, I didn't expect it to be published to be honest. So if you're reading this right now it means that I've actually finished something at last, with the help of others, of course, but in the main it has been a solo effort. Maybe this will mark the start of some real progress in my quest for contentment, and get me the occasional legover. We can live in hope.

I haven't talked about my mother much, funny that considering she's my best mate, and I talk to her every day. She let me get away with murder when I was younger, always siding with me, whatever the evidence said. Women from that era, who'd been through the war and probably lost male relatives, were unbelievably forgiving to their own male offspring, Leonard's mother and Ken's couldn't see a thing wrong with them either. My mother is 81, she still runs around the place, in fact a couple of years ago she told me she was off to Lourdes, the religious shrine in France where people visit with health problems looking for a miracle cure. I asked her what was wrong, she said "nothing" and went on to tell me that her function was to push people in their wheelchairs. You can't fault my mother, that's for sure. In fact this book is for her.

See Ray Roughler-Jones on the telly at:

www.youtube.com/roughlertv

Also available at www.tangentbooks.co.uk

Bash the Rich

Labelled 'the most dangerous man in Britain' by the Sunday People in 1984, Class War founder Ian Bone has produced a book about his days putting the boot into the ruling classes. It isn't subtle, and it isn't any kind of blueprint on how to successfully start a revolution, but it is very funny.

Hartmann the Anarchist

A long-forgotten masterpiece of Victorian science fiction in the tradition of Jules Verne and HG Wells, Hartmann the Anarchist was originally published in 1892 when its author Edward Douglas Fawcett was just 16 years old.

Unsettled

This is the life story of Big Issue seller Graham Walker who has been homeless for most of his adult life after being brought up in a dysfunctional family on a north Bristol council house estate. It's both funny and sad, but most of all it challenges prejudice at every level.